BEYOND THE STAIRS

AN INVITATION TO WALK INTO OTHER DIMENSIONS

SHIRLEY BATTIE

Matador
9 Priory Business Park,
Wistow Road, Kibworth Beauchamp,
Leicestershire. LE8 0RX
Tel: (+44) 116 279 2299
Fax: (+44) 116 279 2277
Email: books@troubador.co.uk
Web: www.troubador.co.uk/matador

ISBN 978 1780882 567

British Library Cataloguing in Publication Data.
A catalogue record for this book is available from the British Library.

Typeset by Troubador Publishing Ltd, Leicester, UK

Matador is an imprint of Troubador Publishing Ltd

Printed in Great Britain by the MPG Books Group, Bodmin and King's Lynn

I dedicate this book to my Earthly family who allow me to be who I am and to my Space friends and Spirit family who have taught me so much and who have not at any time lost patience with me.

INTRODUCTION

In my story, friends come forward from another dimension to assist in self discovery and purpose. Are you ready to take a ride with me? Hold on tight. What follows may stretch your belief. The most important and exciting experiences you can ever imagine all began with meditation. I urge you to take a leap and jump in. I did and have never for a moment regretted doing so.

We are about to enter a gigantic new advancement of the human race, an enormous leap for us all. Are we ready? Much of what follows here will assist you to see yourself in a different way.

Here is a little background just so you know that if this can happen to me, an ordinary person going about life the same as anybody else, then it can happen to you too. I was in my mid fifties, feeling a bit lost having returned to England after an unhappy divorce and starting a new job. I enrolled in a course on counselling where they meditated at the commencement of each session. I'd previously thought that people who meditated were a little weird. The 'beads and bangles brigade' I called them. But these were nice, normal, comfortable individuals. Nothing weird about them, I decided.

Sitting at home one evening I gave meditation a try and had instant contact. What I didn't expect was to have information and pictures concerning the planet and the future of the human species. I took notice. I did not know then that more was expected of me and that all the information I was given had to be passed on.

Soon I had so many clear and exciting visits from other existences that I was hooked. I have come to call these journeys to other worlds and other times 'Mind Walking' or 'Mind Reach'. All that is required is that you go into meditation and let the mind take you where your spirit and soul wish you to be. You **are** there in those other places and feel as alive and real as at home in your time. Meditation is the key that opens the door. Get ready for the ride.

We all have mind journeys. That is for certain. We journey when we dream at night. We journey when we daydream. We journey when we remember past experiences. More importantly, we journey when we meditate. Our inner journeys are vital to our well being and may be, for some, a safety valve from everyday life. These journeys help keep a balance between a spiritual and physical reality.

Journeys through dreams can and often do provide solutions to problems. Many of the world's inventions have come through dreams. Sudden understanding can come while daydreaming. Do you allow enough time to daydream in your rush through your daily routine? Things we cannot face in everyday life are often presented through dreams, interacting with a subconscious desire to find solutions to life so that the soul can go forward smoothly and without baggage. Dreams sort things out in a manner that does not damage us. Dreams will often point the way for our path through life and show us what our purpose is. Scientists and doctors agree that if we are denied dreaming time for too long we may go mad.

However this is not a book on dreams but is about journeys through meditation. What is the difference? In dreams we have no control of what happens and frequently we have insufficient memory recall afterwards, unless we have trained ourselves to remember and then analyse. Otherwise we leave it up to the subconscious mind to sort things out.

At the time of writing, the meditations and urgings from the spirit world have taken me to Zimbabwe, Kenya, and South Africa more than once. I have been to New Mexico, Alaska, Canada, the Antarctic and several cities in America, all over Australia and New Zealand, China, Brazil (what a journey that was) and Borneo. There are many other countries and little islands I have visited without financial recompense, but always there for the work of spirit and our space friends. They are explicit about what they need as the occasion arises, often at the last moment. Imagine, without meditating I would not have gone to any of these countries. Was it worth it? You decide.

My early experiences were valuable baby steps in comparison to what followed. During my connections with spirit helpers I learnt to travel further and further. They are now taking me to heights I had never dreamed of before. I travel to other worlds, space stations and within the Earth itself. I am able to cross time using the mind, and it all began with meditation. Please try it yourself. You will discover who you truly are and how you may prepare for the coming changes and huge leap for the human race.

The journeys have moved into a wider field of interest which covers world changing events. I asked the spirit helpers why they did not do themselves the things they asked me to do. Why ask me to do them?

Their response: "You are very well aware that if change is to come about on your planet the change must come from those who inhabit the

Earth, whether they use their minds or their physicality. You human beings have to make the changes, not us."

Through meditation, by using intention and earnest desire to learn, you not only have control but can interact and work with what is presented by your own soul consciousness and by your guides and teachers. To do this it is helpful to use the method as described in my earlier book *Channelling* which is not at all difficult and is very similar to self hypnosis. The exercise for this is at the end of the book.

Forget the misconception that you have to empty or still your mind. How many can do that? Using 'the stairs technique' set out at the end of the book, it is important to have your mind operating at full stretch, noticing and registering everything that happens. The mind then gets so intrigued by what is going on that it does not stray onto mundane matters.

THE STAIRS METHOD
The journeys described throughout use the stairs method, which allows you to go deeper and deeper. It is very similar to self hypnosis and bypasses the conscious rationalising mind. You go down stairs, turn left into a passage and then go right to enter your space. This is as brief a description as I can manage without going into full teaching mode right now. I have included the stairs method at the end of the book. I recommend you give it a try. You may wish to do this before continuing to read.

A colour may be given or asked for, which by itself can give meaning to what follows. It is helpful to learn and understand the meaning of colour, if interpreting is important to you in your meditations.

The clothes worn and the type of stairs, or method of descent, are presented by the subconscious mind and is not thought of or made up beforehand. They can indicate a theme and give some idea what the journey may be all about. It is good to expect the unexpected. It also proves that you are not making anything up.

All these journeys have been recorded as they happen, except where I state 'reported'. It is a method that spirit has taught me and without which the experiences would have long been forgotten. Recording has the advantage of not having to try to remember. This way it is possible to stay in the moment, truly be there and feel the emotions of each journey. It also has the enormous value of being able to transcribe from the recording later, and read and absorb the true meaning long after the experience. The subconscious mind will never lie and often works in picture or symbolic form, this being a universal language.

Even with today's meditations, if I do not record as it happens then I do not receive as much in the way of information. Worse still there is little memory later as to what has taken place. Having to speak does not allow time for the logical, rational mind to interfere and change things according to how one thinks it ought to go, or worse how you want it to go. With no idea what is coming next, each one is a real journey into the unknown. I am going to share these journeys with you in the pages to come.

Occasionally various people are asked what particular message is being given though these stories. It is amazing how different the interpretations are. I feel that spirit have intended that each draw from the stories what they need. It is for this very reason that I have put them into book form so that you may decide what they mean to you.

Imagine you are taking these journeys yourself. Put yourself in the meditator's place and see what it means to you. Spirit has often said that messages are deliberately presented in ambiguous form so that it might encourage debate and wake up a few minds. I truly feel that the journeys included here are for everybody to take part in and be inspired by. If we are one consciousness then everything that has happened and is still happening to me is also a reality for you. The challenges are there for you to take up if you wish.

I have given titles to some of the meditations when there appears to be a message. You, dear reader, may feel an alternative title would be more suitable. This too is an indication of where it 'hits the spot' with you. Sometimes the grammar and phrasing of the sentence is inaccurate. I have left most as it is, bearing in mind that when one speaks it is often not in good writing order. I have only changed where it is difficult to follow, and to make it more readable. The term 'Being' is used to describe a spirit of high celestial spiritual energy when the identity is not known. Much can be viewed as little tales, similar to parables with a message for all. When there is conversation between the spirit world and the meditator I have used parenthesis " ".

Dates of the journeys are left to chronologically show progress to clearer understanding through the weeks, months and years. So often during the passageway there is room for only one person to enter the inner depths. The squeezing through gaps to begin the experience indicates there must be a real intention to discover and not to give up at the first barrier. The meditations use stairs as a method to journey inwards, with colours, clothing and feelings all giving clues to the meaning and purpose of the experience and which can be an exercise in interpretation. The journeys included here are meant to inspire and encourage you to have them for yourself.

LEARNING TO RECORD

It is to my everlasting regret that when I first began to make contact with the spirit world through meditation, I did not vocalise and record the experience on tape and so cannot recall the words given to me. All I know is that I asked a lot of questions, received answers to all of them but cannot remember them now. They will remain in my subconscious state.

Note: I have audio cassette tapes for each of the meditations in this book.

Previous to the recordings, I had been channelling for some time, all of which was also recorded. Channelled messages give a wider range of information meant for everybody and are not as personal as in meditation. For me it is sometimes hard to tell the difference.

There are other meditations and inner journeys not included here which can be found in my book *Being Human*. To whet your appetite for what is to come I present one journey here that gave me much to think about. I am speaking throughout.

CHAPTER ONE

SEPTEMBER 1st 1998

RELEASE THE GLORIOUS

I go down in beautiful amber. The rails are a bit knobbly, ornate. The stairs are so steep my legs tremble as I go down. I am at the bottom now. My legs are like jelly. I gather my strength, letting myself recover from the effort of going down. After a pause I can go forward a little. My legs are still shaky, as if they might give out at any time.

I totter forward. It is an ordinary passage. Nothing very ornate about this. I must be deep underground. It is very dark and damp. It is a long way down, not much air. I turn off to the left. There are a whole series of openings on the right with metal grills. Oh, I am in a prison. A dungeon, this is a prison of old. I see many cells with metal bars. Very damp indeed, it is not a nice place. I know that in one of these cells (pause). . . there is nothing modern here, no little grill or peephole to see inside, just metal bars. I am not even looking inside to see who is in them. I don't want to see who is in them.

This place is not nice. I go along. There is a man hanging through the bars. I can't miss him. He has been here a very long time. I stop and lift his head, because it was hanging down and I couldn't see his face. As I lift his head I look into the most incredible pair of blue eyes and the most incredibly youthful face underneath all his hair. He is beautiful, he doesn't belong here. He is glorious.

"Why are you here?" I ask. "Why are you here? You don't belong in here."

He speaks: "The most glorious things are locked up inside, waiting for release. The most glorious things are hidden away inside until somebody comes along and lets them out. You are to release me."

I look at the lock and a key is there. He could easily have turned it. But I am to do that. I unlock and pull the door open. He untangles himself from the bars and comes through the door. We link arms. Following behind him are children. I hadn't seen them before. There are lots of little children all trailing like a long procession after him, beautiful, young and fresh children.

1

"Where I go they go," He says. "They cannot do without me and I cannot do without them. They too are wondrous things. But I am the beginning. Take me up to the light."

Years later I still get emotional as I remember this experience. Who do you think this person represents?

THE JOURNEY AND TRAINING BEGINS

I wondered what my family would say if they knew where I went on my inner trips. It was hard keeping it all to myself as I knew they would not understand at all. They would have serious doubts about my sanity that is for sure.

I was slowly recovering from the breakup of my marriage and was regaining my own spirit and self worth. Part of me wanted to keep my visits to the inner world private and the other part wanted to shout from the rooftops. I joined a spiritual circle but still I kept my experiences to myself. Writing this out now is an act of faith for they still may not understand and maybe my friends won't either. But here goes.

FEBRUARY 21ˢᵗ 1992

PANEL OF LIGHT – LEARN

I step down in gold and silver on a modern steel and shiny metal stairway, all the way down, a long way down. At the bottom I see the way ahead is a tube-like passage. I wander off to the left and find a door set into the curvature of the wall of the tube. I run my hand over it to find out how I can open it. It slides open.

I ask to be shown what I need to see. There are panels of instruments. It is very science fiction stuff this. My eye sweeps round the array and is caught by a glowing panel. I sweep on and come back to it, drawn to the glowing pulsating panel of light. I feel I should go towards it to see what it is. I am here for confidence and upliftment, a little confirmation for myself. I am told to step through the panel.

I'm confused: "Step through the panel?"

"Yes, step through the light, it is a doorway." I am commanded.

I feel the need to collect myself. I don't know how to do this. In my mind I pull together a picture of me and how I am dressed so that I can go through. It requires some effort. I have a tickle on my chin and my nose. I step in very slowly and pass into amber light. It is as if light passes right the way through me. I am immersed in light. It isn't so difficult; a nice sensation with a deepening connection. I am strongly reminded to use the third eye.

My mind drifts off onto other things, which is terrible. I must use the third eye. My mind wanders off into all sorts of questions, affirmations, statements of where I wish to be. After a while I realise I am still in the dark, I can't see anything. I have to go back through the door.

I keep getting the words in my head, LEARN, CONTINUE TO LEARN. I step backwards into the orange glow in the doorway and stay in it. I realise that I could stay in this light if I wanted to or I could come back directly from the doorway of light. I don't need to go through it to come back. I feel the light through me and bring myself back to my room, still feeling suffused with the orange glow and wanting it to sustain me throughout the day.

3

CHEST WITH CHALICE AND SCROLL

Sunny yellow is the colour. I am a slithering shapeless form going down. What a peculiar feeling! When I get to the bottom, the feeling changes completely. I take on a stance of determination, almost military. I practically march forward, turning a sharp left, as if drilling. I am absolutely determined. I am walking on sand. I stride forward along the corridor feeling the sand, very solid and firm underfoot. Keep going. Yes, I see a wooden and sandy door; old weathered wood such as you'd get at the seaside. Sand is the theme:

"The sands of time."

I feel energy and am being nudged towards a chest. I hesitate. Chests always represent the unknown to me and I am a little bit fearful of what might be inside. But I am nudged towards it and I know I must go nearer. It is an ornate chest. The theme is sand and sea, treasure trove. That is it, treasure trove within the chest. I feel better about it now. I open it and, laughing, I see a few butterflies leave.

I know it is a good chest; it is no Pandora's Box. I take out a chalice, a beautiful golden chalice. I am awed by it and put it down on the sand and reach in again. I take out an orb. Next there are some papers rolled up. Scrolls! I am fearful of unrolling the scrolls and put them to one side. I am not worried by what might be on the scrolls, I am anxious about my inability to see and understand. I am afraid that if I undo it I will see nothing. I will leave it for the moment. Next there are two candlesticks with candles in to light the way. The scrolls will not be ignored and have rolled over towards me.

I know what I have to do, unroll the scrolls. This I do. There is writing; heavy black words. It is **'PERSERVERENCE, LOVE, TRUST',** it is all there for you. I ask to be shown clearly so that I am not imagining and **'PERSEVERANCE'** keeps coming back. I see the letters on the paper. I know it is enough. I can feel the energy and my ears are hurting. They are hurting and I hear the voice:

"My dear child." I want to cry.

I ponder on how I am going to take all these things with me. I don't have enough hands. I think of leaving them behind. Then I think again.

4

No, the candles are to light the way and it is unforgivable to leave what has been given. So I untie and use the string from around the scrolls, wrap the candles in the scrolls and tie the candles, the scrolls, the orb and chalice together so that it can be carried in one hand, so that I have all these things that were given. I must go on before I go back.

I am becoming very tired and need to lie down on a bank and go to sleep. I am very tired…

*What followed was a long period of deep rest in which I felt very much overshadowed. I felt good. It was not a waste of time and one I could have stayed with, but I knew I had to go to work [the office] and my time was to be limited. My friends, my helpers were very much with me, very much so. I had total absorption in them. A good feeling and one that left me in no doubt that I am getting help. I am quite happy about this and must now go back.

One thing I forgot to mention. While this was all going on there was a lovely smell of incense, quite faint but definite at the same time. I nearly opened my eyes to see if anything was burning.

I still have down moments when I think of my marriage, now ended. My intuitive hairdresser said as I sat down one visit: "You have been to hell and back, haven't you?"

He didn't know my story and it was a comfort to know someone felt for me. I feel this next journey is a spirit effort to jolly me up a bit.

MARCH 12th 1992

BE HAPPY AND SUNNY FOR OTHERS (reported)

Very early in the morning the colour yellow was given. I went down after a little preamble of thoughts about buttercups and cows. I had to look to see what I was wearing and I was wrapped in a gown of sunny yellow. I was wearing sandals. It didn't take me too long to go down and I went along my passage with intent and came to a woven door with a Lloyd Loom type finish painted yellow. It opened very easily, if a bit wobbly. It took me a little while to establish what I could see.

I saw a seat and thought: *well seats are for sitting on,* so I went across to the seat and sat down. I felt the warm sunshine and it was like having a day off work and going into the countryside and just enjoying oneself away from all the cares. As I sat down I looked and saw a market scene with people doing their selling and bartering and going about their business. It was a very ancient scene as if I had gone back in time. It was pleasant just sitting there; feeling detached and enjoying what was going on. Nobody took any notice of me which was lovely and again the feeling of sunshine and warmth and yellow.

Then I realised I was not there just to be sitting and enjoying a nice meditation, there had to be a reason for it. It came to me that I had to go down a street leading off from the square. I made my way down the narrow street. As I got to the end I came to wide open countryside again and saw ahead of me a beautiful sunshine glow. I walked towards it. As I got close I realised it was a luminous, sunny yellow figure. A figure without form, it was just a glow. The shape that was given to it was of a figure so that I would recognise it as a Being rather than just a light.

This Being was a smile, a welcome. I rushed towards it. We rushed towards each other as if we were old friends and held out our arms, if you can say arms for a Being of fluorescent light. We wrapped our arms around each other. It wasn't me being enfolded in it, we were enfolding each other, embracing very warmly, melding as one. We stayed like this, like old friends really pleased to be together.

I was told to bring happiness and sunshine to those I come into contact with today and other days, and to be sunny and cheery and not to be so serious.

6

MARCH 14ᵗʰ 1992

UNDERGROUND CAVERN – UNCONSCIOUS SELF (reported)

I was given the colour yellow ochre and as I thought *I don't like that colour very much*, it changed to a dull gold and then that became burnished gold, very rich in colour. I felt better about the colour then. I had a little trouble settling to start with but eventually I went down. When I reached the bottom it was a tunnel rather than open space. It was underground and I wandered along and came to, instead of a door, one of those openings with a piece of rock across it so that you had to go to the right and then turn left to get round the jutting rock, just like when you have a gate to a field where only one can pass at a time and there is a swing bit in the middle. This was for one person to go through at a time. The opening wasn't easily evident to anyone walking past unless you were looking for it, as I obviously was.

As I got in I realised it was an underground cavern, but far from being dead it was alive. There was life there. There was water and a feeling of being alive. I can't say it was sparkling but there was freshness about it in spite of it being deep underground. I asked why I was there and what was it showing me?

"This is your deep unconscious which is alive. It is not dead, it is full of life and there are many passages which you will explore, which can be explored. There are many directions to go from here to investigate. Some of them will have dead ends and you will turn back and retrace your steps, others will lead out onto interesting scenes, interesting panoramas which may be open fields, another may be open seas or deserts. There are many avenues to explore in the deep unconscious and many things to be learnt."

"How can I take back what I discover?"

"That is easy. You simply retrace your steps; your journey is the link between the subconscious and the mind. When you go back from this subconscious area, you take with you back to your conscious mind by means of retracing your steps. Each time you learn a little more and investigate a little further. Remember it is alive here, it is not dead and is very much full of life and thought and experience."

It was about that time that I began to run my own development circle and had a little group of like-minded friends. Still I couldn't tell them what I was experiencing. What I hadn't disclosed was a contact with what I called 'Bird Man', now known as Osishoo. He clearly was from another planet and all of his information was about the future of planet Earth and our role in keeping the human race in good shape. Telling anyone of this might be a step too far. I have an audio tape of his first contact.

Osishoo transmitted slowly. "I am not of your present race," he said, rather obviously. "I am detached, an observer. I notice the efforts of men being made in all parts of your world. The word must be spread. We are all observers and know what is required for unopened minds and untouched parts of your globe. Word must be spread from one part to another, like a relay. You must use your mind; you must send your messages through the airwaves, through your electrical connections. Use satellites. You can reach all parts through a network of transmissions. Network, linking, many languages."

"Are you speaking of television?" I dared to ask, in my mind. Even then, before the internet existed, he stressed the use of using the airwaves to spread the information.

PYRAMID TRIP FOR GROUP TEACHING (reported)

This is a strange meditation. I linked in as soon as I sat down so I knew they were there with me and I didn't have to go to them.

Having said all my prayers and asking help for various people I was told to make the Pyramid. I was told to put a crystal in each corner surrounding me and as the crystals were placed, a line like a laser beam ran from one crystal to the other, so that they were all joined. As they were joined up the base area was also joined so that it had a crystal base. Then there was a crystal high above me and lines came up from each corner like a laser beam, again to join with the crystal at the top. As that joined the sides glassed over and the sides became walls of crystal. I was enclosed within the crystal pyramid and it was very nice.

The voice came to me that I was now enclosed and although I was sealed off, the world was mine to investigate. If I wanted to investigate a leaf or even be inside a blade of grass, if I wanted to explore another planet I could do that. I could go where I wanted to in my mind within that crystal, within the safety of the pyramid.

It was also given to me to record this. A picture of myself in a hall addressing a large group and actually giving them this very picture for each and every individual there to do; to put the same pyramid round each and every one for themselves. They could then take their minds where they wanted to go. I was to tell them, before they started, what I intended by taking them on this trip. To retain what actually happened so that they could take it home afterwards and examine it and see what it meant to them. In other words retain their experiences, and I had to tell them this before they began so that they would intentionally hold on to what was happening to them for later on.

REMOTE VIEWING OR MIND WALKING

It was much later (2002) that I took a disciplined Remote Viewing course at the Robert Monroe Institute in Virginia, conducted by Skip Attwater and Joe McMoneagle. They would not be too pleased with me now though, since my journeys are driven by where spirit leads me and directs me. Although I do not follow protocol, the training I received in Virginia has helped me to interact more with what happens, to ask questions and to feel physically **there**. I feel I am transported to other realms, other places not of this Earth. More on this later, if I dare!

My attendance at this course was requested and set up by my spirit friends and as usual they expected me to follow through.

PENETRATING THE DARKNESS – RESCUE

It is yellow and as I wonder how I am going to go down, I become a ray of yellow light which spears its way down to the inner depths and travels along the passage like a line of molten metal, molten gold running along in a steady stream. Like a strip of molten metal it just slides through a crack underneath the door, no bother. A molten gleam of light, all yellow. After a long preamble of thought I bring myself back to the scene.

"Why am I here?" I see a shining full length mirror. I go towards it.

"What can you see?"

I see a golden Being which I believe is me. I am a little surprised.

"You can walk through the mirror."

I do this and as I get through a voice keeps saying:

"Turn back." At first I didn't know if I had really heard it.

"Turn back." More forcibly now.

I question: "Turn back?" I was going to do just that when I think: *Who is this telling me to turn back.* I will ask God if I should turn back.

Then: "Look around first."

I look around and see crags and crevasses and darkness. It is the dark areas. Am I ready as a light to go into the dark areas? I ask myself the question. Am I strong enough to penetrate the darkness with the light? Now I understand why I am a beam of light. Am I ready? I decide to reinforce the light by calling for help in strengthening the glow and the light. I pull up the energy within me and call it down from outside me. I feel the increase in the energy and the glow. I intensify it. **They** intensify it to the maximum. I stay with this in a very strong, white hot glow of light.

Then I understand why it is a rivulet of golden light rather than normal radiance. Because the light runs off in rivulets into the crags, into the crevasses. Direct light can't do that; it would shine in a straight line. There is both so that the surroundings are lit up and at the same time the rivulets of molten light are running into the corners and down the cracks. It is very strong and my understanding is that the gold and the light will draw to it those who need to see, to lift them up from the crevasses, from the dark corners.

11

Then the voice: "That is enough. That is enough."

I turn back; I go back through the mirror. I feel much depleted after that and know I have to recharge myself. It isn't very easy at first and doesn't seem to work. I go through the exercise and eventually the energy comes back. I can feel it coming down from my head chakra, down and filling me with energy so that I am recharged. I ask that my aura be reinforced strongly so that I may be of use to those around me as well as to those unseen. I feel it is necessary to recharge before going back altogether. To seal my aura, my energy, what I have done is mentally case-hardened the auric shell leaving *(I laugh)* a one way system, a valve at the top for the energy to continue to come in, but it is a one-way valve so it can't get out again. I am conserving the energy which is there as a reserve.

*

That was unusual, wasn't it? I never know what is going to happen in my meditations. It took about an hour.

APRIL 27th 1992

FINDING LOST SHEEP

I am given the colour deep deep blue, a velvety blue. I feel the need to go within. Velvety blue is with me all the way down. I come to the door which is slatted. I hesitate for some reason before going through.

Somebody says: "Go in, you have come this far."

I go in and ask that I be shown what I need to see. I make out an animal and think: *That is a sheep.* Then, *no, it can't be a sheep.* I ponder on what the animal might be and wonder if I am imagining things.

"Go and look closer."

I go closer. It is a sheep. I can't work this one out. "It is a lost sheep, not a lost lamb. It is a mature soul that is lost."

He means a mature person that is lost. I gather the sheep up, thinking, *now what? What do I do with it?*

"Take it with you on your next stage."

They show me an opening and I go through with the sheep. It struggles to get out of my arms and as I go through it breaks free and runs off quite happily. Looking around I see a nice fresh peaceful scene, countryside. Very restful and lovely. The words come: "Sheep may safely graze." That is very relevant.

"You have to go back. You have to go and find another lost sheep. You can come every so often but you have to keep going back and getting more sheep."

So I turn round and go back. There is a lot of very strong transfiguration with strong feelings. I say to them I wish I could know them and see them and that I feel very lonely. I do feel very lonely at times.

*

My eldest son and his family were also wishing I was not alone and when there seemed to be a possible man on the horizon you could feel their relief. They wouldn't have to concern themselves about me. I got to see the grandchildren more and felt good about this. They were wrong though, and although my friend Stan and I were very much in tune, it was not to be more than that. Our connection was simply to do with our spirit work and nothing more. I learnt a lot from him and will always be grateful.

I began to tell him about some of my journeys. That may have been a mistake.

Stan sat still, stunned and for once temporarily lost for words. "Have you thought about giving up your job?" he said.

"Not a chance. It's no good even thinking about it. I would not have enough money to live on without working," I declared.

He smiled and said something which I missed. He waited for me to reply.

"I'm sorry. What did you say?" I said

"I said, can we work more closely together? I know you have conversations with spirit beings of a special order and I wondered if I could connect too if I was with you when you do it. We get on well, you and I."

This was not what I had in mind. My inner journeys were not the same as channelling, they were more private. We continued with channelling sessions and I was happy to share information that came that way.

MAY 4th 1992

BABY CAMEL – GO INTO THE WILDERNESS

I look around and see a baby camel. I think of Abdul [my guide]. The baby camel is standing by its mother. Abdul has taken the lead and reins of the camel. The little one is trotting behind. He holds my hand as we set out over the sand. It is loose sand, not firm and is not easy to walk on. We come to a rise and I reflect, there is always a rise before you can see a long way. As we climb and get to the top, the view is of a beautiful red sky with the sun coming up. A beautiful red sky, the desert is all lit up.

There is nothing to see, it is vast emptiness spreading out as far as one can see. It is barren and flat with nothing moving. Maybe there would be something if we were closer but from this distance it is just an empty expanse. It is rather strange but perhaps that is what the desert is like. As I think that he says:

"This is not the desert."

What does that mean? I don't understand it. I ask for an explanation, clarification.

"You are to ride forth into the barren wastes taking with you new birth, a new birth of ideas and thought. A new beginning. You are to venture into the barrenness and bring new life."

"What an undertaking! Please will you show me how?"

"You will have companions along the way. Advisors, guides, consultants and you will have companions so you will not be alone. Preparation is being made."

"I keep getting told that."

"Trust is the word, you must trust. We have trust and you too must have trust."

I then have a little preamble of thought and have to bring myself back to the scene.

"When the baby camel grows it will carry you wherever you want to go. You can be independent and you will not need a mother camel. You can go where you wish and the camel will take you."

15

I need to explain that Abdul el Faraz was a guide who had to help me in the early stages of communication. Why did he have to help me? I have been told that we had been together in a previous incarnation in which he had not treated me well. He now has to repay that debt before he can move on himself. I grew to love him and have seen what he looks like. I have even been able to draw him which in itself is amazing since I am not skilled at drawing faces.

CHAPTER TWO

I am learning fast that if I ask a question I get answers most of the time and this moves the experience forward.

MAY 4TH 1992

THE BEAK/BIRDMAN (his first attempt at contact)

My friend the birdman has come. In a very strange voice: "I am pleased to be here to help you, to give you…"

Oh: the pain in my head was too much to take and he left. Obviously I am not ready for him yet. [this was Osishoo one of the first to make contact with me from other planets.]

MAY 10ᵗʰ 1992

CHILDREN UNDER DARK CLOUD

I can see a playground full of children, happy and laughing. They are not in an enclosed space, they are all ages and I can see no adults. There is a big cloud growing larger over the sky. It is very black. It is coming over. It is growing dark. The children notice the dark and are puzzled. They don't know what to do. They are looking for guidance; they look around and hold on to each other for comfort and security. There is no dwelling for them to go to and there are no adults to show them what to do. They are concerned and worried by the darkness in the middle of the day. I have the strange one [Osishoo] with me.

Speaking in a strange voice: "I have come from another time and another place unknown to you." It ends.

MAY 24th 1992

DISTRIBUTION FROM STOREHOUSE OF KNOWLEDGE

After a little preamble I am given pale gold and lemon. The scene is the colour of gold. Spring and autumn, both colours. The stairs are granary stairs with dust and husks from ground grain. I ask to be taken to where I need to be as I don't know where to go. I am taken down and along to a wooden door, half and half door.

Inside is a mountain of grain, a store house of the harvest in a big heap. It's an enormous harvest all ready for use. There is an old man taking me around this heap, showing me. Here the concentration of the third eye is coming in. Very intense!

I have a picture of this very knowledgeable man who says:

"It is no good keeping this here to rot. It must be distributed to the starving thousands, millions who are starving for knowledge, for insight and for love. The grain is the harvest of love, work and wisdom. It must be distributed to those in need. There must always be some reserve for times of greater need. Further work must be made to ensure a continuation of supply. A certain reserve is necessary for times of winter, but do not allow the mountain to remain and rot."

I am getting my usual dribbles down the side of the mouth when it is an old person, an old man speaking.

He continues: "Think what one must do to obtain such a harvest. The first steps, prepare the ground, sow the seeds and nourish with air and water and light. Remove the invading weeds that would choke the goodness. Do not allow goodness to be strangled at birth. The harvest must only be handled with clean hands; it should not be contaminated, for fear of spreading contamination to those who would feed from this storehouse."

I ask to be shown how to go about distributing this wealth. I am taken to another door, an exit from the storehouse. It is bright sunshine outside and a fleet of lorries are lined up. That is alright, but there are no drivers. None of the lorries have drivers.

"It is symbolic. Movement must be taken to points where it is required."

Still no answer on the drivers! I get the feeling that I am to drive but I can't drive them all. Then I notice on the back of each lorry there is an 'L' plate. Learner drivers! What does that mean?

"People will come who are willing to take a load, but first they must learn how to use the vehicles. We will leave the rest up to your imagination."

I just notice something further. On the bonnet of each lorry is a flag, each one different. Different nations, and there are many. They are all standing in the bright sun, ready and waiting for those who are capable of steering and finding their way and managing the vehicle with the load. I have a very strong feeling of emotion over this scene. A very emotional feeling, not sad but I feel like crying.

I am given the colour of yellow, my colour. I am going down taking the sunshine and the light into myself. It is strange because I am walking on golden coins, real golden coins. It is also strange because as I walk along I am trailing a yellow light behind me, like phosphorous which is lighting everything up as I go. I come to a door covered in daisies. I am almost afraid to open the door for fear of damaging the daisies. I go inside but I can't see anything, so I am asking to be shown.

A voice from somewhere: "Over here."

I look around but I can't see.

"Over here."

I turn round. There on the floor is a dark Being. I can't clearly make it out as it is not lit up and is small. I have a feeling of a hobgoblin; it is that sort of Being. I am unsure! I turn round to face it and maintain a feeling of love, knowing that it transforms everything.

The hobgoblin takes my hand and wants to take me one way but I say: "No. We are going there." I can see a light in the opposite direction.

I repeat: "We are going towards that light", and I walk along, dragging the hobgoblin by the hand towards the light. He is pulling away but I continue. The light is a doorway, a bright light shining through the doorway. I push him through ahead of me. I have to push because he doesn't really want to go. But he goes through and I follow to the other side. I cannot see, the light is all I can see. I cannot see the hobgoblin…

Oh! He is no longer as he was. He is a tall beautiful Being, as one might imagine an angel without the wings. Beautiful, glowing figure and I know this is the same hobgoblin now transformed in the light. Beautiful, loving, a feeling I cannot describe. I feel very earthy and very ordinary in front of him even though I am yellow and previously glowing with light. I cannot be compared to him. I am very ordinary in comparison to this Being. I ask if there is anything he wishes to say.

"Go your way in confidence and trust and know that you are being guided and directed. Walk always in the way of light and truth. Walk always in the pathway of love for others. Have confidence and all will be well."

The glow is fading and I know it is time to come back. I retrace my steps in what now feels to me to be very dull and ill lit in comparison to the brightness of that Being. Back to the realities of earthly life and the greyness that requires illumination. (Here some of the original, for some reason, didn't get recorded.)

I know there are many messages coming from this experience.

MAY 27th 1992

BEINGS OF GRANITE SUPPORTING ME

Pink: a colour of gentleness and affection. Nothing violent. I go down and ask for guidance, to be told what I need to know. After a little drifting around I am shown pink granite. Beautiful it is. Smooth and not cold granite, it is warm and feels warm to the touch. Pink granite! Strong firm and solid and yet warm, gentle and pleasing to the eye. I think they are telling me that is how I must be because it is in answer to some of the questions that have been floating around in my mind.

Oh. This is lovely! Out of the granite face are stepping Beings, a variety, many. They are all coming out of the granite wall towards me. Oh, this is a procession and they are all coming out to help me, to assist. They are letting me know that I am not alone and in my dealings with others they will be there. They come from the foundation of strength and solidity, a rock to lean and depend on and yet a rock with compassion.

WRITING MY BOOK OF LIFE

A very deep magenta, which to me means knowledge. This is in response to asking to go to my very deep unconscious. I go down with a little apprehension, not fear. It is like treading into unknown uncharted territory. I go into swirling clouds. Looking through the clouds I see a figure sitting at a table. That figure is me. I am meeting me.

The figure [me] says: "I am writing our destiny. I can write whatever I want. I can make the story whichever way I choose. Whether it is acceptable to the publishers will depend on the quality and the grading of what is written. You have to act out this story. If the standard is low it will not be accepted and you will have to rewrite. Consider what attributes you would like to see in the heroine or main principal figure within a novel. What gives you pleasure and a feeling of attachment to such a figure?

When you have decided, apply those qualities to yourself and write them into the story. Other characters will be there, all the characters of an ordinary novel, those that tempt, those that aid and those that are part of the family and those who lead one astray. It is up to the heroine to choose what connections are made or disconnected. You can if you wish, in composing this story, put the ending first and weave your story to arrive at that ending. In this way you can…" My alarm clock went off to tell me to go to work.

As it did so the figure stood up and closed the book as if to say: "That is all. Time has run out for you on this occasion."

HALL OF MIRRORS

I go down very speedily though I have a lot of difficulty keeping my mind on this meditation and I wander off into tangents. Eventually I manage and go through into a perfumed room. It is as one would expect to see a hair-dressing beauty salon, heavily perfumed. I look around and notice that all around me, on the walls, are mirrors reflecting back.

I am to look into each mirror in turn. The room is round. I go to the first one where there is a tall, smiling young man. I feel I know him. That is all I can see. Strangely I can't see myself as one would expect. I go to the second one and there is a little girl, a little girl of about twelve, looking a little unsure. There is a country scene behind her. I go to the next one and see a very old man, slightly bent but certainly not ailing. It is just an indication of age. He looks at me with very penetrating eyes. Blue eyes that look straight into you, not unkindly, but he knows everything that is going on.

The next, oh yes, a very tall, mature woman, not old but mature. She is one in authority, who knows how to manage things. She is in blue. She is knowledgeable and is a no nonsense type, but kindly. The next one…my goodness this is quite a parade! I can see a dog in this one, a large dog and he is with another man with dark hair and glasses. A strong upright figure and I feel he is on a different level to the others, almost in by mistake, perhaps not meant to be there. That is a strange thought. It is as if he has taken the place of someone who should be there. Not a stand in exactly, but he has found a vacant spot and stepped in. He shouldn't really be there.

The next one. I feel sure this is one of my guides. I feel sure this is Wang Lu. Yes, it is Wang Lu, although I can't see him distinctly I know it is him. There are many more, a long succession of mirrors reflecting some part of my experience.

ONE FROM OUTER SPACE

I hesitate over this next one because he is so large that he almost doesn't fit into the mirror frame work. In coming up so close the mirror isn't large enough to get it all in. He is not in recognisable human form but is a living Being, a real Being though I cannot say man or woman. It has a very large bald head, round, pear shaped. Very unusual, no eyebrows and eyes that are different and not as one would expect. The whole shape of the face and head is like an upside down pear drop with the fat part at the top and narrowing down very much at the bottom. It is difficult to read any expression. He is just there looking at me. I think the expressions are difficult because it is not what we are familiar with. Sloping shoulders more than us, very sloping. I can't see all of it because it is too big, too close. This one is meant to be there but it is a surprise and a puzzlement.

CRYSTAL FROM EARTH

The next one shows an empty scene except for a tree in the distance, a solitary tree. I am invited to walk into the mirror and walk towards the tree. It is a mirror door. I walk through it. As I do so I am moved to experience the physical feeling of the environment. The ground is hard and not quite rocky but bare. You might almost say dead with nothing on it. I walk. It is still, I cannot hear the wind or a rustle; it is still like holding one's breath in a vacuum, unreal and dreamlike. This is a strange experience, like being here and yet part of me is not here at all. I don't know which is unreal, what am I in or what? I am making my way to what looks like a tree. It is strange that it is on its own.

Something moves beside me, some little thing. So it is not empty after all. I keep going and have the feeling, though I cannot see, that on either side of me are whisperings, watching my progress towards that tree, like a bank of whisperings on either side. Shadowy Beings I cannot say I can see, but I know they are there and as one would just catch something out of the corner of one's eye and then on turning to look it is gone. It is like being watched by the unseen. I am still walking and have come a long way from the violet smell.

Close now to the object and I see it is not a tree after all. It is of the ground risen up. What is it? It is solid, solid, a bit like an obelisk and although it is part of the ground it doesn't appear to be natural. It is like a giant long crystal with a point. That is why it is of the ground and yet has the appearance of being cut, pointing up. It is enormous.

I look into the crystal from the outside and can see on the inside what appears to be slopes, pathways up. I know this isn't so but that is the appearance…one can imagine mountain scenes and pathways and even Beings inside the crystal, and yet my mind tells me that can't be. There are paths going in different directions, going up all the time encased in this clearness. It is blue, not like any blue I have ever seen. I cannot describe the blue as it is not like any blue I have ever seen, I could almost say an ultra violet blue, an unreal blue.

From the top, the point of this crystal is a beam, pure dead straight and not wavering. A beam straight up; white. Those whispering Beings are around me on the ground. I have only just noticed them again. They are no longer hiding, they are all around and observing my observations and my reactions. In fact I am not reacting but am just absorbing and noting and wondering. It is wonderment at the enormous great crystal springing from the Earth in an empty landscape, at least to my eyes at the moment, though there must be more I can't see.

There is more but I am not to see yet. This crystal is sufficient and it is sufficient to know there are Beings. It is sufficient to know that they know that I am there. It is sufficient for the moment. I wish I knew what this is telling me. It is sufficient, they said to register for the moment. I keep getting told 'it is sufficient' so I feel I must retrace my steps. In fact I don't need to retrace all the way, it is a long way. I am back in the room, stepping through the mirror and stepping through the room of violets.

I have been sent on that journey and others are there to make sure I come back. They were watching over me to make sure I return. I am back and I don't need to continue around the room, though there are other mirrors I haven't looked into. I feel I mustn't yet. It is sufficient to know that there is more to come. It is like starting school and knowing quite well that each year and each course as it is taken leads to yet another course.

"The knowledge that there are more courses is sufficient. One cannot do them all at once. One step at a time."

I still don't understand why I got that scene.

"Don't try to understand it, register it and hold on to it. It will be clear at a later date."

*

I have just been brought back to reality by the sound of the washing machine working. That really has brought me back. Though they are still with me and the power is still there. Well, I am back and the whole thing took an hour which surprises me really. It didn't seem that long and I still do not understand. No doubt they will explain it in due course as they said they would.

JUNE 20th 1992

GUIDANCE SINCE THE DAWN OF MANKIND

I go down a staircase covered with animal skins and am wearing an animal skin. I ask where it is leading me.

"To the dawn of mankind, to man's early beginnings."

I go through into a cave and look around. There are, as one might expect, groups of humans from early times. There are babies, families, and standing in the midst of them is a glowing angelic figure. A glowing smiling figure which says:

"Even at the dawn of time we have been here watching and guiding. Even in the early beginnings of mankind there has always been guidance."

I ask: "What am I to learn from this?"

"There is no area of time or place where we are not present, where we are not watchful and sending our love. There is no time when this is not so from the dawn on."

I ask if I might approach and be embraced by his light and his love.

He smiles: "Look down, you are already encompassed with the light, you already have the love."

I look and my being, not only my clothing, my being was glowing with an orange light. There was a glow from myself.

Then, a very sobering message; "You are to go where there appears to be no light into the dark areas. You are to go and make it possible to see."

I reflect on this for quite a while and think, *What do I do? What do I do?*

"You will know when you are ready."

JULY 6th 1992

LIBRARY OF PAST EXISTENCES

A beautiful sapphire blue. I go a long way down. I go along my passage and turn off to the left. Instead of my normal door on the right there is a heavy dark door at the end of the passage. It is solid and I must try to open this door. It won't be easy.

In fact it is easy. I just walk straight through it. It remains closed and yet I walk straight through it. I ask to be shown what I must see and feel a tug on my clothes. I look down and see a little girl. She is tugging me and is going to show me where to go. She holds my hand and walks me along. I am moving like a rusty tin can. Clunky and jerky. How peculiar! I am just like a rusty piece of machinery. As I thought that, the words:

"And He anointed my head with oil," were spoken.

I then had a mental picture of somebody with an oil-can as I walked past, putting oil on my head and it was running down. They are still keeping the theme of machinery up because I am walking through what would be the equivalent of a car wash. It is a narrow pathway through with jets coming out from the sides, but this time it is oil. It is very non literal this, all symbolic. They are oiling me up for smooth movement. On the other side of this I feel quite loose and at ease. Ease of movement and I see it has been necessary for there is an opening not a door. I must go through this small opening. It is necessary to slide through, which I do.

I am in an enormous library, round shaped with a domed ceiling with books as far as one can see. It is enormous, galleries running round it with books right up high. Everywhere the eye turns there are books.

"These are records. They are your records. They are all yours."

That is funny because I always imagined the records would be in one book only and these are in many sections. A book for each existence. Goodness me!

I am reminded that I am writing the latest book and it must be worthy of all the others.

"It must be of good quality."

I notice in the middle of all this there is a table. Somebody is sat there, an old man reading. He is reading the story that I am writing and it is ME. It is my original ME, that is what I feel.

He says: "And how are you going to work out the situation this time? How are you going to solve this particular presentation? You write it, write it correctly and with satisfaction. It is all in your hands and nobody else's. Do not expect others to write your book for you. They are too busy writing their own, even if they are not aware. You alone are responsible for the content of the pages, you and no one else. You may utilise reference books. You may call on others for ideas; you may do a little research to get the facts straight. You may look up old records to see how things were done previously but you in the end are the one to put pen to paper."

I wonder why I got the picture of a rusty old machine being oiled.

"The machine, as you call it, has been in existence a long time and the moving parts have not been used to the full extent and have become a little stiff. We are attempting to ease the movements of the various sections of the body and the mental processes. All parts were in perfect working order at the outset when the machine [body] was created. We are attempting to restore to perfect working order and to put into action the assets and the gifts you were given at inception of time."

*

I would have liked to have stayed there but I had to finish to go to work. I thanked them and came back. Rather hastily, I have to add, because I suddenly realised that I had been with this one for quite a long time. I finished only just in time to leave for work.

My job at the office was becoming an interference in my mind, but earning a living was essential.

JULY 17th 1992 *(my 58th birthday)*

CHILDREN LOOKING TO ME FOR HELP AND PROTECTION

The colour is silver and I reflect on this and have a little wandering away in thought. I ask myself what I am wearing and see that I am in a shining silver coat of armour. Soft, not hard, this is very strange.

"It is not symbolic of protection; it is symbolic of a knight going forward."

I push open with my shoulder the door I must enter. It is quite gloomy inside and I look over to the spot where I expect to be shown something of enlightenment.

"Lay down your arms. They are not needed here."

I realise that I am there to give protection not to be protected. I feel and suddenly realise that I am surrounded by little children tugging at my garments for attention and trying to be close. There is a baby further away. I go towards the baby. A peaceful, bonny child. I pick it up and am swept by a wonderful feeling: a feeling of love and protection with the protective instinct of mother's love coming out very strongly. All the children are clamouring to be close and each of them individually wants my attention. I wonder why they are all there.

"They look to you as a child looks to a grown-up for supply of the things that are needed in life. They look for comfort and warmth and love, as well as education and supply of creature comforts. They look to you for nurturing, guidance and the knowledge that they can put their trust in you. You have in fact been entrusted with many lives, many souls' development."

"I don't understand the suit of armour, the chainmail."

"The garments you are wearing are symbolic of invincibility. It demonstrates to those souls gathered around that you are invincible and cannot fail to win through and so their trust is reinforced. They feel protected and strengthened."

"What must I do with these people, these children? I can't leave them here now I have found them."

"Take them into your heart and your thoughts and hold them within. They are representations; they are turning towards truth which is as strong as steel, invincible. They turn to truth for their own pathway."

31

I look up and suddenly I see a glowing light. A Being is with us, a Being that will help in my endeavour. I am not alone. There is Greater Protection, a Greater force that encompasses all of us. This Light, this Being is keeping watch.

I say a prayer, asking for help and feel a great presence. As I finish I notice all the children have laid down and are going to sleep around me. They are at peace and all is quiet. I am left with a feeling of a Presence.

Emotion hits me as I leave.

ALL CAN ENTER THE LAND OF TRANQUILLITY

I am travelling up in what appears to be a moving column of a sunlight beam with dust particles in it, or as gold dust, suspended within this beam. It is as you would view a shaft of sunlight with dust in it. It is moving upwards as if on an escalator and I am part of that beam, one of those dust particles and I travel upwards with all the others. As we reach the top it levels off and spills over onto the ground. I pick myself up and look about. Immediately I see a hole, a gap. It is such as you might find in a river flowing into an underground cavern, a mouth type hole with the star dust pouring like water into the hole. I know as I look into the cavern that I have to jump in, go into it. I can't see where it is going. It is going to take a little faith to just jump and let myself go into this deep cavern.

After some hesitation I jump. Immediately it is like being in a water chute, being swept along the twists and bends. Not at all unpleasant. I tumble out at the end, quite safe into glorious light. There is fresh golden light, a scene, an expanse of beautiful countryside, golden and peaceful and calm and clean. Clean is the feeling, absolutely clean and fresh. No pollution here, no blackness.

I realise that two helpers have helped me stand up. They have been there waiting to catch me as I come out at the end of the tunnel. They made sure I am alright; they are not significant in themselves but are there to help.

"Dear God, where must I go now?"

Looking down I realise that my feet are in flowers. A nice soft feeling on my toes. Spring flowers and I know I am not hurting them. I stand there looking down at my toes and the flowers pushing up around them. I am afraid to move in case I break any. I am rooted to the spot and I wonder how I can move without breaking off these lovely things.

"Move! You cannot break and destroy the beauty and the soul of these pretty flowers, for their roots are firmly embedded and cannot be damaged by you or those who tread on them, for they will spring up again with fresh shoots and fresh beauty no matter what tramples them. No matter what passes over them the roots and growth cannot be stunted or damaged in any way."

I move off, feeling the coolness under my feet as I go. I look back where I have walked and it is as if I have never been. No mark of my passing. That is rather nice in a way. I wonder why I am here, what is the purpose of this visit?

"This land of tranquillity, glory and beauty, this experience is available to any who have the courage to enter into the golden tunnel of light, who take the plunge into the unknown without fear. They too can pass into the area where they may be given peace of the heart and of the soul."

I thought that was rather nice.

I wondered what my office colleagues would think if they knew where I went when I was not at work with them. I also knew that the spirit world wanted me to 'come out of the closet' so to speak. I was not ready for that yet.

ORIGINS OF SELF

Green is the colour I have. I immediately think 'pea-pod'. A bit strange!

"All alike in the same shell, but in fact unalike and none identical to the other. We are all in the same casing of a body, each casing is slightly different to the other, and no pea is actually like its brother – each pod is attached to the branch, and each branch is attached to the main stem which is grown from the Earth, the Earth with all the elements for life reaching down and drawing what it needs to provide nourishment."

With that thought I slide very quickly back through the corridors to origins of myself, back through the corridors to my beginning in the Earth.

"I give you a picture of the original seed being placed in the Earth by the hand of God. So it is not your original beginning, it is yet another beginning, from the pea derived from the pod, from an earlier time and so it continues. You have been placed in the Earth for growth, in a particular position chosen and prepared and well manured so that growth may be healthy, strong and reaching up and so the fruit from the one seed may provide nourishment to those who partake of it.

You are but one seed, but as you grow you produce many more, many more companions who will grow alongside, portions if you like of yourself, who will in their own turn branch away and become either nourishment or the origin of a new plant that will serve its purpose. There will only be a handful of seeds for continuation to produce yet more."

*

I wonder now, in my current time, from that last sentence if they were referring to the changes about to happen on the planet.

AUGUST 13th 1992

THE REHEARSAL

The colour is yellow and I go down in a lift wearing rustling silk. I can hear it as I move. I have gone through a bleached slatted wood door, bleached almost white by the sun. As I look around I see yellow on the floor. I try hard to see what it is. It is yellow corn that is laid out, not threshed but as flattened corn in a field. It is yellow, not dirty or brown, but a beautiful sunny yellow. I must walk over this which is not easy because my feet sink into it. It is not too difficult but I must keep my balance. I walk over it trying to not fall over and to keep a balance. It goes on quite a long way until at last I am on the other side and I can walk on firm ground again. Nice solid wooden floor, firm and clean on the other side of this corn. My clothes have stopped being rustling silk and have become a nice filmy material. Though I am still in yellow it is softer altogether, one might almost say feminine. It is diaphanous; it is the only word I can use, lovely.

There is a tug at my clothes, if one can tug at such flimsy material. I look down and there is a little figure. It is difficult to tell if it is a little man or little boy, a little imp, a little gnome, pixy, I don't know what to call him. A tiny little adult that is what he is. I don't feel I should take heed of him and keep looking around. There is a figure, a big dark figure, only dark because he is silhouetted in a doorway with the light behind. He is a figure of strength and energy. I feel that is where I must go. If the little man wants to come then that is his decision but I must go to that figure standing in the doorway of light.

I walk towards the Being. As I get near I can see he is smiling in a benign way and is welcoming. He stands aside and allows me to go before him, out into the light that is coming through the doorway. I go out into the golden light and know that he is following and feel his hand on my shoulder. It is a hand of energy and the energy goes through me. I feel charged, charged in more ways than one, like plugging into an electric socket, not unpleasant. I am also charged with responsibility.

As my eyes become accustomed I see that I am on a floodlit stage, I cannot see beyond the light but I know standing in the light that I am on a stage. Beyond are faces and ears, waiting. They are waiting for what I am to say. At this point I don't know what I am to say but I have his hand on my shoulder. It is a support and I know that while it is there I can remain calm and confident and wait for what is to come. It is sufficient for now to stand and feel towards these faces a great love and a great yearning to help and to give them what they have come for. There is a feeling of expectancy but neither I nor they know what it is that they will be given.

The Being pulls me directly in front of him and puts both hands on my shoulders. His light wraps around me also and we are both standing wrapped in the same energy field. I am drawn into his energy field and in doing so am protected and endowed at the same time. This is a preview, I feel as there is nothing forthcoming that this must be a rehearsal, a preview of a future event because I turn around and walk back through the doorway into the area where the corn is lying. I see that the little figure, that little man is still there looking a little dejected but had decided not to go through the door. It was open for him as well but for his own reasons decided to stay where he was with the grain.

BLESSING ON THOSE WHO TRUST

I have a picture of a little girl with straight hair leading two big dogs. The dogs are almost as big as she is. I can't think why I have got this. I hope they are going to tell me why. The dogs are leading her, although she thinks she is in charge of them as little girls will. They are large, amiable dogs. They are leading her down a steep slope.

They take her down through a wood, it is quite a steep path and she has to hold on so as not to slip. It is very steep indeed going down, but the dogs have boundless energy. They get to the bottom where there is a pool. The dogs jump in and are full of fun. The little girl is uncertain what to do. She doesn't know whether to follow. She doesn't want to go back the way she came because of the steep climb up. She is definitely very uncertain, but she feels they are happy so it must be alright. She takes her shoes off. She is a very old fashioned little girl, shiny patent shoes with buttons, white socks. She is very neat. She removes her shoes and socks and her little dress and goes in and splashes about. She takes hold of one of the dogs and climbs on its back and is beginning to enjoy herself. I still don't know the purpose of this scene but I will wait.

The dogs are going to the far bank so she has to leave her clothes behind. She gets out the other side with the dogs, still holding on to the back of one. He tries to shake himself but he realises that he mustn't because of his burden. They start to climb up the slope. It is a climb even for the dogs, especially for the one with the little girl on his back. There is no question of her getting off and walking, they know that and they go up through the trees slithering and scrambling a bit until they come out into a little copse, a dell I think you would call it.

They break cover and come out onto flat grass where the sun is warm. There on top, a little way off is a very familiar welcome figure, smiling and waiting for them to come. The dogs rush up, going mad, mad with joy and happiness. The little girl also runs towards the figure. She takes the hand of this wonderful person with absolute trust. He places her on his lap. The child is being blessed by the Creator, which is wonderful. The child becomes golden, a special soul, golden all over and it is only so because she followed, braved the water and crossed and had trust with no fear.

"All souls are able to do the very same, all souls who have courage and trust and the love of their fellow companions, be they human or non human. They too may make the journey to receive the blessing and receive joy. Remember material trappings and burdens that would hinder you may be left behind so the passage will be that much smoother and unencumbered. You may always, if you wish, return carrying gladness and joy with you to tell others of the journey you have made. Tell others that they too may so easily reap the same rewards and be filled with light that will remain with them. Indeed they may prefer to stay in darkness with all their encumbrances and remain burdened. Not all know of the journey that can be travelled with joy."

It is what you would term a happy scene. There is a picture now of the pool and you can hardly see the water for people crossing it. Word has got around and it is absolutely chocker block full with people. They have seen one child go and are not afraid.

AUGUST 14th 1992

EARTH CHANGES

I see tall mountains like the Alps with snow, but it is no longer snow.

"It is the red sand of the desert covering the tops and smoothing the sharp edges, filling the crevasses. They will be unrecognisable, no longer will they be scaled, no longer will they be subject to storms and high winds and the eagle shall be no more."

The sand is running down like sugar poured over, it is as if it is tipped onto the mountain tops. I see birds flying over the Alps. They are not eagles but are of wider wingspan.

"They are the vultures that appear out of nowhere as do the flies and the tormenting insects. They arrive apparently from no direction, no beginning, no growth, but immediately, as if they had been waiting. They will be well fed and will multiply. It is not a scene of despair, it is a scene of hope. You may think that very strange with the picture you have before you.

Remember my child, this one area is but a postage stamp upon the face of the Earth and there are many lands that will prosper and flourish where there was once desert and waste land. A reversal of positions both of a geological nature and of peoples. You might say, if you had the humour with you, that it was 'musical chairs' with which you are familiar. A change of position, a change of peoples, a change of culture. It is for the benefit of all, a humbling, a levelling and a great learning, an advancement. This must be for the good of all."

I have a picture of skin taken from a healthy part and removed to be implanted and to grow over a damaged area. It is just a symbolic picture.

"Implanted by skilled surgeons, we may add, in whom we have great trust."

The one speaking has a strange face. It is a very strange feeling as I would almost say he has no neck. It is just an impression I have. I can only see his eyes.

AUGUST 15th 1992

THE GROWING DISC

Purple is the colour and after a little wandering in the mind came purple and royal. I go down. At the bottom I wrap a purple cloak about me very tightly and a crown appears on my head. I wrap the cloak all the way round me as if I need it all the way round. The crown isn't mine but is given me to use. It is a little askew, looking a bit crazy. It is mine for the purpose of this visit only.

There is a door with a little panel of glass in it so that I can peer through before going in. I don't bother and just go straight in. Over on the right I catch sight of a vase with a very slim stem, more like a goblet really, only very large. I don't know whether even to call it a vase. It has a very thin stem like a goblet with handles. It seems to beckon me; I must go towards it and reach into it. It is very tall and being short I have difficulty reaching up and getting my arm down inside. I do this with difficulty and am feeling round on the inside. Standing on tiptoe my fingers just reach. I scrabble around the bottom. There is something round and hard there and my fingers manage to grasp it by using two fingers because my thumb won't quite reach as it is that difficult to get there. I manage with a little manipulation and persistence to get the object up the sides until I can grasp it with the thumb and pull it out.

It is a shiny — I hesitate to use the word coin because it has no monetary value but is a coin of sorts, a disk perhaps, I don't know! As I look at it, it is growing larger and thicker and heavier. On one side there is a beautiful man's face, very alive and moving and smiling. It is superimposed by thought upon this object which is now as large as my hand. It has grown. This beautiful Being is on one side, beautiful and very much there. I don't want to turn it over to see on the other side because I don't want to lose the sight of this one. I keep looking and it is making me smile back because it is having that effect.

I am moved by it. It is a smile, one of love and warmth, everything. Everything a person could wish for in another being. The disc is getting larger and larger and I can't hold it any more. I have to put it down as it is getting so heavy. It is filling my arms. I lay it gently to the ground with

41

great care and tenderness. It is still growing; it is becoming a platform, a dais so large. The face is just in one corner, the corner? There is no corner but it is telling me without words to stand on this, this platform, this dais. It is growing and filling the area that I am in and I know that I must step up on to it before it becomes too big for me to reach up. I have to climb up because I cannot just step on.

So I climb up on top and at once I feel different. I am also caught in the magnification. I am growing with it. It is not unpleasant and the face of the man is no longer just a face. It is a Being standing beside me. He has just straightened my crown which is slipping a bit and the folds of my cloak have loosened and they are draping softly, not wound tight, it is more natural. The man's arm is across my shoulders in a protective gesture, like being under his wing. I feel rather insignificant beside him and wonder where this journey is ending. I look down in answer to the question and see we are standing on a map of the world. It is spread out and is covering all the areas of the entire globe. As I look down the map moves beneath our feet. Rather as clouds scud over the sky, the picture of the world is scudding over the surface of the platform, to cover all the corners of the Earth. We are looking at it and standing on it. I am feeling a little giddy as one does when one stands at the sea's edge and the waves come in and out. Your feet are on firm ground but your head becomes a little dizzy with the movement below.

The crown on my head is now a firm fitting and I notice that at the far back edge of the coin/platform there is a flight of steps leading off. I feel I must go down these steps. Not many of them, just enough so one doesn't have to jump down. It is easy. We go together and walk down the steps. There is no floor as one would expect – it is into clouds, beautiful dreamy clouds. The clouds are illuminated, lit up by a glow. It is almost gaseous and penetrates everything that enters it. It is all colours, changing colours. It is hard to grasp as it is wispy, difficult to catch hold of. I know it is alright because I still have the hand on my shoulder and we are going together. We walk into cloud, a vapour of colour. Harmonious colour I have to say. There is nothing harsh. It is gentle and soft and dreamy, very dreamy.

At that point I know I must come back and although I know that if I carried on I would reach heaven, I mustn't carry on. I must come back to where I came in. My time is not ready for heaven, my time is not yet over and I must come back. I did so with a big sigh.

42

POOL OF VISIONS

After some preamble I am given red and green, both very strong in colour and vibrant. I get the feeling it is Earth and the energy of the Earth. That is very good, I feel that is right. My stairs are green grass; cool to the feet, a luxurious feel of soft thick grass under the toes. As I go down there is a beautiful feeling of red energy field, hovering, it seems, over everything. This is a vivid strong red aura one might say, over everything. I am going down to the heart of the Earth. As I go deeper the darkness is illuminated by colours of red and green. Everything is reverberating with this colour; absolutely everything that is visible has this aura which lights the way for me. All I need do is follow the light, this strong deep colour.

It is all closed in. It is not open and I am walking through tall passageways of rock, no end to the height which is coloured. I slip my way through and eventually find my opening which is a slit in the wall. I slide through this quite easily and find myself in an expanse which I can investigate with my eye and see what it is I am brought here for. There is a reason for me to come this way. As I look around words came to me:

"I am spirit."

Then follows a thought that I must remember to see what I am wearing and it came again.

"I am spirit." There is nothing in the way of clothing to see. The energy field is strong in my head. I can feel this both consciously and where I am. It is extremely concentrated in my head and I don't feel alone. I am being guided.

Over in the far corner in front of me is a gushing stream of water, gushing out of a cleft in the rock at a really fast speed, flowing down the rock face and settling at the bottom spreading out as a pool. Quite a tranquil pool considering the force of the water. Everything still has the red and green glow which illuminates everything. It illuminates dimly, not bright. It is a dim illumination and if it were not there I wouldn't see anything.

I am fascinated by the pool of water. It is important I feel. I walk towards it. It is quite contained though there must be an outlet somewhere or it would flood the entire place. I walk over to it and the water is dark due to the lack of light but it provides a good reflection. *I am losing my words here for some reason.*

I must bend over and look and use it as a mirror, it is perfectly still. As I bend over I see a face, a lot of blond curls on a square face. A man's face, tight blond curls, longish hair. It is difficult to put an age but it is not my own face I feel. That I see because it is smiling at me as if to say hello.

BREATH OF GOD ON CARGO OF SOULS

As I was finishing with the pool of water, another hand, a different hand came and drew a finger across the water. It wasn't my hand. The water broke into a thousand pieces and didn't settle. The picture was on the water in its broken state of a ship, a full galleon ship driven by the wind, driven hard by the wind. It was in no danger; it was speeding, going at all haste with its cargo of souls to its destination.

"Where is its destination?" I ask.

"The final destination is totally dependent upon the minds of the men within. It may be washed on a deserted shore, it may be brought safely into the harbour of the land of plenty and sun and joyousness. It may be broken up on the rocks beneath the waters and the ship and the men within scattered to all points of the compass. It may ground gently upon a land that requires long and arduous cultivation to provide a living. The destination will be dependent upon the minds and thoughts of those carried in that vessel. It is not our dictate; it is according to THEIR will. They direct their own destination."

Then a wonderful thing happened, the hand that had created this picture, an enormous hand, reached over and plucked the ship off the waters, the entire ship in its palm and held it gently. I knew that the ship was breathed over, blown gently upon. I could see the breath and the mouth. It was a soft gentle wind, a breath breathed over the ship [*the Earth*] with its cargo of human souls and placed gently back on the water.

I feel it is a blessing from God upon humankind, a helping hand, a desire from the Creator that these souls utilise their wills with love. I feel emotional about this because it is so beautiful. A breath of God on humankind, what more could we want? This has made me cry because we all need it.

I try to regain my composure so that I may continue, but how can you follow an act like that. It is not possible. Suddenly I notice that the water has disappeared. It is bare rock but the glow is still there and a little brighter. I feel that that indeed must be all I am to see and it is certainly quite sufficient for anyone.

AUGUST 17th 1992

MY PAST DEATH

I am given purple and my first thought is, Purple? Not again!

A voice said; "Yes, purple my child. Accept it. Accept the spirituality of the colour."

I do and prepare to go down my stairs. I go straight into a hall of purple. I see one of those very tall gallery type halls that one gets in stately homes, seemingly endless. The ceiling is so high that I wonder how they manage to get up there without scaffolding. I walk around and down the gallery- that is what I shall call it, looking at all the pictures on the wall until one in particular takes my attention. It is the eyes of a man in the picture that holds me. It appears to be of the period with large hats. I'm not sure if it is the Cavaliers, I always get them mixed up.

The most gripping thing is the way the eyes look, most intense and following. It is almost alive. As I look I see a scene in the eyes and I take myself into it. It is a village, a street in the village with houses and cobbled streets. It is not of this time. It is back in time. I hear carts noisily going over cobblestones and sounds of children playing, women calling and the murmur of men as they gossip on the corner. A quiet, peaceful, natural village scene, quite peaceful.

I ask myself, *what am I doing here, why am I here?* I see a doorway and since it is brought to my attention I know I must go through it. I go in and there is a flight of stairs. It is quite dark and unlit. I go up the stairs and turn round at the top. There are bare boards. I go along the landing to a room at the far end. In the room there is a – I am not sure if it is a man or a woman lying on a bed – a sick person. It is a woman. She is very sick; it is difficult to see her age as she appears to be wavering before me between old age and middle age and then again a younger woman. I cannot pin the changing picture down. She is looking out at me with old eyes.

The eyes have seen much and suffered much. I go over to the bed and kneel down beside her and take her hands in mine. They are strong but very tired hands. I hold them and they feel good to hold. I release one and put my hand on her head and stroke her brow and whisper a blessing on her that she may be peaceful and enjoy the rewards that are her due for all her striving. She smiles at me and I feel sure that this woman is me. It is strange. I feel it is me.

She quietly closes her eyes and relaxes, happy and peaceful, and drifts off into what I feel is her last sleep. I pull the clothes up to her chin and get up. I see there are other people watching; standing in reverence with their heads down, so I walk out of the room, back down the stairs and into the sunlight. I don't know why I have been brought here, what the purpose is other than to give this lady peace and a happy end.

Suddenly I notice a well in the middle of the square. I go over to the well and draw up the bucket. There is just ordinary water inside. I take a drink and it is cool and refreshing. There is a little dog by the side of me so I cup my hands and he too has a drink from my hands. It is nice to feel his tongue on the palms of my hands. It is a contact with an unsullied soul, one who trusts without question.

I am still seeking for the reason for me being here. I feel that nobody can see me except the dog. I am still in my clothes that I am in waiting to go to work. I have not changed my costume and I feel like a visitor, an unseen visitor from a time not of this scene and I know I must come back and go to work now.

My need to earn a living and continue with my job began to take precedence over meditations. I frequently began to question the time it took not only to meditate but to transcribe everything that happened. Often a large part of my weekends off were taken up with the task. Then I had a dream. It appears that spirit will always find a way to prompt further action.

AUGUST 19th 1992

BENEATH THE SEA

I am dressed in pale green and go up holding on to a silken hand rail. The steps are clean and smooth with hard edges. Everything is very clean cut. I go up and up and up. When I get to the top the floor is shiny like glass and the walls are also shiny – hard lines. Nothing soft except the colour. It is like walking through musical chimes.

As I walk I hear the sound of chimes, like tinkling wind chimes, musical, gentle but clean. The overall feeling is clean, absolute purity. Even the sound is clean and sharp, but beautiful. I ask myself, *how can one hear a sound yet not hear it?* I could hear the sound in my head but not hear it with my ears. It is like a memory of sound.

As I walk on, the scene in front of me is a vast ocean. That is all I can see, the ocean as far as my eye will go and nothing else, an enormous expanse as if that is all there is in the world. I am to go in the water. It is strange as there is a tunnel into the water. I enter the tunnel which is not an earthly tunnel. It goes in under the waves perfectly safely. I follow my eyes and go in perfectly secure knowing that the ocean is above me. I am well aware that this is not a natural state to be in.

I keep walking. It is translucent so on all sides one can see the water but it is perfectly secure from the pressure. I keep going. I notice that there are corridors off on both sides. I keep going until I see one which is lit. Obviously that is the one I must go into.

I turn a corner and there spread before me is a living area: tables, chairs, different from the normal. It is for my eyes but not necessary. It is to make me feel comfortable, no more. There is someone; I cannot say a man, I cannot say a woman, it is a form that I recognise. I recognise it as a Being, I cannot say what. It is vibration at top speed, if it were to slow down I would see the shape, it is a vibrating mass of something, someone that is real but is spinning too fast for me to see its form. The form tells me not in actual words but tells me by thought that:

You are a creature of the water; you can make connection between the deep and the conscious any time you choose. You can come and go at will when there is a need for reflection in the quiet and to be undisturbed. The pathway is always open. You can visit and remain in solitude with your thoughts, your questions and sit quietly for communication. There will be no disturbances and you will feel perfectly at home as if it were your natural environment.

This was in answer to my question, what the purpose was for this visit and that is the response in thought from this Being.

He continues: "You may visit this quiet place at literally any time even during your working period with others present. You may in an instant transfer your mind here for the peace and tranquillity it gives. You have but to direct yourself."

There are loads of questions going on in my mind, one of which they answered. *What can I learn from being here if I have a certain problem?*

"Look through the walls of this room."

So I do and I see that the wall is a giant reflective surface of pictures and that I can see, as on a television screen. On the walls are answers to my questions, or at least some direction so that I may arrive at my own answers. I have a picture of Brian who I am sending healing to, sitting up and rubbing his eyes as if out of sleep, getting up off his bed and, strangely picking up a golf club and striding off. I should explain that Brian is a friend was recovering after a heart attack and still in hospital.

I mentally ask if they would shut me down in time to go to work.

They smile: "You have but to ask, that is all that is necessary. You have but to ask at the outset to cease this transmission at the time you require to close."

I think: *that's handy!* They then present me with a swivel chair, very comfortable so that I can swivel round and face any wall to have a change of scenery if I wish. It is to make it as comfortable and as convenient as possible. I can even go to sleep here if I want, if I feel it is necessary.

Then he says: "Too many questions at once, centralise your thoughts a little more, my dear. Do not throw them all in one heap and expect coherent answers. You would not do that to anyone with whom you were discoursing. You would never throw questions of all varieties and all sizes and all complexities at a person in one go, so why do it here? Concentrate your thoughts and ask at least one question in turn after another in an orderly fashion. You will learn."

49

AUGUST 21st 1992

A dream – QUEUE FOR ASSETS

I am in a queue at a bank waiting for my turn. Someone points out that number 29 is next and I looked down and realised that I am number 29, I hadn't noticed that they went by numbers at banks but this IS a dream. So I go to the cubicle right at the end on the left. The lady there is looking round to see who is going to come. She looks at me and smiles. She is not what I expected and not as I imagine a normal bank teller would be.

She asks: "How often is it that you come in?" It is clear to her I don't know what to do about this number business.

So I say: "Oh, not often, once or twice a year". I explain that I work and can't come in the week. She starts explaining about social get togethers, guitars and things and I think, *well what that has got to do with the bank?* She asks if I play the guitar and I think, *what a funny question.*

There I am in a bank and she puts her finger under each of my eyes and says, "There is a light here under your eyes," and then starts to give me a reading.

I realise that she must be a medium or psychic or something when she stops.

I say to her: "Don't give up."

A little voice says from somewhere: "**You have**."

That really upsets me and I protest: "No I haven't, I haven't. You have got it wrong, I haven't given up." That is when I woke up thinking, *what a funny dream.*

My interpretation of this at that time is that the Bank teller is in the position of giving out assets. I am waiting not realising it is my turn because I don't go often enough to know the routine. I am not going to receive the goodies, the information, sufficiently enough. The communications are the assets so it is not money, it is esoteric help. She starts giving to me but then stops because I am not using them or accepting them.

AUGUST 21st 1992

BABIES BLESSED

I have a picture of babies. The whole area is covered with new babies, all lying in little cots, moving their arms and legs, perfectly happy. Many: a sea of them. There is a golden light that I have been drawn into and which is spreading over them all. It is as if they are being washed in the golden light for a special reason.

"They may appear as babies but in fact they are not as they seem. They are the promise of a blessed beginning, each covered and bearing the mark of the golden envelopment. They are each and every one marked with the blessing that is to protect them and envelope them in a purpose for their next existence. Those ones who at this time are leaving incarnation and are glad to do so, these ones too will receive the golden aura that is being bestowed."

I have a picture of all the starving children that are dying at the moment and I feel that it is these children who will be blessed.

AUGUST 29th 1992

WIND OF ENERGY

The colour is pale blue silk and the stairs are wide clean marble. At the bottom is a very wide passage, clean and un-encumbered. The main route, very wide such as you would see in the entrances and exits to an underground station. Totally uncluttered and clean and there is my opening to the right. No door, everything is easy. I turn into this. There is a great energy with me; it is coming in very rapidly like a great wind. I must join this force and step into it and be swept along with it. The energy is also within me but I am to enter the main rapid stream that is flowing past from left to right.

I step in and immediately am swept forward. It is as you would feel if you were in a strong wind and the wind was blowing from behind. You would be pushed along without being able to resist. No effort, just go along with it. The journey goes on a long time and eventually I am shot off to one side and dumped rather unceremoniously into a lit area.

There is a man waiting, an old man. Waiting it seems for new arrivals and I am one such. I walk towards him; this is the one I have come to meet. He is very venerable, very kindly, but must be treated with great respect which I have no difficulty in feeling. I stand before him and wonder what I am to do next. He says not a word.

*

Stupidly this is where I ran out of tape and now a day later I am having to recount the events which is not the same as when it happens.

Any time I could enter the force of energy to receive words of wisdom. I have to say I can't remember much more which is stupid, isn't it? This just shows the importance of recording.

52

AUGUST 30th 1992

FUTURE MOTHERS

After being given rosy red and feeling the energy build up and swirl all around me, I am given the picture of a lot of little girls in school uniforms running down a hill, running fast. One or two slip and fall and slide down, pick themselves up and carry on running. They are not frightened but just in a great hurry. I don't know what this is meaning.

"They are running to listen to a speaker and are anxious not to miss the beginning. They want to find themselves a place that is favourable to them hearing every word. The words are for future mothers, those who will nurture the new ones, the leaders of your planet, and those who have been chosen to help humanity through difficult times. There will be as much importance attached to the mothers of these little ones who will become great in stature and will be of great value to all. The words these future mothers are to hear are of vital importance. Those who instruct the mothers such as this speaker, must choose their words wisely. They must choose words so that they remain within the conscious mind and are not forgotten and buried."

I have a picture of nationalities from all over the world, young girls of all races in giggly groups, gathering to listen in their own areas to speakers chosen for them. They are but giggly youngsters at this moment but the words will reach their hearts. They will appreciate the importance of their future role which they are to play, all races.

I have a picture of somebody going around and looking at great gatherings of children and pointing a finger and saying 'that one and oh yes, that one, this one' and choosing from among the gathering, those most fitted and most suited for this role of encouraging and nurturing and instructing their infants.

I have been asking many questions and have been to the high levels of vibration. I have someone with me now, someone who I know but not by name.

WORKING ON THE PLAN

I am in sea green and have slid down, deep down into myself with the sound of water. Right the way down. I am being edged forward by a surge of water at the bottom. It is like a watery tunnel. I am pushed along and swept into an opening where there is a throbbing, steady throbbing. It is the engine room to make things go forward, it is a concentrated effort for smooth running. As I look I see little figures dotted about all working away, all knowing what they are doing, all intent on their task, making preparations, working hard for the project. It will be one project, the result of the efforts of these individuals who are there to help. It is all to be put together.

I look around as a visitor, one might almost say a prospective client come to see how things are getting on, not as an overseer but as one who will use the end product and so have an interest. I walk through and enter the office area which is well lit. There are older Beings, heads huddled, discussing the project and putting their ideas together formulating the plan. They see me and motion me to sit down. I feel I am merely the executor of the plan. It is the plan that holds importance. That is where the attention must be put.

As I sit here I feel un- it is difficult to find the words – as I am unaware of what they are discussing I sit here looking around and trying to find something of interest in the surroundings, trying to look intelligent one might say, because I don't have the knowledge to understand what they are discussing. I am merely there for their purposes.

I know that there is trust in me and that when the plans are completed then attention will be given so that I execute and carry out the plan according to the programme. I will be entrusted with the final stage. At this point that time is not yet and there is further work to do, I must merely prepare myself.

SEPTEMBER. 5th 1992

THREE GUARDIANS IN THE OASIS

Corn yellow silk is the colour; the walls are white rough walls. I go along to the only door with a handle and go in. I feel sand beneath my feet, a sandy ground. I am not in a closed in area but in a green desert oasis; a green island with shade and water and peace, solitude and quiet, no disturbing noises. It is very tranquil and I am here to take my ease.

I am not alone. I have with me my three Tuareg guardians. They are forever at watch, quietly monitoring and controlling many happenings. They are there as a support, a protection and as guides. I can depend on them and cannot continue without them. I can see them making more preparations, gathering things together, watering the camels, packing things on their backs and generally being very busy.

I ask: "Is there anything you have to say to me, anything I should know?"

The one with the eyes looks at me; I feel his eyes are lovely. He imparts a sense of trust, that I can trust in him and must simply put my faith in them and they will lead me to where I am going. There is nothing I need do at this moment.

I ask: "Is it so that I must do this alone?"

He replies: "You are not a partnership, you are alone."

I knew he meant alone in my work not totally alone because they were there to guide me and to lead me and to safeguard. It is only I that has to do the work.

A great bird flew up, I can't tell what bird but it is a large bird, very large, an eagle or a falcon, something of that nature, very large. It flew up intending for us to see it.

SEPTEMBER 8th 1992

HEAVY CRYSTAL – BETHSHEBA

I go straight in. No stairs this time. I am in a very busy street with cars all coming towards me. I am trying to keep on the pavement. There is a lot of noise and clamour and a lot of fumes from the vehicles. It is extremely busy: cars, people and a lot of fumes and pollution. This is Manila, I just know this is the city of Manila.

After a lot of pictures I have been going back in time, like going backwards into a tunnel, back and back and back and I ask to be stopped at the right place.

I am a woman and into my hands and in my lap has been given an enormous crystal stone, all faceted, round, reflecting all light. It is put into my hands and is large and heavy. It must be rested on my lap or I could not bear the weight. Bethsheba is the name I have. I ask about my life's purpose, my soul's purpose.

"Use the stone to light up many lives. Each facet will light up a life to which it is directed."

*

At this point my nose and ears were filling up and broke me out of that. What a nuisance! I have to finish here as it is too much hay-fever.

56

SEPTEMBER 8th 1992

SNOW EVERYWHERE

I have been asking for a picture. I have had many thoughts but the picture given is of snow, falling hard, heavy and thick. It appears to be English countryside. The ground is covered thickly with white snow and is very deep. There are people struggling through it, trying to move about. The roads are paralysed. I don't know why they are showing this but there is a lot more coming.

"This has created paralysis in transport and deliveries and general movement from the workplace and the schools. In fact it appears to have paralysed the country."

I have asked when this is and they have said:

"It will begin early and finish late, it will affect Europe as well as your own country. Widespread transport will be disrupted."

SEPT 10th 1992

THE MOON'S EYES

I have a picture of the moon and of man standing on the moon and the weightlessness and the dust and the craters that are seen as eyes. It is strange because I look at the crater eyes with the movement of dust, and the eyes open like doorways, circular shuttered doorways with the shutters acting as eyelids. As they open one could go in to the interior. That is strange isn't it?

SEPT 11th 1992

FOOD FOR THOUGHT

I am recounting this slightly later, although I am still in the meditation state. I have been given yellow and have gone down what was at first wooden stairs. Then they became stone, going down ever deeper in a spiral, similar to what you would have going down into a circular narrow tower. Very dark and underground and I know the consciousness is very high above me. I take a little time for reflecting as I go, and I find a door which is huge and heavy. I realise that I must slide the big heavy wooden bolt to get in. I go through and again my thoughts play around in different areas and I have to bring myself back.

I ask where I should go and see ahead of me a dark passage to the right. I go down there and it suddenly opens out into a wide area. I look around and see two pillars, just two pillars. I know something is behind the pillars and so I look – this is very amusing – a hand is extended with food, a container of food. You might almost say like a lunch box packed up. As I am wondering about this and what a strange thing to be given they said:

"The food you have been offered, that you have been given, is food for thought, food for your mind and food for your soul's development and food for your spiritual body. It must be ingested and will feed and nourish your spiritual body. It is food for the mind and the spirit."

While they are saying this and more I feel a great upliftment; a soaring feeling and a lot of energy pouring into me, a good feeling. As I ponder on all this I realise that the food is all packed up for me in a nice little parcel and has been handed to me from the pillars, the pillars of the temple. Just handed to me and I know that they are referring to all that was given to me on Wednesday. It has been given to me from the spiritual source to be ingested by the spiritual body. I feel very good about this. Unfortunately I must now leave.

SEPTEMBER 11th 1992

BUILD UP FOR WAR?

I have a picture of a row of houses similar to those you get in the Cotswolds, looking all peaceful. It is a typically idyllic country scene and then a whole line of tanks come rumbling down past them. A convoy of tanks. What a strange picture to get! They are all fully armed and fully manned. It is not just an exercise, they are on the move; deployment, a gathering together of forces for deployment of action. There are tanks and armoured vehicles, lorries; it is a massed movement of troops from various bases around the country.

They are not in white or sand coloured; they are in ordinary army colour. It is not for the desert. They are all heading south, it is building up and building up and filling the whole picture. If it were not on the streets and in the countryside I would say it was similar to a military fly past- a parade – an army demonstration but it's not, it is for real. There is every conceivable type of preparation, bridge building, and the lot. It is incongruous because it is rumbling past a peaceful row of cottages. I have difficulty shaking that picture off.

I have a very beautiful loving person come in who shows me a picture of children playing in an orchard in what one might call an idyllic setting. Little children playing and completely oblivious to the cares of the world.

"The little children will not be affected by all this movement. They are to remain in blissful contentment and will not be traumatised. They will only be vaguely aware of the events going on around them and they will be protected. They are the important ones."

SEPTEMBER 11th 1992

WATCH ANIMALS SENSING VIBRATIONS

I am getting a picture of cats and dogs. I really don't understand this as there are a lot of cats and dogs. They are quite orderly. All colours and shapes, almost like a school crocodile all filing past. I ask what this is all about.

"They are living creatures, trusting, completely trusting blindly, in perfect faith. It matters not if they are unseemly or beautiful, it matters not."

What I am getting is that they are going the same way [direction].

"They have entrusted themselves to the care of humans. Both cats and dogs have much to offer in return for their trust. You do not avail yourselves sufficiently of the benefits to be gained. You should be more perceptive of the vibrations and should be more watchful and attentive of the attitudes and instinctive reactions of these animals. They will tell you and teach you much.

"Note well unusual behaviour, note well in the coming years. Note well bizarre behaviour. There are signs to be watched for which will act as an indication of unnatural occurrences. There are many of these animals all over the globe and will serve a useful purpose to those who have eyes to see and understand. They are more in tune than most other creatures. They are more aware of the difference in normal occurrences and that which is out of the ordinary and are readily accessible to those who are about them. The creatures of the wild are also aware but are not observed. This is intended to be of use."

I asked about horses.

They said: "Horses aren't in your living room." It is funny, I get the most bizarre pictures and they lead into something meaningful. There are a lot of smiles going on 'upstairs' today and it is a job not to keep grinning with them.

UNITING

Purple is the colour, purple slippers and a purple cloak over what appears to be a jumpsuit, rather incongruous but that is what it is. I know my inner self is down there in peace and quiet and that the self is serene and contented, simply waiting to be contacted. I come to a great big wooden doorway, though that is not the right description. It is more like a wooden entrance to a courtyard such as you get in Italy and France. There is a little door at the bottom and I go through this, which opens into an enclosed tranquil courtyard. There is a little fountain in the middle. Very peaceful, an oasis, even though there is hubbub and activity going on all around, this little area is in isolation and tranquillity.

I approach a figure sitting with his back to me. He is by the fountain in the middle, on the seat that runs round it. This is the one I have come to meet. I look a little incongruous in the cloak and jog suit, almost a ridiculous figure. Then I realise that the one sitting down is wearing the same garments as me, but it is a man and it doesn't look stupid for some reason. It looks quite fitting. The cloak is right and what on me appears to be a jog suit, on him appears to be perfectly natural – what can I say – it is a tunic and looks perfectly right. He stands up and turns round. He is very virile and all knowing.

He has an air of confidence and serenity that comes with knowledge and peace of mind. He takes my hand and leads me over to the far corner of the courtyard where there is a little door which we enter. It is dark inside. He is holding my hand so I don't bump into anything. We work our way through what appears to be corridors and passages going deep into this building, winding our way round things. I have absolute faith that he will not allow me to hurt myself on this journey even if it is in the dark. He doesn't need lights as he carries his own light.

We come at last to a very large room which is lit. It is right in the heart of a complex of buildings. It is the centre, throbbing with light and energy, like a powerhouse almost, strange, a powerhouse but with peace. It is a quiet strength, quiet but strong and vibrant. The walls of the room are shimmering. They are solid but there is a shimmer coming from them, a crystalline shimmer, very much alive. It is very old and beautiful, a place of absolute peace; that is the overwhelming feeling. Peace but with strength, energy and purity. It is unsullied.

We stand in the middle of the room, facing each other. As we do a big shiver passes over me and we merge into one. We become one being, neither man nor woman but a complete whole. We are strengthened, complete and the word is 'sanctified'. I have to use it as that is the word. There are no other words that can describe it. As I stand here I am viewing the room from the centre. The shimmering walls of tiny reflective crystals are sparkling and shimmering as I look all around.

The crystals are there but the sparkle and light is coming from us/from me. We are now the centre. The walls fade from vision because they are viewed through light which spreads out and out, almost pushing the walls outwards. With the light that is expanding from us the walls are forever pushing outwards and outwards and outwards, as would a ripple from a stone thrown into the water, so these walls are going out but they are pushed out with the light. One could say dissolved with the light which is forever growing larger as a circle, out and out, beyond. By the size it must be beyond this building. It is such a wide far reaching light. We are just standing still and being, no more than that, being with the light. I cannot describe. After a long session of standing there I know I must come back, I have to leave, and I have to return.

TEACHING ON MEANING OF MEDITATION

Silver is the colour. A thought on what meditation is comes to me and I feel I should put it on tape as a teaching aid perhaps. It is about meditation and the normal technique of relaxing the body.

"It is simple. Be unaware of your body just as when you watch television or read a book. When you are engrossed you are unaware of your body. Meditation is similar to being so totally engrossed in what you are reading or watching or imagining, so engrossed that you enter into it and become one with what you are absorbing, whatever it is. It is very much like becoming a child again, entering fully into your imaginative games.

"Imagination is all important and allows you to become a child again, that blissful existence where imagination is real and very much present. In that way you can tap in to your real selves and to your helpers by becoming a child again, but with the experience of an adult.

"How many times do you say, 'Oh, if only I knew then what I know now, I would have done things differently?' This is an opportunity to go back into the 'then' with the knowledge of the now and affect the 'then' with your thinking, and gain from the 'then' so that you may bring it into the now. It is a wonderful tool.

"Do not worry if you cannot relax your body. Providing you enter fully and become engrossed in your imagination and where you take yourself, then your body will automatically relax. It may appear to be after the event but it will happen, providing you have total absorption.

"That really is the secret of meditation. It is not the same as raising your vibrations, that is a slightly different thing and we will go into that later. I have to add that we are talking of guided imagination, guided with a purpose, imagination with a purpose and then your inner self, the child within you will take over, and being much wiser will lead you into many realms."

SEPTEMBER 14ᵗʰ 1992

NOT TIME YET

I keep asking to go where I want to go and they have said I am a persistent thing. I will never get there. They take me to doors – that is not the right word – portals is what I had better say, of where I want to be, but the doors are shut and they say:

"This is not the day, this is not the time to enter."

So obviously I am not going to go where I want to be, not today.

It is all pictures. I have a very high mountain with snow and there is a ski slope with somebody skiing down it fast, very good. I really don't know what that is supposed to mean. Let's see.

SKILLS REQUIRED FOR BALANCE

"It is a controlled and expert descent at great speed from the heights to the normal plains of living. For such a skier, much practice has been required to avoid a tumble and a breaking of bones. Such a one as you have seen is well versed in the skills in managing the slopes, which were needed to be scaled to enable the descent and to experience the exhilaration felt during such a run.

"Much hard work and endeavour is required to reach the peak but one must be able to descend safely and swiftly. It is not enough to reach the heights. Much more skill is required to regain your feet on level ground and is equally necessary. One cannot live forever on the peak, but having climbed the internal need to experience yet again, the exhilaration will forever be with you and you will not mind the climb."

Someone said laughingly: "There is always the chair lift!"

But that was a bit flippant because immediately they came back and said:

"There are no chair lifts on all peaks and those less frequented and at times never visited do not have facilities for chair lifts."

Looking back on this episode a year later I think that they were trying to tell me that I wasn't yet skilled or experienced enough to go where I had been pestering to go and wouldn't have been able to bring myself back safely had I gone. It has taken me a year to realise it.

SEPTEMBER 14th 1992

CHILDREN READY FOR BIRTH

I have someone I want to go to but they keep stopping me with pictures. I have another one. I have a picture now of a whole line of beds, like in a dormitory of sleeping children. Children again!

There is someone moving along the line very gently and saying, "Come on, come on wake up, it is time for you to get going."

They are shaking the children very gently from their sleep and saying: "Come on, get started now."

They are not here, not yet. They are to become children; they are to be newly incarnated souls, all coming together or as near as possible.

As they get up they are all, all of them surrounded by their own bright lights. I say lights because they are in varied colours, like little fireflies all darting about. This is an inadequate description

SEPTEMBER 20th 1992

ASKING AND GIVING HELP TO SICK SOULS

I have who I believe to be Raman the Rajah with me. I have been asking for help and direction. I feel that channelling is on hold.

I change my thoughts and I am now going downstairs in all nature's colours. As I go, I feel very sad and ready to have a cry. There is a great feeling of sadness. I go in and along my corridor and am having difficulty not to have a good weep. I don't understand it. I have a vision of myself, my head bowed on the table on my arm in sorrow, in sadness, I don't know why. I feel that I want to be sick, a real feeling of nausea. Then I have a vision of me leading a whole bunch of people who are in need, mentally and physically; sad sick people. I am taking them all together and am allocating rooms to them, settling them each in a separate room where they can be looked after and helped. It is like a soul hospital; they have come and have been directed to the area where they can receive help. Others more spiritual than I can take over from there, I am merely the director bringing them to the House of Healing.

MEDITATE DAILY

Once I get in they present me with a feather that I am clinging to. The feather is carried aloft by a white bird. I see a picture of me in a little white outfit, gown or whatever you want to call it. I am wandering up and down almost impatiently saying:

"Where am I, what am I doing, where am I going?" I pace to and fro. "I don't know what I am supposed to be doing. What am I here for?"

I know what I want but what will they give me? As I ask, a door at the far end opens and somebody there says: "Come in. It is open now, you can come in."

I go to the door and enter. Inside there are many tables. They are consultation tables and have somebody sitting at each one. Which one must I go to? As I look I get the feeling of a beautiful person with me, a smiling, gentle soul. She is both with me and at the table.

"You don't need to go to a table. What you need is within, it is with you."

I ask the question that is in my mind always: "What am I to do with my time to prepare?"

"Merely be. Do your meditation daily and allow your vibrations to increase and we will make the necessary arrangements for the next stage. Make yourself available. We ask for nothing more."

SEPTEMBER 25th 1992

CHOOSE CORRECT TOOL

The colour is green and purple – spiritual and earthly. Going down I am treading on what seems to be plants that have produced their fruits and their seeds, and have now been pulled up. I am walking on old pea pods, stalks and the sort of thing one has when one has cleared the garden out. It is not bad, just a strange thing to get.

"They are going to provide good compost which will give goodness to the garden for the next year. What is grown returns to the Earth to continue its benefit. It is pulled up and seemingly discarded, but is not so. It is adding to the quality of the soil for further growth."

I go along my corridor and lift the latch in a very tall wooden door and go in. It is a real jumble inside with all sorts of things.

"All the tools of the trade," somebody says. "But they are not in order. They are all thrown in anyhow. If you were to tidy this up you would see your way clearly to the tool that is required, instead of having to search for it."

I think, *how true*.

"You would choose the tool that you know how to use. You would ignore those you are not familiar with. Get your thoughts together and tidy up all the knowledge that you have. Arrange it so that it can be easily brought out for use. Polish up where the edges are rusty and blunt. Clean off all unnecessary mud and usage from previous times. It doesn't take long, all the tools are there at your disposal. It is a matter of arranging them into some sort of order ready in preparation for the next harvest.

"The dark nights and winter time is the right time for this task. It is the time for preparation, for ordering next year's stock, for ordering seeds for planting in the spring. There are one or two new tools that you will need. Make sure that these are of good quality and will not let you down."

I ask about my job and he says: "If you are not working you will have more time for your garden." This was a very symbolic message and clearly they want me to prepare for something.

SEPTEMBER 25th 1992

WOMEN'S ROLE

I think it is an African I have with me. He is black, or dark anyway. Rather tall with a large, rather tall head. A woman is bent over doing her washing in a stream and she is not English or European, I feel Eastern. She turns round to look at me. She has a nice gentle face, not old: yet very wise and very gentle.

"She understands from a woman's point of view. That is why she is presenting herself doing the washing. She understands the different attitudes given to the woman in comparison to the man. This has been the way of things going back many life times, many ages to the beginning of your own reality with the origins of your religion. But there have been previous times when regard for women was of a different nature. It will be so again. It is of importance that influence upon offspring is greater, present even before birth. It has a profound effect upon the subconscious thinking and subconscious mind. This naturally affects the subconscious of the male child as well as the female, but it is the female that will in turn influence yet further generations."

I ask why she is telling me this.

"Many women do not recognise that they are vital, indeed vital to the welfare and future of the Earth on which they live. Vital to the minds. They need not strive for positions of authority, for positions of management within the realm of men. They have authority of a greater importance."

It is more thought than words here; that the men provide the balance that is required, they provide the stability.

"We know that men are referred to so often as men of the Earth, the salt of the Earth."

A man came behind the woman and helped her up and in a supportive way helped her, not that she needed it. It was a gesture of support. He walked her away from the river. They are giving me the earthly connections with spiritual growth, the woman's role irrespective of social standing.

69

SEPTEMBER 25th 1992

HOSPITAL LIGHTS

They are taking me to the Healing Corridors where there is soft diffused light. Nothing is harsh but is gentle and peaceful, none of the bustle, none of the packed corridors as our earthly hospitals are at present. None of the rush and bustle but quiet orderliness, calm and peaceful. It almost seems deserted but it isn't. There are areas to which one goes according to the light that is most beneficial. There are different shades of colour. Looking down the corridor one can see the glow that is coming from the different entrances, all different colours.

"You go to whichever colour is required for you."

VIBRATION AFFECTS ALL

There appears to be, and it is on the edge of my hearing, music, but it is not music that I can say is a tune. It is more a vibration of sound which is pleasing to the ear, like music that I cannot describe. It is almost a sound that is beyond the reach of the ears. It is *just* caught, it is beautiful. One tries to hold on to the sound, a striving to catch the whole beauty of it but I can't bring it into full strength.

"The vibration is real whether you can perceive it audibly or not, it has the same beneficial effect as the music that you are able to hear. The vibrations affect just the same. There are many vibrations around you, even on your plane of sounds of which you are unaware but which have an effect on you none the less. Indeed many of the sounds of which you are aware are not so beneficial and do not help. Too many of these sounds abound. Blessed are they who have difficulties in hearing those more strident noises but even they are affected by the vibration upon them."

The corridors, they go on and there is one person that I can see more clearly. The light is changing, I was about to say purple then it changed. It changes according to the position of this Being in the vicinity of a particular doorway, almost like a chameleon. As this Being, a woman, passes the doorway, the colour changes rather like different coloured lights when you watch someone on a stage and they have different colour lights played on them. This Being's own light is there nonetheless and has its own individual colour. It is able to take on the light that is required for any given person and so it is with many. This lady is a very gentle Being in facial appearance as well. One moment young and the next moment old, then back. A kaleidoscope of love.

"A face of love has many faces, many aspects and takes on many colours. It shows great patience and great compassion for those who are not able to love or to receive love because they do not recognise it for what it is. Feel pity for those souls for they have greater need. These souls here do not have any more protection of physical ills, the protective cloak that they drew to themselves to cover the ill within. They do not have the barrier, the protective casing against the hurt or the damage they have inflicted upon themselves between that and their conscience, their souls. It is our aim, our work to enable these souls to rectify and put at ease the ailments within them."

As she passes each doorway she changes colour. It is lovely and as she turned round a beam, a ray of strong red came from her directly towards me. She might recognise me from that. I feel as if I am catching it in my hand and if I put my hand up I could direct that ray where it is needed. I can feel it.

My spirit helpers had not given up on their desire for me to leave my job. *Alright for you,* I told them. *You do not have to pay the bills.*

CHAPTER THREE

OCTOBER 1st 1992

LEAVE JOB TO TOTALLY COMMIT

Colour orange, gold and warm, one that makes you feel warm and cosy. I go down and through a door. It feels like a homecoming. I go into a warm rosy glow and as I stand there a lion comes towards me, a male, gently padding towards me very softly, solid and reassuring. We greet as old friends. I put my arms round it to hug it, pleased to see the lion again. I feel the dust from his mane; he is a little older than he was. I debate whether to get on his back or whether to walk beside it because it is going to take me somewhere. I hesitate between the two and in the end decide to walk alongside and hold onto his mane. He takes me back the way he had come; back down the passageway, almost a tunnel through. It is lit up in golden light all the way, reflecting on the walls. I go through with him. I come out into just this big glow, I can't see anything, just the light for the moment.

The words: "You have come so far, you have come this far, why are you hesitating?"

"I don't feel I am hesitating."

They repeat: "Why are you hesitating? It is all there for you, total immersion, total dedication."

I know I must give up what I have been doing up to now and concentrate fully on the work ahead. Immersion, study and dedication. Put my trust in them. I feel this means I must leave my job. That is nothing new!

OCTOBER 2nd 1992

OLDER ONES NEED HELP TOO

I have a picture of hospital beds, which changes to a picture of old men bent over. It is an exaggerated picture of old men bent over walking. I try to dismiss it but it won't go away. All old men walking about with sticks and trying to stand up straight.

"Because they cannot stand up they cannot see forward, they can only see the ground. They walk on but cannot see where they are going. They rely on others to make sure that they go in the right direction, in the direction they intend. It is too painful to be forever keeping their heads up to see from that position."

I don't know why I am being given this.

"As they get older they require more assistance than in their prime. They require others to lead them."

I still don't know why I am getting this. I am asking.

"It is not only for the young that you are required to assist, to teach and to make aware of their direction. Also the old require direction and guidance. Do not assume that because of their age the elderly do not need your help. They do not know everything. The number of years they have lived does not signify that they have learnt more than those who have spent fewer years in this incarnation. There are those who learn all that is necessary within a short space of time and those who do not arrive at knowledge necessary for the good of their growth until their last days.

"So do not assume that age has anything to do with the need for education and awareness. Much concentration of thought has been given to youth, the new ones and those yet still to come. That is good but do not forget others who are about to depart. They require as much, if not more, of your time and thought. They require much gentleness for they are reaching a new beginning, a new change. Each individual knows this and is a little uncertain and apprehensive also. And those who feel that the end of this life for them is the end of everything have the greater need because their fear and trepidation is the greatest. We are sure you will remember these words."

73

OCTOBER 2ⁿᵈ 1992

SPINNING RUBY

I have a picture of a great red ruby; it is all I can see. It is a happy beauty, one that gives great joy to look at. I know the meaning of the word 'breathtaking' now.

"It is truly breathtaking. One could look at this forever and never grow tired. In each facet one sees a reflection. Each reflection demonstrates what is needed to be seen, each face depicts a scene. If you have eyes that can see, each of the facets narrows when looked at. It is an illusion, look again. Thoughts fly across the mirror of red. Where are they flying to? Where have they come from and why are they rushing so? It is no more than a reflection of life and the questions posed by those within that life, the same questions looking for an answer. Look on."

He is showing water drawn up, pulled up by some invisible force.

"A force none the less. Not all forces can be seen but they have great power and can change and alter."

He has just spun. He is spinning into a continuous surface, liquid.

"You may enter."

I can see a Being on all sides looking back at me, indistinct but real, observing. They are spinning and I am central and in one spot.

"Riddles. Many riddles to ponder upon. Will you ponder or experience and forget? Ponder on the questions in your mind and ask them at a later date. Think of the possibilities and seek the answers."

OCTOBER 3rd 1992

RED HEALING FROM RAJAH

Green and gold is the colour. I make my journey down beneath the Earth, a long way down. Going along my passage I nearly miss the door as it is earthen like the walls. I just notice it in time. I am trying to find a way of opening the door. It is strange, there are no handles so I just push with my shoulder. It pivots open and I go in. I can see nothing. As I stand, there is a red glow on the ground beneath my feet. I am standing in the light and the red glow that is shining through from the Earth, as one's hand does if you put a torch on the other side.

It is eerie but not unpleasant. The glow spreads upwards through me so that I too am caught in the light. The whole ground is suffused with a red glow. As I become more accustomed to it I notice that it also indicates the way. I follow the glow. It is a lit up path, guidance of direction. I follow. It is strange, no heat just a light. It gives the appearance of heat but it isn't, it is quite normal.

"The red glow is also a healing light and all who stand in the light are receiving healing. It is enabling the body and the soul to function perfectly, as was intended."

At which point I get a tickle in my leg which I have to scratch, which is rather off putting to say the very least. I realise that the Rajah is behind this because I can see him at a distance. He is distant from me but he is there in full, not just his face, in the clothes that he wears. It is he who is showing me and giving me this healing in answer to my request to see him. But I am not to see too close.

He is a distant figure, there and real. As I watch he draws nearer without apparently moving a step, he just becomes closer and closer until I can see his eyes. I have a feeling of excitement, a churning in the insides of anticipation.

The tape ended here and I can't remember the rest.

75

IMPORTANCE OF CLAIRVOYANCE

"Clairvoyance is very important if you are to waken the minds of those who do not believe. It is an initial step to allow the mind to be opened to undreamt of realms. Like peeping through the key hole and then finding that the door is open and one can walk in. There is no need just to peep through the keyhole."

I have a picture of somebody peering through because they have an idea something is going on behind the door and what they see is not quite enough. They don't want to admit that they have an interest and when the door swings open they can't pretend that they haven't been looking. It is all laid out in front of them. It is rather nice.

I also feel that meditation is a key that opens the door to greater knowledge.

OCTOBER 4th 1992

PRACTICE FOR PERFECTION

Silver: each step is hard and clear and firm – the hard edge of truth – I know my guide is with me every step. I go down knowing he is with me all the way. I come to a door which is hard, clear, sharp and silver. I go in, no handle, I push open. I ask to be shown the truth.

"Look around."

As I do so I see work benches and somebody, it is not important who, is working away busily at each work bench. The benches are all the way around. As I turn round to look there is activity and work going on at each one. Then we come to the finished product. They show me a shoe, just a shoe but all the many various activities that go on to complete the shoe.

"At first it is not a perfect shoe but it is wearable. In time each work desk will become more practiced and the end result will be a perfect shoe, even more comfortable and will last much longer. Practice is required for each facet of what goes into the making of the end product."

There is a beaming man standing over the final production of the shoe. He seems to be well pleased, irrespective of whether what is before him is perfect or not. There has been a final product and that is enough for the moment.

I ask again about my job.

He answers straight away: "Why practice the arts to an end where there is no product, where there is no use for you? Why waste your energies in this direction? The time spent could be spent perfecting various skills needed for your shoes. Think of it as moonlighting while serving an apprenticeship. One does not expect to be well paid during an apprenticeship and we understand the need for supplement, but your time as a result is not totally dedicated to the task."

I feel from this that they are determined that I put all my efforts into their work and what they wish me to do. It couldn't be clearer.

STUDY THE HANDS

I have pink and go down a clean pink marble staircase, right down, down. I go through a waving curtain door and immediately all around me are glowing lights, red crystal lights, all around in a circle. They are all glistening and glowing, clean and shiny. I am lit up with the glow and I feel my guide with me, very much on me. I ask her to impress me with her thoughts, to tell me what I need to know.

"We would like you to study hands."

I start to think about hands, hands in pockets etc. and feel I must study them more; not necessarily just the lines but hands in general. Then my alarm went off and I knew I must get off to work.

*

What followed this was a local talk by Robin Llown on palmistry which really inspired me to learn the skill. I took them up on the suggestion. I studied and put it into practice with everyone I met. It has paid off.

OCTOBER 7th 1992

NECESSARY OPERATION

I have a picture of a girl, a mature girl being taken by the hand at quite a fast speed. I am being led by my thoughts to the second major operation I am to have soon and I am told that the girl is me being dragged to the operation, but that it is necessary for their programme. I have a picture of a lot of people walking towards me. I can't see individual faces. They are walking towards me in a bunch. I don't know what this indicates.

*

I was told in a later meditation that they would make full use of the operation. Rightly or wrongly I immediately took this to mean that I might have a near death experience. I looked forward to this since I had heard that it frequently opened up avenues of spiritual and psychic contact that could normally take years.

On coming out of the anaesthetic I knew that something had happened, but I didn't know what. I knew I had nearly 'gone' during the operation. However the doctors said nothing and I remembered nothing. I felt cheated and knew without doubt that I had been somewhere. I also felt an extreme nostalgic sadness for the star that was my home.

I lay in my hospital bed wishing I were elsewhere.

OCTOBER 8th 1992

BUILDING SITE

I go down in green and red. The wooden stairs are with rough walls. It is very steep and a long way down, almost like a downward chute, very steep. At the bottom is an extremely narrow, wood-slatted passageway. I go along until I reach a boarded up opening and just manage to squeeze through. It is like a hoarding, all boarded up. I keep getting the words, BUILDING SITE. I am on a building site. Over to the right I see some Porta cabins, a contractor's office. I go over towards it, up the steps and go in. Inside there is a table with plans scattered all over, quite orderly really but spread out. Then I notice a man sitting in a corner in a chair having a quiet nap, having a rest from his work on the table. I ask for an explanation because I don't understand.

"Do you not see, we have the site? The site is prepared, which is you. We have the plan, which is your programme. We have the workers, they are your helpers. But even workers need a rest from time to time. We at times need to wait for materials and the construction must proceed in an orderly logical manner. We cannot build a roof before the foundation is laid. But all is in progress; all is going according to plan. There have to be periods of waiting, reviewing and passing of various stages by those qualified to do so, so that we may proceed with the next stage. There is no cause for concern."

I ask that there be many access points where people may come and go, as well as ideas. I ask for the building to have many rooms and many facets open to people so that they may learn and be helped. I ask that the skylight be open to God and that the light may pour through in every room. I ask that there may be peace and quiet in all the rooms, and tranquillity and healing love. The man in his chair wakes up and rubs his eyes and gets up. He goes to his table and starts to study the plans and that is when I must leave.

OCTOBER 11th 1992

IMMERSION IN THE MIND OF THE GUIDE

I ask for a colour and get an explosion, a kaleidoscope of colours immediately. It gradually all settles down and becomes pure white. I go down in moonlight. Each step is lit by moonlight all the way. A beautiful light that is clean and pure. I go through into my area which is lit by the moon. It is a beautiful restful and still feeling, an extraordinary experience. There is a pathway of red, a lovely red through the moonlight. I walk along to what I can only describe as the mouth of this red ray. I walk through into what is a surrounding, a complete immersion in red. I give up trying to make sense of it and just let myself be lost in red.

Total immersion and total exclusion of thought. I am in the mind of another, I am immersed in someone else's mind, my guide's mind. It allows no clear thought of my own. I can't break it to say what is happening at the time. I stay with it until it eventually diminishes and withdraws very slowly, very gently and leaves me as I am. I withdraw and walk back along the red path until that fades and leaves me standing in the moonlight where I am now. It was a good experience. Now I am feeling chilly and cold and so I must come back. Ooh I am so cold!

OCTOBER 12th 1992

CUSHIONING

I am given pink and straight away I am walking down a cushioned stairway, everything is cushioned. I think of those who are cushioned in life and I realise it is even more difficult to walk down the stairs to your inner self on cushions and soft living, than it is to walk on bare boards and a firm surface, something firm for your feet. It is more difficult for those who have had it easy and obstacles are more difficult to get round.

"The feet are protected but for the rest the balance is not so easily maintained. The going is slower, one can move much more quickly over a hard surface. With soft going the end goal is much more difficult to achieve."

I have difficulty in getting through the door; it is hard to find the entrance. It is like being in a padded cell, where does one find the door? It is so difficult to find. A door swings open for me as if I am being allowed to enter by some outside influence. Inside there is a classroom; adults, young people. All well clothed and well nourished. They are in a classroom and I am not clear if I am a teacher or a student.

"The picture is awareness of differences between those who have a cushioned life and those who do not."

OCTOBER 14th 1992

BROKEN GLASS – disorientation

I have pale yellowy greens, yellows, all mixed up. There is a feeling of glass and I go down on crushed glass, all reflecting different lights. It is not difficult or painful but just IS. I get down, it is a strange feeling. I come to my door which is a sheer sheet of glass. There is no way of opening this door until I realise I can walk through the glass. I just walk straight through it, like walking through nothing.

On the other side of the door there are reflective surfaces. Whichever way I turn there are surfaces all broken up. They are reflecting and it is rather disorientating. I can't quite get a grip on anything substantial. There is something down by my feet but I can't get myself together

"Operate your instruments of recordings and make arrangements for presentation. It will merely be necessary for you to impart what is given."

All this is in answer to my unspoken questions. As I reflected on this, a heavy wooden yoke is put on my shoulders. It is significant. It has a comfortable feel but is very heavy and I feel weighed down. I ask when all this will begin and I get September floating about in waves in front of me. Somehow I don't feel that it is this September. I can't help but feel that this is September next year.

I had the words given: "Keep your own council and allow others to come to you."

I take that to mean I must wait for those who need help to come here and not for me to give it out all over.

"This doesn't necessarily mean where you are residing but means where you are in yourself. Wherever you may be, allow people in need to come to you wherever you are."

I have just received and I have to repeat it because I could not come out of the state I was in to say it before. I went in to what I felt to be a hypnotic state.

They said: "You cannot open your eyes."

I tried and I couldn't. It was self induced I feel and then I was given a series of affirmations [on tape only] I have my arms full of things and they said:

83

"You are now receiving the assets from the bank. Use them wisely."

I now recognise why I had the dream. I am being given all these things and I am to use them in the way that it is intended.

They then said: "You can open your eyes now." Immediately I did and now I am recording it, though not exactly in the same way as it came through.

OCTOBER 14ᵗʰ 1992

NEW STRUCTURE OF LAND AND GENERATION

I have a picture of sharp pointed rocks, crystals – I don't quite know what they are as they keep popping up out of the ground at random. It is in movement and is not still. It is as if the crystals are forcing their way up to the surface, a constant movement of the forcing up of crystals, the points of rock, and all kinds. I don't know what this is trying to say to me.

"The inner is becoming outer. New land formations, formations and structure that have not been seen before. It will be new to the eyes of man."

I asked, "When?"

"When this new generation is full grown."

OCTOBER 18th 1992 3.00am

JOURNEYS AFTER DEATH

After a long session in silent communion they said to go on my journey. I was about to go down when they gave me purple. The purple clothes I have got on are hampering me on the steps and I am tripping over the cloth and making slow progress. After a little while I decide to cut some of the cloth off at the bottom into a manageable length. The going is much easier now. As I get higher it is busier with more activity going on than where I have just come from. There are buildings and centres and habitation and a lot going on. It is like going into a city rather than coming out of it. I am going into the hub of work, an extremely busy place.

"If you think when you leave your earthly plane that you are going into realms of idleness and dreams, then you are mistaken. You are going into a realm where work is more constant, more active and more important in other respects. There is no idleness unless you wish to be idle and if you do nothing you get nothing in return. On your earthly plane it is possible to do nothing and others will take care of you. There you find there are many who rely on other people to get them through their lives.

"This cannot be in the realms which you are visiting now. You alone are responsible for your existence here. You can turn to others for inspiration and guidance and, most of all, for love but you alone must do the work, must put your own efforts towards what you wish to receive to enable you to go where you will. You will not be carried there, you go under your volition and will, and if you do not have sufficient of either then you will remain where you are. This can be very boring for you and in time, if this period is too lengthy, you will become extremely dissatisfied and your will may then modify itself; self motivate.

"You understand that I am not speaking only to you as an individual here. I am speaking to all those souls who will enter these realms and who will, in time, visit. We say visit as it is not a permanent residence; it is merely one step along the way. One might say it is a first step according to whether you as individuals are well travelled or stay-at-homes.

"For those who have never ventured abroad it will seem like a great step, a great adventure, a new experience. For those who have already visited many times and seen and learnt and wish to visit again, to visit yet new lands, will pass quickly through the first stage and be eager to go on to other areas of knowledge and experience. For what is travel but new experience, new ways of looking, an opening of the eyes to what is possible outside the familiar domain.

"You will have among you intrepid explorers constantly looking for new challenges, seeking out the hardest route to go where few travel. There will be new endeavours, new experiences, greater heights of achievements. There are not so many of these and this on its own is part of the attraction. There are others of you who would be perfectly happy to travel safe routes where there are many like companions. Not quite so exciting but none the less it is travel and in good company and travel which can be enjoyed without too many frustrations and stresses.

"There are still others who have an aptitude; a tendency to find and meet difficulties, whatever is presented to them. However well arranged the journey they will view all preparations in the light of difficulty, almost as if they had been put there especially to make life hard for them. They feel grievance which is in reality their own doing. Yet more will go ill-prepared for venture into lands they should not enter without due preparation. Still they go and having done so need to rely on their wit and good fortune to get them out of trouble and face the unexpected.

"If you look upon your journey through life as a traveller and look at all aspects of travelling, you will find that your own journey through your many lifetimes is not so very different from the comparisons we have given. Prepare well, learn your route, mark well the signposts, have an open eye to absorbing new experiences so that you may learn and understand more fully. There are many ways that you can ponder this point and that in itself is learning."

It is becoming noticeable that the information through this style of meditation is to be spread wider and is not just for me alone.

OCTOBER 26th 1992

NUGGETS OF GOLD

Rosy pink – I go down and ask if it is really necessary and they say, yes. So I keep going down but it is in a lift, a miner's lift passing many levels.

They say: "You will know when to stop."

At the bottom I get out and again it is a mining theme. I walk along and follow shored up tunnels into a large opening. I ask to be shown what I need to see.

A voice says: "Look around, my child."

I look at the walls and ceiling and see little gleams of gold everywhere among the dark black face of the rock. Everywhere I turn there are little gold nuggets.

"Yes, there are nuggets of gold all around you, waiting to be discovered. Everywhere you turn there are nuggets of gold of purity, endurance and of value and worth. You must find them and dig them out and bring them to the light. Each individual has the qualities that we are looking for. You must polish and bring to realisation the worth and value that have been buried for so long. This is your task."

I feel a little overawed by this because they are so deeply buried and scattered and I could be here forever doing this job.

"You must make a start. Looking at it won't do anything. You must get going."

I am quite happy about this because it is an answer to my question at the beginning of my meditation: whether the idea of starting a development group was a good one.

"Think of gold fashioned into useful articles and items of beauty, which are acquired by others who then carry them abroad and into circulation."

OCTOBER 28th 1992

INTERVIEW FOR THE JOB

Green and blue. I go down in what seems like a spiral passage, very quiet respectful colours, such as you would find in the interior offices of someone important. That kind of feeling, men's club feeling – a round and round spiral going down, going down wondering when I am going to get to the bottom. It seems worth noting that I am going anti-clockwise down. At the bottom I eventually come to an opening. I can't help but go into it because of the narrowness of the passage. I follow. I try to get away from this because it is not what I expected, but the scene won't go.

There are a lot of bespectacled clerks. It is over-exaggerated to make me realise this is an office with all the activity of an office. There is even a little junior fussing around with bits of paper. It is a busy office. I don't know why I have got this and I have tried to change this scene but it won't go. I am a bit bewildered by it all, when a man looks up, sees me and beckons me over as if he has been waiting for me. He takes me through into an inner office. I go in and sit down.

I am here for an interview. He is interviewing me but I don't know what for. Strange! As I look at him he begins to change from the office personality to a beautiful person with a lovely face and a lovely glow. He is no ordinary man, he is a Being and he looks at me kindly. I want to cry.

He says: "Are you capable of the work, do you think you can handle it? It is for you to say now if you are up to the job."

I am just so taken in by the warmth and the love from this person that I know that this is where I want to be.

I say: "I have the will, I have the application and I will learn as I go. I may not be expert at first but I will apply myself to that end. This is where I want to learn and become practised in the art of helping others."

He continues: "It is a big organisation, many departments and you will have to inter-relate with many of them. Communication is very important in a smooth run office, as it is in all matters. If you need any help on any particular thing do not be afraid to ask and help will be given. In time you will progress to become one that others turn to for help within the organisation."

Feeling very new, I know I am accepted. I still want to cry. It is very difficult not to feel very emotional about this meeting. Then I feel elated because it has suddenly dawned on me that I have been accepted and I could skip out of his office whooping and hollering for joy. It is a lovely feeling. I want to shout it from the roof tops. "I HAVE BEEN ACCEPTED".

Then I know I must finish because I have to go back to work, the earthly office this time. *Ending on an emotional state with tears streaming down my face.*

This is plainly to do with my spiritual teaching work. It is becoming clear that I rarely have to do the stairs as much. However if I get stuck I can fall back on that method and I am on a roll once more.

OCTOBER 28th 1992

JOINING THE MONKS

I am on rough and stony ground. I don't know where I am going and am just walking. I am with a high vibration. I am going for a rendezvous. Yes, to a group of monks on a mountain. I am on a high mountain but it is flat ground and is not cold. There is a group of brown robed monk figures ahead of me. I have a lot of tickling round my face and intensity in my head as I go with this. The monks are conversing with themselves and do not see me at first. They are in a discussion and as I come up to them they turn and open their circle to me. I join in quite naturally as if I do this all the time. I don't feel new and they take it as perfectly natural.

OCTOBER 30th 1992

ONE ORIGIN – MIND TO MIND

I am in an open roofed, V shape passage. It is difficult to walk along the bottom of it because it is such a sharp V. I am walking along with a foot on either side of the sloping walls of the passage. Running down the centre is liquid. You might almost say it is a conduit. It is red, not blood or anything horrible. The liquid is running along the bottom. I am going up a slope. It is a very awkward thing this, holding on to the sides which are almost too wide for my arms to reach, so I am lurching from side to side. Very odd! I daresay they will tell me why, in time.

"It is a conduit through which many substances flow. Communication, transportation, evacuation and anything you can think of travels along a conduit. Go to the head of the conduit; be at the source so that you can add your own contribution to that which flows out. One normally thinks that there are separate conduits relating to separate individual items to be transported or sent. In this presentation there is one conduit for all manner of things. For all manner of reasons we are utilising one means of conveyance. **Mind to Mind**."

"Why is the colour red?"

"Life blood, it is the lifeline."

I am getting a picture of all the cords that attach incarnated souls, joined into one cable, joined to **one origin**. That is the lifeline.

"The communication is for those who are still connected in their incarnation. It is their means of communication."

I never thought of it like that before! It is like all the wiring coming from a giant switchboard, all channelled into one conduit.

OCTOBER 31st 1992

HOW TO MEDITATE

I have just been given an explanation of how to help people to meditate; how to explain it to them.

"It is wrong to feel that you must empty the mind, because the mind cannot be empty. The idea is to keep the everyday mind occupied while your inner self makes contact with your subconscious, your soul. It is giving it something to do, keeping it out of the way so that the real objective is obtained."

I am getting a picture of someone being kept occupied while someone else is slipping in round the back door and down into the cellar. The mind hasn't noticed because it is occupied with something else. And that is meditation, keeping that part of the mind focused on something else while you get on with the real work. Control of the mind and not allowing the conscious mind to dominate your thoughts where you don't want them to be. That is the gist of it.

NOVEMBER 3rd 1992

CEREMONY IN CAVE

I am given green. It is jungle green with a jungle feeling, all palms and tough spiky leaves. I go along very carefully, treading on soft undergrowth. I am hemmed in on either side by a wall of vegetation. The strange thing is I don't seem to be going down, though I want to. It is flat and level. I go along for quite a long time, asking questions in my mind. "Why am I here? What is this all about?" I come to a cave. I can't avoid it as it is right in front of me and there is nowhere else I can go. I go in. It is very dark. There is a definite somebody overshadowing me, very strong and determined. There are tickles all over me.

I feel almost at home in this cave. It is a comfortable, warm feeling, not cold or damp. A living area, an area that is used is more correct. It is quite familiar to many but is not an animal's lair or anything of that nature. I keep wanting to say, "Ceremonial," is what it is used for. As I look I realise there are flashes of blue coming down from above. It is flashes rather than shafts; electric blue flashes as if the sun is suddenly catching something, reflects for a moment and then is gone, that type of flash. There is something shafting briefly down for a moment in blue.

It is a special place this. Then I feel hands on either side of me, walking me gently over to stand beneath the shaft of light. I go quite willingly. As I don't know where to stand they take me and put me there. I stand in the light of blue flashing over me, some long bursts, some brief and short. I must stay there for a bit. I have a very weird feeling that I am to one side of this activity and yet it is still coming down on me. It is like a double me. It is coming down and I am under the lights, yet also to one side. Two of me! A weird impression, I know it can't be and yet it is so strong that it must be. I can't quite work this out. Now this is extra strange. I have a blue ___ gap in recording ___

I now forget what followed, which emphasises the importance of recording. I leave it to readers to fill in here, especially if they take this journey.

NOVEMBER 3rd 1992

CHINLESS ONE

I feel I have someone with me who appears to have no chin. It is a highly evolved being, one who does not have exactly the features that we expect to see. The face does not possess the chin or the normal jaw structure. It is strange for me, the energy is very high.

I will recount as there isn't much in the way of words but more of feeling. A lot of high tension feeling and transfiguration. There are a lot of thoughts but nothing you can call channelling, I almost feel it is a new stage. They are still with me but I feel it is sufficient.

NOVEMBER 7th 1992

BACK THROUGH MISTS OF TIME

Colour is deep violet and with that colour came a very strong energy. After some time I go down through a cloud of violet smoke. I don't know what you would call it, very wispy stuff.

Somebody just said: "Back through the mists of time."

It is like going back very speedily through a tunnel, with past events flashing by. Past a little girl, past the Cathars, past little groups of something you know you have been through, and then it is gone. Like passing through a tunnel at speed. I have asked to go back to where I need to be.

OLD TROUBADOUR

There is an old man walking with a stick, he is having difficulty walking. I think he has arthritis or something, or he is just old. He is walking along. He is not poor, neither poor nor rich, just old. There are children coming to him and pulling at his clothes and pulling for attention. They want him to tell them a story.

He is good at telling stories but in the stories are truths and that is why they like them. They don't know, they don't realise that they are being taught at a high level. To them it is an enjoyable invention, one they can enter into. They are absorbing the real meaning, the real teaching without realising it and it will stay with them all their lives and influence their actions.

All learning for those young in years should be perfectly natural and enjoyable for it is the pleasurable things that are held and remembered throughout the lifetime. The old man is an aging troubadour, one that has spent his time in his youth entertaining on his travels. Now his age limits him to the occasional words of wisdom.

I ask my helpers: "Am I doing this right, am I relating this as it is?"

"Yes, go on you are doing fine."

"Well, who is this man?"

"He is yourself. That man had the ability to pick out among those children those whose abilities were beyond the norm. He was able to bring capabilities and gifts to the surface and nurture them into full growth through the use of their imagination. He was responsible for many great achievements in his time, by the simple use of relating stories that produced the desired stimulation.

"You might think a story-teller does not have much influence on fellow-kind, but you would be wrong. The influence is far-reaching, even to the future development of races still to come. It is a humble beginning with far-reaching consequences. Each chain has a link, each link is extremely vital to the continuation of the chain. There is not one that is unimportant."

Just then the man looks up. He has twinkly blue eyes and a merry face. It is a young face in an old body. The soul is alive and full of energy, even though it is housed in an old body, the light shines and the love and kindliness shines. This is felt by the children and all those who come near. He's twinkling at me. That's the only way I can think of it as he looks. A man with a twinkle in his eye.

NOVEMBER 8th 1992

AT HEART OF THE MATTER

I have very deep red. I play around with the colour for a bit, I just think deep red, imagine it, you know, but I get a lot of energy coming down and then instead of doing my normal slow stair process down and all the rigmarole, I just go straight there, I can't be bothered with all that. I find myself in an area of pulsating red, warm, and I get the feeling of heat on my knee. It keeps coming and going as if wet, you know when you get something wet and warm on your knee. It keeps coming and going.

I ask, "What's that?"

"It's blood."

I say, "That's strange! It felt like something wet and hot."

"Don't worry, it's blood that is for the good. It's for a good purpose, this blood."

"Why on that knee, my right knee, that's a funny place?" Then I realise I am inside the body and there is me right down in the corner, tiny, tiny, like a little pea down in the corner, with all this mass around me of pulsating red, like internal organs and things.

"What's all this supposed to be telling me, what does all this mean?"

"You are at the heart of the matter."

"Sorry I'm thick, but I still don't understand what I'm supposed to take from that."

"Whatever happens to the body, you are at the heart of the matter, you are the one that controls it."

"Right, in that case, I want the coming operation to be used as a means to gain higher vibrations. Take the opportunity, use the opportunity. I don't mind if it means I would be able to function at a higher level to be able to help others."

*The meaning was very much accepted I felt. I thought, *if I'm controlling the body and they're controlling the rest, they ought to be able to put two and two together.*

This was referring to my major operation due any time.

NOVEMBER 13th 1992

EVERYTHING ENDURES – WHEEL AND WALL PAINTINGS

I've been given the colour of blue; harmony and healing. This is a little strange. I try to go my usual way down the stairs, but it is as if I am at the hub of a wheel and I have to drop down from there to the rim which is slowly turning. I do this, and the rim is my deep subconscious, it is the bottom. Then I climb up the outside of the rim until I come to an opening which I drop into. Having dropped into it I am alright. I am where I have to be. I can't see anything at first.

"Give yourself directions. Look about".

As I look about me I see what appear to be wall paintings on rock.

"Everything endures. Every apparently insignificant thing you do endures forever. It doesn't go away with the passing of time, but it has an effect on those who follow and look upon past deeds. It affects their thoughts in one way or another. It is therefore up to you to ensure that your deeds are worthy of being looked at and that they have a good effect on others' reactions. Be remembered with affection and pride."

This is strange, I am passing from one area to another and all I have to leave behind is the memory of me.

"The new areas to which you are going will need your imprint upon it. It is fresh for you to make your mark upon the wall of time. It will be for you to influence through deeds and words."

Then I think, *I really do need to know when.*

"No, you don't really need to know when. It's not necessary. Be content that it will be. When is not of prime importance. It will be."

NOVEMBER 13th 1992

HITCH HIKERS – NO EASY RIDES

I have a picture of two horses both side by side. They're very restless and tossing their heads. I don't know what significance they have. They are dragging a litter behind them. It's not a carriage; it's a litter, very wide. They're slow at telling me what this is about.

"Those who attach themselves to this conveyance will have a less than smooth ride. They would be better to proceed under their own steam. They're hitching a lift. A litter is for the infirm and not for those who are able. This is for any who look for easy passage without even attempting by their own efforts to go forward – they are hitch-hiking. They do not develop their own muscles and as a result become wasted."

Then two people come up and cut the traces, just slash through them and leave the litter on the ground, as if to say: "That's enough of that!"

"Unless achievement is self-achievement it is no achievement at all. One has to work and progress under one's own initiative and searching. They may use any means to obtain insight, to further the practice of abilities, but actual achievement must be attained by each individual. There are helpers who can point the way, many who can educate and advise, but the work still remains for self progression. There are those who believe they can ride on the back of another."

I can see a Chinese pagoda, a cross-section view. It is a cross sectioned view inside that one doesn't normally see.

"There are students on the ground level, there are many levels. The numbers thin as they go up."

I can see students, I am sure they are students, many at first level and at the top only one.

"He has reached the pinnacle and from there he may leave. There are many who have to retrace their steps and start on the ground floor yet again. There are those who would take the lift little realising that the lift does not have exit points and they must return down the way they went." He thinks that is amusing.

The man I have here says: "You have now got the message. It has taken a long time," laughingly. He is one who comes to assist in the teaching of those who would learn and who will be present again.

FORCE OF VIBRATION- UNSTOPPABLE

[Osishoo]

I have a picture of children who are having joyrides on two horses, just for pleasure and fun. Somebody is putting them on and they are taking it in turns. The pagoda is still there, but black clouds are coming, darkening the sky and drawing nearer.

"The lights will have to be lit if we are to see. It will be time to light the lamps when the darkness descends. The place is shaking. It is similar to when you have a blast of noise, vibration moves all in its path. It cannot be stopped by human hands. It is a natural consequence of force through sound, the sound that is not in tune. It cannot and will not diminish.

"The pattern has been set. It will be a shaking no more [ceases], but one that will have been noticed and one that will cause many to fear and question and to wonder if this is the beginning of something greater. It has been indicated to you before. Do not fear. All is in hand to bring about a healing and a change in attitudes; attitudes of those who would not make their own adjustments.

"If the plan for all the universes is to proceed without disruption, then we too must make our own arrangements and adjustments to produce a rebalance. Preparations are proceeding. The education of those who will assist in maintaining calm is in hand. Continue with the education."

He has gone. I keep seeing snow everywhere coming down, a lot of snow. He has gone. There is a stepping down of vibration. It is really cold round my legs. I am taking that as an ending.

I think for one minute I have Abdul back, when I realise it isn't Abdul at all because he has a different headdress. He is on a horse and I now know who it is [a Tuareg] though I have never seen him on a horse before. He says few words but oversees and is very much in charge. He looks very grand. I know he oversees and is keeping his distance. He has a moustache __ almost hawkish.

"You must do what you tell others to do, note detail. Come up close, look into the mirror."

He comes up right in front of me, really close but I don't know if I can hold it.

"Remember the Arab boy." [This refers to a regression in which I was an Arab boy in a past life]

This man is so strong and I know him – it has gone really cold. I have a falcon, a hooded falcon. It was still but now it is turning its head round as if to see, even though it has the hood on it.

"I am ready to take the hood off so that sight may be used to full advantage." He takes it off and the bird realises that it can see. He is released and takes off but doesn't go far. The bird returns to the arm of this man, the Master of the bird. The bird will always return even though it has freedom.- – - The cold is too much I have to stop. It is enough.

NOVEMBER 15th 1992

THE EAGLE TO FEED ITS YOUNG

I am given purple, deep purple and instead of stairs I have a hole, a purple hole. They say: it is going into myself. The hole becomes a tunnel, not a firm tunnel. I walk along and see a picture of someone drawing. They have a large sheet of paper and are drawing with their right hand so it cannot be me [I am left handed]. Then they hold the sketch up. It is a sketch of peaks, mountain peaks, very tall and straight up. No gentle slopes here. It is an outline sketch with the tallest peak to the right, the top is in the clouds; in fact you cannot see the top. How one reaches that I don't know.

Someone says: "You fly like an eagle. That is how you get to the top."

"That is all very pretty, but what does it tell me?" Immediately they take me to the other side of the cloud with the eagle perched on the pinnacle, feeding its young. The nest is there and it is supplying the baby eaglets with bits of sustenance to help them grow so that they can fly when they are matured enough.

"They too will build their own nests in time and feed their nestlings so the chain may continue."

When?

"You must first fly up and build the nest in preparation. You must fly many times with bits of twig and all the materials to make it firm and solid, a safe nest. Then the nestlings will come."

I feel this is referring to preparation for the development classes.

SHOWING KINDNESS

I ask to be taken to the higher vibrations, one of purity and truth. I have been told to visualise a staircase going up. It is a many stepped, clean staircase. Wide with nothing on either side, just all white steps. I follow a red beam going up which is ahead of me, like a carrot for the donkey. As long as it is in front of me I can follow. It is just a beam, no more. As it draws me up I follow with the thought, *when will I get there?*

"Soon."

I feel energy round my eyes as I come to a platform leading to the right. I walk along the platform which leads to big doors opening in the middle, curved at the top. Big clean marble like doors. They open for me; I don't have to open them.

I ask, "What must I do now?"

I notice a group of men in white robes huddled together talking to each other, not looking my way. I must go towards them. I am dressed the same as them. I notice for the first time that my clothes are as theirs. I draw close. They sense I am there and open their little group. I join them quite naturally. They are all very kind, all knowing. Very kind in a non-contrived manner, it is natural to them. They are not being especially kind to me as they are just kind in general, as they would be to anybody, to anything. It shows in their faces.

As has happened before, the kindness that they give makes me feel emotional, moved by it. I feel I want to cry again. It is strange that I should want to cry at kindness, but I am touched, very much so.

One of them who is reading my thoughts says: "Imagine how much help you would be giving to one who needed some of that affection and kindness shown to you, and how it would reach the core of the heart and stir some response within the heart that one had considered dead and armoured against all ills. It is a way to reach and warm those who need that warmth. Just be kindness, there is no need for words or action because what you are will show itself to all who wish to see."

At this point my words become a jumble as there is so much I want to know. I need help and guidance and I need to be shown more direction. My thoughts are jumbled, but they know I am sure.

I feel I am slipping away from the centre of the group. Not wishing to, but my mind is going off elsewhere. They put their arms out and put them round my back and gently draw me back in so that I am brought back to the centre. I am grateful because my mind was wandering away and I was losing them. Which would have been a pity having managed to get here.

I ask, perhaps foolishly, if they would show me my future. They show me a suitcase with me standing by it on a railway platform, a departure point of some area, travel, on the move.

"Travel can be very tedious. When you arrive it is alright, it is the travelling that can be extremely wearing. Do go prepared, armed with books and matter for the mind to occupy those tedious moments so that time is not wasted and is not spent worrying about connections etc. Use the time to your advantage. Also use it as rest between the work for which you are travelling."

DECEMBER 16ᵗʰ 1992 4.00AM

BRINGING PEOPLE OUT OF DARKNESS – RESCUE?

I have brown, not a colour I would choose. I am going down. I go along a tunnel similar to a burrow and through a gap on the right. I just have to push through a pile of earth and break out into an area with walls showing a glint or two. It is not all plain earth.

As I look around there is a stone slab table. I go over to it. It is long and large. I run my hands over the stone which is not smooth but fairly rough. I get the urge to stand on it. I want to use it to see further. I feel the need to stand on it and I hear:

"Follow the urge."

I climb up onto the stone slab. Turning round slowly to look I see a sea of faces, people. I couldn't see them before because they were all low down from my viewpoint. They were too low. Now I see all the faces waiting, a little fearfully it seems. In the dark all huddled together. They are all in the dark. I don't know what they are waiting for.

"Each word you utter will be as a light. You must bring light to their darkness so they can see where they are going and needn't remain all together in the dark. They can stand up, stand up on their own feet and go where they wish under their own will. You must bring light to them by words and they must see that the words come from one who is real and not a figment of their imagination or a figment of their dreams."

I ask, "When must I do this and how? How will I have knowledge of what to say?"

"The time will be. We are showing you what is to be so that you know there is a plan and you are not stumbling along. There is no end to your journey but there is a purpose. We will make it clear."

DECEMBER 24th 1992

LION AND THE LAMB AND TRAVEL

Green is the colour. I am walking down a grass terrace. Everything is covered in grass. I am dressed in a gown of fresh pale green. At the bottom there is a swathe cut through tall grass which I am walking through. The grass is high above my head on either side but there is a way cut for me, so I know where I must go. There is an opening on the right which I go through. As I do it is like breaking out into a wide open space.

Peaceful! There is a lamb at my feet. I look down at it. As I think that a lamb shouldn't be away from its mother, a lion appears. It comes up and stays with me. Now I have the lion and the lamb together. I start to walk forward and they follow. I don't know where I am going. I just keep going so that I may see what is over the horizon.

I keep walking, so do they. I reach an incline at the top and can see beyond. Beyond is the sea. I go down to the edge. As I reach the water I notice a boat on the right. It is a large boat which is ready for me. It has the gangplank down, nothing special just a plank. I go onto the boat and the lion and the lamb come with me. As I get on, the plank is brought in and the boat moves off. I don't know how, it just moves off and I am quite happy. It is so calm, dreamlike.

A voice says: "You are going to far off lands where you will see many things."

I ask what this means.

"Distance, travel."

At this point I have the feeling I should bring myself back and finish this, there is no more.

CHAPTER FOUR

JANUARY 5th 1993

HIGH ONE COMES HEALING SOULS

"Try to continue with healing of the soul. There are many who require your assistance in pointing the way to a better and greater understanding of the natures of those who are troubled; troubled as a result of their thought patterns. If these patterns could be of a happier nature then their own pathways would be so much easier. It is for you to open the way to enlighten and show how attitudes can enhance the lives of troubled ones.

"That is all that is required, an attitude that is not based on hate, fear and worry but one that is based on hope, acceptance and love. Where love is not possible at least have an understanding, compassion and a feeling of pity for those who apparently are doing so much wrong. For they too will suffer and will have need of pity for what they, in turn, are to endure. Awaken the minds of those steeped in bitterness and so much suffering will be alleviated.

"Not everyone will listen, not everyone will wish to change their pattern of thinking. It is always worth the effort, even if it changes but one, for that one in turn will change the attitude of another. Those such as you are always asking what you can do. What is our next step? How can we make a difference? How can we serve? And we say to you, put your attention on those who have hate, fear and bitterness in their hearts and show them that these feelings are not necessary.

"We come not from your plane, not from your world. We come to assist, to alleviate the pain that exists upon your world. We come to add balm to sore and troubled spots. It pains us to see these eruptions and distress. If it is at all possible we aim to make suffering easier. We do not have these discomforts."

At this point I can smell something rather pleasant. This one doesn't have any hair, just a smooth head. The face isn't from this planet. There was a beautiful feeling with this one.

JANUARY 8th 1993

JOURNEY FROM TAKE OFF SHAFT

I have a picture of a star which is not a real star; it is the sort of star you would get on a stage. It is not a real star. It is sending out what appear to be firecrackers, like fireworks going out in all directions. I have the words 'paint your wagon'; why I don't know. They are inspecting my documents. You know how you get passport control, looking at you, looking at the passport. It is that sort of scene and the wagon is for the journey. It is making sure you have the right papers. There are quite a few Beings here who are conducting this. It is a journey. I don't know whether to describe what I am getting or whether I should wait for more because I am getting little stages of the journey. I don't know where it is all leading. I am very puzzled.

Have you been on a tabletop? We are not talking of a table; we are talking of a mountain, flat and high without the peaks. It is larger than a helicopter pad but is like a take-off platform. There are people standing around. The people are thick set and heavily gowned, older people and white gowned. They remind me of big heavy Russians. They are all in white and with long white hair. It is almost albino white, not even grey. I can't see any colour at all.

What are they waiting for? I feel they are waiting for something, standing around in little groups expecting something. A shaft has come down onto the open space. You can't see through the shaft, it is agitating. I need more words. It is like dancing molecules, which is the only way I can describe this. Can you imagine dancing molecules? They are all rapidly moving inside the circular shaft. There is an opening in the shaft. I have stepped out and am walking along but I am not on anything, there is nothing around. I am going towards somebody there waiting, not like anything or anybody I have ever seen.

"It has been arranged. It is the link between you and them. They are not like you; you wouldn't recognise them in the form they have. There is a lot I mustn't say to you."

JANUARY 8th 1993

A MEETING WITH SOCRATES

I make my way inwards in my usual way, using the stairs. I ask where I am going when I see in front of me a lovely face, a wise smiling man. A smiling, gentle man and I know it sounds absolutely crazy but I must say it: the name came – Socrates. I have no idea what Socrates looked like but this man has a round and merry, kind face. I didn't think he was a particularly kind person, was he? This man is wearing a coat down straight to the ground, with an edge to edge front and long sleeves, the sort you can tuck your hands into, and slippers. He has a sash from his left shoulder over to his right, purple. I have itchy eyes.

He looks at me and says: "I am glad you are reading my students' work. You will learn much from the writings and will disagree no doubt on many points, but that is good. To agree with everything is not my way and should not be the way for those who read what is written. One should exercise the mind with the minds of others. It is that in my work, opinions are not stated as facts, they are put forward as ideas for debate to be considered. The object is to awaken the minds so that all angles can be investigated so that we all learn much. This process still goes on. There are too many who blindly accept and do not pursue their own brain cells and thoughts. How dull it would be if there were but a few herdsmen imposing their will on a lot of sheep.

"Words that have been put down from my time were deliberately unconventional, creating debate and opinions that differed. In this way, controversy energised the subject of the matter and from this evolved true import which established itself. If I may say, in many cases my own views were acceptable, but not blindly so. There was controversy before acceptance but this very act established it in the minds and books of many others, as established reasoning becoming grounded in the history of thought processes.

"There is nothing eventful or unique in stating that a surface is black. It is more controversial to state, for example, that a given surface has all the colours upon that surface at one and the same time, irrespective of the colour that is perceived by the eye. You can imagine the controversy that that would erupt. You see my point?"

"Are you still active?" I ask.

"My now is very real but I exist at more than one level. I am here now and am engaged in thought processes every bit as important. I am also elsewhere and utilising the delights of my existence. I am in a position of being able to oversee my other existences. It is very amusing for me and am enjoying myself hugely.

"No thought pattern is ever lost and my brain as you would term it − I am still a thinking Being and as such, that which I emit goes out and is not contained within myself. Those who have an interest in debatable subjects and subjects of the workings of the mind will attract these thoughts. It is necessary to have one who has an attraction for thought and debate. One who investigates and delves into the workings of the mind will attract any thought, not only from me but also from others."

I feel I am merely being used here. My eyes are funny.

JANUARY 9th 1993

DO NOT WAVER

I have with me White Owl [guide]. In answer to my thoughts he responds:

"There will come a time when your words will be sought; when they will be listened to as being of value. We will ensure that this time arrives for you. It will be communication from those who have words of importance. They will be imparted to you for onward transmission. This time will come. It is naturally the result of your efforts and application.

"We look to you not to hesitate and stumble. We look for determination of purpose and trust and faith during times when there appears to be no assistance. Accept these periods as necessary pauses for consolidation and fusing of the links. Connections must be made and secured. Do not waver, be sure and all the rest will be taken care of.

"There will be a time when you do not have so much put aside for your pleasure. It is to be a working environment in the realms of communication. In turn you will gain much for yourself and you will grow in all directions. Much will be learnt and understood. We will ensure, do not waver and be trustful."

JANUARY 18th 1993

AFTER THE OPERATION

The recovery period from my operation came to an end. I returned to the office and the panic situations that were always present there. There followed a long gap in recording my journeys through meditation. This is mainly because I could not find the time or energy to transcribe.

I attended many talks and gave some myself. There never seemed to be enough time as I followed through with instructions from the spirit communication. I did, however, do channelling each week and this had to be transcribed also. There are just so many hours in a day.

However it appeared that my spirit helpers also had this situation in hand. Some time later, after my return to work, I was asked to go to the personnel department. It was sympathetically explained to me that several people were to be made redundant. They were sorry but I was one of those. I was shattered. My world was turned upside down and my security lost, and to a Cancerian, security is everything.

My last days in the office were in May 1993. My spirit helpers had my full attention which they had intended all along. The meditations continued.

AUGUST 24th 1993

LOOK INTO FUTURE – BIRD MEN

I have been given silver after quite some time and am in a tight fitting, silver suit. Very unusual and attractive. I wouldn't mind having one of these. How different it makes me look. Quite a lot younger, I don't mind this at all. The stairs are very modern in a modern setting. At the bottom it is clean and empty of any clutter. I go along the passage in a businesslike way, in a 'knowing where I am going' manner. I turn off to the left, press a button and a door slides open for me. Very science fiction stuff it seems. You can't see my hair because it is enclosed in the tight fitting outfit even to the head.

Someone says: "It is a step into the future."

There are others here. I get a shock as they turn round because they are Bird Humans. Human bodies but their faces are, while not birds exactly, you immediately think of birds when you look at them. It is the features, the face and the eyes are piercing, bird-like, eagle-like. I have my own seat there at a console. In front of the console is a large screen. I press some buttons and there is a scene of other times. Of the 'now' time, I know it is the now time because it is a familiar scene of Earth.

I recognise it as being of Earth, landscape and trees and all that one views as familiar. I can't see any people. There are just clouds and trees and a wind blowing. There is a strong wind blowing, in fact it is growing in strength and blowing across. It seems to be turning into hurricane force, getting ever stronger. Things are being blown across the ground; trees, hedges, all sorts of things. I ask myself: *Where are the people, where are they?*

"Those that remain have buried themselves in places underground, have barricaded themselves in strongholds. They are securing their survival, those that remain are holding on tight to their existence. They do not wish to relinquish their hold upon their known Earth and will fight for survival of their known existence, for they do not believe there is anything more."

"Why I am seeing this?"

"You are watching the last of the old kind, of the old thinking and of the old beliefs. You are seeing the last, for the new that comes will

114

bring insight. Minds will turn in new directions and will know that there is no need to fight for survival. There will be peace. There will be peace."

It is comforting to know that way back in 1993 we were being alerted to the changes due around 2012. All is in hand I feel.

SEPTEMBER 10th 1993

TEAM WORK UNDER HIGH COMMAND

In this meditation I went in rather fast and did not wait very long. I soon connected with a wise Being. It was the start of channelled information and a new beginning.

*

A voice speaks, "Although I have been given command, I am not a superior Being to those who work under my command. We do not consider ourselves one above the other. It is simply a field of experience that places us in certain positions where our expertise can be utilised to the full. It is simply a matter of choosing the right tool. I am no more than a tool of those who have higher command. In their judgement the placement of me in this position ensures the most positive result attainable.

"We work as a team. The team is vast, much greater than you can imagine. It is, shall we say, a larger contingency than if you had put all your experts together, and by this we mean **all** your experts upon your planet. Our contingency of teamwork is larger. It will give you some idea of the scale of the operation. We work under a higher command you understand, one which you have reached at times, one with which you have had contact at times.

"If you wish to do this yet again you must allow yourself a longer period of time for the connection and do not be in such a hurry to reach a certain stage. We are merely a stage point, quite able to give you some information. If you wish to reach those who are able to give you a yet wider view, then you must allow yourself more time for your adjustment to be made. But it is well and we are satisfied, though we do feel at times that you yearn for the familiar contacts that you have had in recent months.

"Now you understand why we stress the importance of not being attached to a particular entity, to a particular name. This very attachment would make it yet more difficult for you to release your ties and reach yet further. Every attachment you make anchors you. That is what attachments are. It is logical, is it not? Now you can see the importance of not becoming so reliant upon those you call your guides. They are still with you and they are still important to you, do not misunderstand our meaning.

"There is a time for everything and the time this evening is not for that level of communication. You may call upon your familiar ones whenever you are dealing with matters concerning your physical plane and concerning matters of your astral plane and even beyond, for they will assist you if you have difficulties in achieving this level. We simply say do not become so attached that you cannot release an attachment at will. Consider it if you will as casting off the rope from the quayside when you wish travel out to sea. You cannot travel beyond the quay if you remain anchored and tied up alongside what is familiar to you. I think this analogy has made this quite clear. You will be able to return naturally to your quayside and we are grateful that you do this. We hope to present you with more information according to what we feel to be a necessity for clarity of understanding.

"We can feel a question you have. We understand you are concerned with why, in giving your messages and readings to others, you progress into the future and progress in forecasting what may be. We wish you to continue in this manner. We state it is important that you continue to relate what you feel is in store for any individual who comes to you. You will find that the context of matter given will be ambiguous as to time. It is important that you continue, to work upon your development and to work upon how you react and inter-react with each other and with the experiences that are presented to you.

"We do not wish that any soul goes into a state of non action. We are searching for the correct word for you, … of non …we nearly said of non existence but we feel this would be too strong. [state of] Resignation. This would be of great detriment to you if this were so and it is for this reason that we do not go into details. You are still in charge of your evolution and you are all still in charge of the evolution of your planet. You are still to be responsible for your futures. Each and every one of you, how you act and react NOW has an effect; will have an effect on what is to be for each and every one. So do not feel you have no control. We state this most firmly.

"We give you the picture of a family who moves into a residence that is not their own and they are aware that they are to be there for a matter of six months. So they say to themselves, 'It is not worthwhile to decorate this property or to maintain the garden or to perhaps put up a

few shelves and make it more habitable, for we will not be here for long.'
So they live in this way, live in discomfort and do not enjoy their
surroundings for it is not to their taste.

"They move residence as predicted, as they have known they would.
They move to yet another temporary residence and they continue in the
same manner and this goes on. Later they look back over the years.
They say, 'we did not enjoy ourselves much, we lived in run down places
which were not to our liking, and we never grew anything because we
were not to be there long enough.' And so it goes on and they see that
their lives have been wasted and they have not enjoyed themselves. Does
this analogy make things clear to you?"

INTENSE COLD

I am aware that my chest is hurting and tension is building in it. My
head is filling with the power and the energy. My upper body is ice cold.
A Being puts an arm out and extends it towards my chest and touches.
It is ice cold. I stay with this for a long time and the cold reaches down
into my stomach. The cold is like being frozen, like an anaesthetic cold
where one cannot feel anything. I must stay with it. My arms are feeling
numb as if being drained. My throat is beginning to ache and tighten
and I don't know if I can speak much more. I find after quite some time,
my mind coming back to other things so I know that it is finished and I
can't hold it any longer. I am brought back still feeling cold.

*

I was told later that this process was to raise my connection with spirit to
a higher level. They were pleased I stayed with it.

I am told many times by spirit that taking me into the cold is a
means of changing and raising my vibration, so that I can communicate
with higher vibrational beings. It indicates a change in my physical form
and sometimes I am seen to disappear from view. I wish I could see that
– ha ha!

CHAPTER FIVE

NOVEMBER 1st 1994

SPECIAL CHILDREN IN CIRCLE OF TEACHING

I have green and am in a cave of green crystal; beautiful translucent green. Smooth and soft to the touch, the sort of surface one wants to put one's hands on and stroke. Solid crystal rock is all around me, through which there appears to be a glow. Translucent light with a subdued but fresh feel about it. I ask what I need to see. I notice a little further off in the distance a circle of. . . I think they are children sitting on the floor playing over something. They are quite intent on what they are doing. They don't notice me at all but are just getting on with what they are doing. I go over to investigate.

The children appear to be studying a map of the world and seem to be concentrating their energies on the world in general. As I realise this, I see for the first time, standing behind them, are what I can only describe as Light Beings. They stand behind each child forming a circle of light around them, enclosing them, watching over them and quite probably influencing their thoughts as well. So they are getting help.

Now a strange thing, from a far corner come a stream of animals and birds and creatures. They too are surrounding the circle and arranging themselves around the circle of children and Light Beings, settling themselves in a ring, as if to say, we are involved as well'. All sorts of animals and creatures here, it reminds me of a Walt Disney film with all the animals getting on with each other.

I still don't know why I am being given this because I have asked to be shown what I need to know and what I need to see and what my part can be. As I ask again, someone is pulling my tongue out making it extra large and wagging it up and down.

I can only take that to mean that I must speak and have a wagging tongue. The tongue gets larger and larger and goes over the top of all the rings that are formed around the children and in to the middle. The tongue has become a chute, a slide. The tongue is now pointing into the centre of the world. Out of my mouth comes a jumble of words and letters, the alphabet, bits of paper, just tumbling down a chute, with papers and words all jumbled up and sliding down to the centre of the world. As it continues it forms a little pile. It is spreading and spreading and is now covering the entire world so that one can't see what is underneath.

The children are clapping their hands in delight. I think this has told me what I must do.

I ask now, "How must I do it, how?"

They give me the song: 'Buses Planes and Trains'. I assume that means travel and speaking. How am I to know what I am to speak about? How am I to be able to be represented? I tell them I need to be told how, what and to whom I am to speak. I need to know how and who to approach. It is an important part. In answer they have put the book in my hands and opened the pages, and it is the book that will do this. The book is only a catalyst, only a beginning.

NOVEMBER 3rd 1994

CHRIST AND BISHOP BLESSING BOOK

Deep purple. The stairs are in the same deep rich and soft to the feet purple. Actually it gives it a gloomy air because everything is dark with deep purple. The light is not reflected at all but is absorbed. I go down loosely dressed, not tightly dressed at all. I ask for an explanation to my dreams because I have had several and they are all interesting. I keep going down. It is just as gloomy down here as it was at the top. At the bottom the walls are rich, again in gloom. The door is a strange door because it is embossed in gold, like hammered beaten gold into figures and designs. Very ornate, the sort you would get on a church door. It has a ring handle. I turn it and go in. It is a church, a very quiet, dark church. One feels one must speak in a hushed voice in here. The pews are along the sides. They must be the choir stalls or whatever they call them. All carved in solid wood, very old this place. I don't feel it is an English church. Everything seems to be in wood, rich solid wood which has been there for oh so long, it will be there forever. Rich carvings, on the seats, on the stalls on both sides and where the altar is.

Oh, there is a figure kneeling at the altar. He is a serving dignitary of some sort, a serving member of the church, not a member of the public because he has a tall mitred Bishop's hat on. I feel he is somebody important. Rich clothes hanging down from his back, all vested up. He is kneeling for his own prayers, not for the public, it is for himself. He is lost in his own deliberations, making his prayers.

I want to know what this has got to do with me and my dream. There doesn't appear to be any connection whatsoever at the moment. I feel as if I am observing something special, something of importance and not a run of the mill service. Something so special that it has to be done apart from the routine stuff that goes on in churches. I move round to the side of him so that I can see, though I hardly dare to for fear of invading his private thoughts. I do not want to intrude but I must see.

He is kneeling and before him is a rich tasselled cushion, the sort that is used for presenting an object on. On it is laid a book which he is blessing, but the strange thing is that as I watch the open book, the pages are turning over as if fanned by a breeze. Gently, slowly and with deliberation the pages are turning as if by an unseen finger, page by page. This is going on while he is lost in his prayers, his dedication. He is in fact offering it to be blessed. The cover is in a strong clear blue, a rich shining blue.

The rest sounds a little bizarre but I have to say it because now in front of the Bishop is a seated figure of Christ. He is sitting in a half sideways position, He is sitting there just watching and smiling.

This is the strange part. The book which is now closed gets up as if it has little legs. It walks, moves, I don't know. It goes to the figure of Christ and appears to climb onto his lap. It has got little legs as if it is a person or the person is the book, I don't know which. It is a living thing. Perhaps that is what they are trying to tell me. It is living with a heart and mind and feelings of its own, so it can go to the Christ and it can feel to be a child of the Christ.

That is what it is, a child of the Christ; what Christ represents. It has settled itself down on the lap and when it does that it starts to open again and the pages start to turn again one by one, little by little. It is for the Christ to see the contents. I feel very reverent and hushed about the whole thing. The Christ holds the book and looks down at it as the pages turn and then makes the sign of the cross over it. He is giving it a blessing as well. I wonder what is to happen next.

From here my mind starts to come in with all sorts of ideas which seem to be absolutely stupid, so I allow this scene to fade because I think my own mind is interfering now…They [spirit] are still here. Perhaps I am not so silly. What is it? The book is being sent to the post office. It doesn't make sense! It is being despatched, wrapped up in brown paper and sent to the post office. It has had the blessing, the approval and now it is being despatched. I thank them, though I still don't see the connection with the dreams.

DECEMBER 16th 1994

I ask White Owl to show me where I must go. I am climbing up a rocky hillside. It is a steep climb, almost vertical holding – on – by – the – fingertips climb. There is no stairway or path. I must pick my way to the top of this rock. I do not know where I am going. I go quite steadily and although it appears difficult to any onlooker, in fact it is really quite easy. There are plenty of footholds. It is a question of stamina and strength, I have both.

I get to the top, which is an open space. There is nobody else up here. What is the purpose of this climb? I turn round and look all around me. The peak I am on is high above everything else. I can't see any other mountains. I suddenly realise that standing beside me are two figures. They are not of this Earth. They are not physical as I am. They are spirit entities. They have come to lift me up. They take an elbow each and rise up with me. It is an odd feeling. I can't see their faces; I only know what they are doing. They are two males, I have to call them angels, without the wings, it seems. Two messengers; that is the correct word. There is no effort on my part because they are making the effort for me. I just have to allow myself to be carried. I wonder where we are going.

As soon as I wonder that, I find myself alone, standing in a big hall with a smooth polished floor. I have arrived. I need to know more than I know. I need more answers, more information and more insight. I walk forward across the floor. I am at one end of the hall and must reach the other end. Again I am alone, I can't see anybody else. The hall is empty except for me. I can hear my footsteps echoing and making a sound on the floor. It is a lonely sound, as if the place is deserted. I know that can't be, otherwise I wouldn't be here. I have now reached the other end. I go through a tall doorway, no doors. It is simply an opening into somewhere else.

I step through and as I do it explodes into light. It is as if everybody has been hiding in there. It is a surprise for me. It is as if a party has been arranged, one that wasn't expected. Everybody is laughing, waving, smiling. They are coming forward taking me by the arm. They are hugging and kissing me. It is a surprise party. I am totally overwhelmed by it. What is the party for? They take me forward and emotion is building up in me. I am almost too overwhelmed to speak. They are pulling me forward.

Waiting is a man. A father figure, the father of them all; kind, loving. He holds his hands out to me, pulls me into his arms and hugs me to him. He kisses the top of my head. I am very emotional about it, especially as I do not know what this is all for. I am released and step back. I want to know what this is for. *What is this all about?* I wait.

"You have passed a certain stage. You have successfully completed a phase and are ready to go on to the next. You have earned the right to one who will be with you at the next stage of your journey. One who will be with you at all times. He will be one with whom you can communicate and who will uphold you in times of need and guide you in times of doubt."

I do not know who this is. I am getting a picture. I am feeling giddy and a little woozy, a little physically uncomfortable. It is as if I am under an anaesthetic.

CHAPTER SIX

1995

This was a time of post operation checks in hospital and although meeting with family members more, I was still unable to speak to them about my connections and conversations with spirit. It was hard to keep it all to myself. There was a little discord because I was not paying as much attention to the grandchildren as expected and was not a normal grandmother in their eyes.

JANUARY 21st 1995

I have been given silver and am in a silver armour suit, like chain mail. It is quite flexible and easy to move in. I am going down. There are brick walls on either side, rough and unadorned. They seem old yet the bricks are new. I don't know why that is. I skip down quite gaily, quite rapidly. I go down confidently, not hampered or hindered at all by the suit of protection. I haven't got a hat on. My hair is free and loose. The feeling is of abandonment, confidence. It is strange that towards the bottom the steps are much steeper. It is not quite a climb down but is more difficult now. One can't run down the last few steps, they are so steep. There are only a few like this, almost as if one has to be determined to carry on through these last stages. I mustn't be misled by the ease that I started out with. Determination and confidence has to follow right through. I can't go any deeper now, I am at the bottom.

It is dim down here, very dim, though light must be coming from somewhere. I walk ahead in the gloom which has a brown tinge to it. I look for an opening in the large brick walls. I can't work out if it is brick or stone as they are large slabs put together. I come to an opening that reminds me of the slits in castle walls. Narrow at the outside and wider inwards. I can just get through this with a squeeze. I have to go sideways as it is too narrow to go face forwards. I squeeze through and don't hurt myself because of the armour. As I get inside it is warm and lighter. I almost hear a noise, a sound. I can't catch what it is. People, music? My ears are hurting like mad. The tension is building in my ears and my head. Oh! What am I to hear?

There is a figure I must go towards. He is very special. He looks like a Master in white. He is waiting for me. I feel extremely emotional. I can't see his face. I can only half see. I feel insignificant and a bit earthy in front of this one. There is a glow of absolute love and understanding. What am I here for? I suddenly realise that all around me and behind me are other similar beings, glowing and in white just standing there. There is a wonderful feeling coming from them. There are several here. I am between the circle behind and the one in front. What am I here for?

"You are not alone. We are in front of you and behind you and around you. You are never alone in your endeavours and enthusiasms. We wish for your aims to work for mankind to be realised and will take advantage of your offer of service. It may feel to you that you are working entirely without help. But this is not so. For where we can, we move certain situations into favourable positioning. You should realise that although we have influence, we cannot alter another's will, even those which may be contrary to our thought transference. If one we wish to connect with denies their intuitive feeling then we are powerless. Please be patient. The ultimate aim is that you shall succeed in your desire to assist and to complete your mission upon the Earth.

"For your own journey, your desire, application and perseverance in the face of doubt, distractions and other influences will benefit your soul when you continue in spite of difficulties. Indeed perseverance and continuation against difficulties have a beneficial effect upon your own soul growth. We wish you well and ask that you do not be overly anxious as to whether your movements and decisions are correct or not. While you act according to your heart's desire to assist, then even misjudgement or appraisals which are not quite true, do not count against you. They are merely symptoms of inexperience. You cannot be held accountable for inexperience. We ask that you continue to work together in all your mind states and unite your consciences and your consciousness together.

"Your soul knows what it is about, but this too has a certain amount of inexperience as well as experience in some other areas. This final stage is completion of a cycle of learning, which would not be necessary were the experience already contained within.

"We say also do not be confused by the names applied to your soul for there have been many. It is not detrimental to apply yet another, providing you have a point of reference which is easy for you. The name you have been given applies to a past incarnation at a time when your wisdom came forth in a recognisable way to others. All past incarnations have required a cloak of anonymity for the current period of incarnation. We do not wish this meeting to be taken up with explanations regarding past lives. Our main purpose now is to make you aware that you are surrounded by love and influence. Do not be concerned with your physical ailments for you will not be allowed to depart just yet."

I notice now that the ground around me is all silver. I am not only standing in a silver suit but I have silver all around in a circle. To any onlooker there is a silver circle in which I am standing, surrounded by a circle of white beings, the main one being ahead and slightly raised. He doesn't appear to be standing on anything but is raised. It is as if he is standing in space which enables him to look down. The others are on the same level as me. It is a very clear picture. Something more must happen here. I don't know what it is.

I have coming in from both sides. I don't know how to explain this. The horseshoe of white Beings is behind me and one in front. There is a gap between him and those on each side of the horseshoe and through these gaps other Beings are coming. They are not in white, as are those behind, but are depicted as guides, different nationalities, different personalities, recognisable as my guides. Dr. Po, the Indian, the Rajah and even the Tuaregs and many others besides. They have all filed in and have formed in a half circle, another horseshoe between myself and the white shining ones. They have come in, not to speak, just to be there. They are showing support. I feel they are to act as intermediaries. It is a symbolic representation. I feel I want to turn round and greet them all and hug them, but I mustn't because it would break up the feeling of ceremony. But it is what I would like to do for they are my friends. They are all my friends and there isn't one who would not work with me. That again makes me feel very moved and emotional.

"I don't know what I must do and why have I got this coat of armour on, flexible though it is?"

"The silver suit of truth that is impenetrable to the arrows of disbelief and criticism and any other aggressive force. The suit is for your protection, yet it allows you to move freely. It will not hamper any action."

I thank them for that. Once again as has happened before, I have to put my tongue out and one of them has placed a drop of mercury on the tongue which I then take in. I am getting tired, very tired. I should leave, the energy is going.

JANUARY 23rd 1995

UNITE TWO SOULS

Everything is in a beautiful, deep, ruby red. It is a quiet, deep colour. It feels clean and pure. I have been given a ladder which is laid flat so that it spans as a bridge over a gap. I have to go over. It is a long gap, so I go along on all fours as the only safe way to go. It is not easy or steady so I have to make sure that I am well balanced and do not lean to one side or the other, or the whole thing could tip up. I am trying to be as central and stable as I can be as I go. It is not comfortable on the knees or hands. It is not the easiest thing I have had to do. It is high up and narrow. I certainly don't want to fall off.

I reach the other side safely. I crawl off the end of the ladder; I don't want to stand up yet. As I clear the ladder I stand and am on rocky ground. It is bare rock with open space and very high up. Everywhere appears to be rather barren. I can't see any trees or grass. I don't want to stay near the edge. I walk away from it as far as I can. I wonder what I am doing here.

"Why am I here and where am I to go?" As I walk I go down a slope and over a rise I can see what was hidden before because the land falls away. I am coming off the bare rocky surface now and things are beginning to grow as I go down.

There is someone sitting on the ground looking out over the scenery in front. I go up to him and sit down beside him. He is the only one around so he must be the one I am meant to be with. I don't sit too close. I want to look at him from an angle. He has a lot of curly hair, quite long, bouncy and what one might call, unruly. He has a youngish face, not immature but full of youth and vigour. Not an old man. Virile, a straight nose, almost Grecian. The eyes are beautiful and kindly. Again blue. A nice round mouth. I wonder if he knows how much I am studying him. He is what one might call a beautiful youth. I have seen him before. All this observation takes place very quickly. He looks at me and is doing the same. I know he is doing the same.

So now we know each other. We know each other well. We are old friends and are comfortable without speaking. We both put our hands out to each other and hold hands and join. This is a union with each other. The hands feel good and warm and strong. It is a good handclasp. Having done that we edge a little closer. Still no words. We stand up and embrace closely in a warm hug. It is a comforting feeling, a homecoming. He is a lot taller than I but it is still comfortable and I feel good about it.

We go down further into the valley. We walk side by side holding hands because we are joined and are meant to be so. As we walk ahead of us we see another figure. This one is old, older than us. He represents a father figure, a wise man, one much wiser than us. We walk up to him. He comes from another time and puts a hand on each shoulder. He bends forward and kisses us on the forehead in turn. What are we here for? I want to call him father.

"What are we here for, Father? What are we to do?"

"You are to work together. Unite your two sides, your two characters into one, forming a balance and use the combined force for the benefit of others. The joint effort will enable you to fulfil your mission in absoluteness, providing you are not deterred by obstacles and interferences placed in your way. Know your objective of teaching others to understand the Spiritual Law. Know your objective of preparing men for their next stage of existence. Prepare the souls of men for the knowledge that they have been ignorant of up to this moment. Your work is to teach and to awaken minds in understanding. You are to use your combined force so that what one lacks the other supplies. This is true from whichever point of view you regard it. You will be unsure as to the validity of what I am saying. It is for you to decide. It is your choice. We say that if you decide other than what is given here there will be other choices offered to you. We say that combined force is greater than one as a separate entity.

"There is much for you to dwell on. There is much for you to understand. We will endeavour to place before you situations which will enlighten and make clear. Do not be over anxious. Continue with your endeavours. First you must attempt your own understanding. Go now and be blessed."

JANUARY 25th 1995

MEETING WITH THE MASTER

I have green and silver. I am reminded of the green of the forest and the silver of the leaves. I walk through the forest and come to a swing. I get on and begin the movement to and fro. It goes higher and higher. I am not very keen on swings that go high but it seems to be alright as the ropes are quite taut. I go really high and the ropes are caught by someone. I am wondering where I am. I stand but I am not at the tops of trees but in a separate place altogether. A solid floor. I walk ahead trying to make sense of this. There is a little door. I bend down low and squeeze myself through. It is such a little opening; it might almost be missed except that there is nothing else to see. I am through now. It is dark inside.

Something is moving around my feet and tugging on my clothes. There is more than one here. I must be careful how I move my feet in case I tread on these little beings. I must take care with them. They want my attention. I feel a bit like Gulliver for I am a little too large for where I am. They know what they want but I don't understand.

I ask Andreas [my guide] to stay with me. We go joined as one in the direction of the pulling. We could resist if we wanted to, but why should we resist? We come to another opening which is lit on the other side. The light is shining through the opening. This is where we have been pulled to. We go through. We squeeze through the small opening. Inside there is beautiful light. The warmth of it is like a warm spring day, comfortable, comforting warmth, a good to be alive feeling. It is not telling me what I want to know at all. My throat is tightening up and I want to cry now. Why is this so? Oh, the throat is tightening so much.

Arms are being put around my shoulder and I am led gently forward very kindly. I have an intense feeling of tears, emotion. It is so difficult not to cry and I don't know why. They are so gentle, so gentle. I sit down at a table. It is smooth but empty. Opposite me is a very large person, kindly but with great authority. A father of all, not just ours. One who has charge and I am just one of the children. He pushes something towards me. It is a book but the pages are not empty. I can't read it. The pages are full of gold lettering. What is this telling me? Now

130

he is piling other books on top, one after the other. Many books. Is this to read, to write, what? He pushes them to one side because the pile is high and he wishes to see me. He takes both my hands and looks at my fingers. He is studying them. He puts the two together as if in prayer. He holds them in that position. This is very moving for me. One of those who brought me here now brings some length of cloth and binds the two pairs of hands round and round so that they are joined together. It is symbolic of receiving from the hands of the Master into my hands. It is a heavy responsibility and an honour at the same time. The figure is beautiful and has the face of a beautiful Master. Kindness and love overwhelms me.

"Father, how can I go about the work that is there for me? I need guidance for this."

"You will be supplied with all the help that is necessary. You will be led into all areas that we have in mind. Situations will be placed before you and you will deal with them according to your own growing wisdom. We will not let you down. We will be supportive for the very reason that you have offered yourself in service. We will take advantage of that offer. Do not doubt that we will take up the desire to be of help to those who have less understanding. It will be clear what you are to do in connection with those who group themselves around you.

"You are to keep this message to you close so that you may be reminded in moments of uncertainty and doubting your own abilities. The matter of names will be clarified in due course, for we understand confusion has arisen. Now you have experience of why we denied you access to names in your early attempts at communication. Confusion is caused. You may use whatever name you feel comfortable with, irrespective of the true one given from the spirit world."

The hands are now unbound. I sit there not knowing what to do. I don't know whether to get up or not. Two from behind put their hands on my shoulders and help me to rise. They escort me back to the opening, but I don't really want to go. I want to stay there even if there are no words. But I cannot do my work here and I must go back into the darkness. There is a little light now. I have the feeling that you have when one is given good news. A lightness of heart and happiness inside. I go back through that first opening and out. I come back here having been given more confirmation. I must keep this message close to me.

JANUARY 27th 1995

THE HAWK

There is a great white Indian, all white. He stands there very strong. He steps forward and points to the ground. I look down and see a pattern in the earth. The pattern marks out a circle, in the circle is a maze. In the middle of the maze is a jewel. I look down and can see the way clearly, the entrance and the ways one must go.

"When you look from a distant viewpoint down onto your puzzlement, when you look from above, you can see clearly the route you must travel to capture the rewards that are waiting at the centre of things. Look from above and not at ground level for you can see nothing but confusion at ground level. Raise yourself so that you may look from a distant viewpoint."

"That is easier said than done."

"You will find answers by removing yourself into a higher state of being. That much is obvious. Continue to do this until the way is clear. Persevere until you have perfected the art. When you have succeeded in raising yourself above your situation it is then that you must direct your enquiring mind and ask in that moment what it is you wish answers to. It is you who will find the answers. It is yourself that will see where your footsteps must go. The effort is yours."

"I am feeling that this is a mammoth task."

"It is not impossible. It takes application, dedication and perseverance. That is all. So, allocate to yourself more time than you have in recent weeks and months. Do not be distracted from your task. There will be events happening which will require understanding and it is when these needs arise that you must withdraw yourself to a higher state. When you have succeeded and discover you may seek your answers with ease and with no difficulty, then you may proceed to yet greater communication. The ways will be opened. The vibration of others who have wisdoms to offer will be felt and will join with yours. Wisdoms of The Masters. It is then you may teach others and lead them into awareness. First you have your own task to accomplish. You are to resume the intense application given at your first awakening."

I feel intense heat and pressure on my hands which is good. I feel it is good. I feel the presence of the Indian very strongly. I feel pressure and weight upon my hands, an energy that was not there before. I look down on the maze for he is pointing again and the jewel in the centre is glistening and glowing. It is like a miniature fireball. It is worth having. An energy source, an oracle. It is not to be taken with ease.

The Indian raised his arms sideways. They are now wings. He turns his head and has become the Hawk, the bird. He is now immobile before me. I am left with the maze and the jewel and the intense energy on my hands. I am told to raise my hands to my head.

FEBRUARY 2nd 1995

SACRIFICE FOR CAVE DWELLERS

The colour is silver. There is a silver chute and a double figure of me, like a shadow me, has slid down the chute and shot out at the bottom. I land on a mat. I stand up. There are steel walls, steel floor. It is like being encased in a biscuit tin. I walk ahead. Everything is very solid and shiny. There would be no breaking into here. I turn off; there don't appear to be any openings, no doors or windows. Nothing, just shiny metal steel walls. I walk along and at last there is a door, like a panel. I press a button and it slides open. Very modernistic, this. I walk in and am immediately back to ancient times. It is like being back with the cave dwellers, not quite prehistoric but in the cave dwelling period. There are lots and lots of people here, families, babies, all living here. What an odd place to find them! They don't appear to see me because nobody takes any notice although I am dressed in silver. It is as if they can't see me.

"So, what am I doing here and what am I to do?"

"You are to observe and note their actions and see what is in their minds for it will be obvious. You are to guide and impress them with solutions to the difficulties they have, for you will see clearly. You are to show them by means of your mind what their actions are to be. They will learn by the discovery which will be felt to be from themselves. You are to bring them forward from their limited thinking into a wider field of seeing and understanding."

"I am wondering how on earth I can do this? How can I project my mind? It sounds easy but I don't see how."

"You are to observe their difficulties and see the solutions yourself and then enact the solutions in your own mind so that the picture is complete in your understanding and then project this package to their mind area. Leave the rest to us. These beings are still existing from day to day on a minute by minute basis, with no thought for the future and no projection ahead of their existences. It is required at this time that thought be given to consequences of actions. This is what we are referring to. Actions now in preparation for future events."

"I still don't know how I can help them. My knowledge is not that wide. I need to be given help in this, I think."

"You will be impressed as and when necessary with what is to be given through you. You will be equally impressed from another source to enable you to pass these impressions onward. Do not be concerned at the moment. Do be aware that these beings have nothing to offer you. They are oblivious of your existence. This is to be a sacrificing of yourself with no recompense from those for whom you sacrifice."

SETH – NEW GENERATIONS OF MAN, MAN TO CONTINUE

The colour is a deep indigo blue. I am dressed in a long gown which is sparkling. It is a midnight blue, sparkling like the stars in the sky. I am reminded strongly of the Magician's cloak. This gown is long and draping. I must go towards my space. I am not sure whether I have to go down or straight. I must find out. I walk along a passageway which is narrow with high walls on either side. There is just room for one. I look so small at the foot of high walls. Walking along. This is like a cleft, it is that high. I can't see a ceiling. I suddenly realise there are pictures all along the walls, but being so close to them I can't take them in. To see a picture clearly one needs to step back and I can't do that here. They are very close to me but I can't really say what they are about. The passage winds around. It keeps reminding me of something but I can't think what it is. I have just realised what it reminds me of.

It is as if I am walking round and inside a tube of rolled up paper and I am walking at the bottom of the long tube. The paper has loosened around the roll. I am walking between the spaces where the paper has come away from being tightly rolled up. What an odd thing! An upright tube with me at the bottom walking round and round from the outside in. I am walking around to the centre of the tube. Now I see it. I am walking around the inside of a magazine or paper, rolled up with lots of different articles and pictures that I can't see because I am too close. What am I going to find in the middle?

I arrive at the centre. Sitting on a stool in the middle is a person. He has the domed hat that I have seen so often before. The strange beehive shape that stretches up, quite elongated. He sits there and his nose seems to follow the contours of the hat in a sweeping line. He is obviously of some rank because of the clothes. One knows that he belongs to some high order. I shall describe his clothes. There are rings round his chest going out to his shoulders like a cowl. It is of quality and heaviness. It is not a working outfit but something special, official. He has a chain round his neck with a great circular pendant. In the middle of it there is a ruby, but that's not all. Circled around this ruby are little gemstones in an amber colour. Round that is another circle of stones in blue. It is very big, this pendant. There are many circles of jewels round the outside of the middle ruby. It is hung on a very strong chain.

He stands up when he sees me and puts his finger on my forehead, tracing across in a circle. He turns me to face the walls of the space we are in. Now we have seen space. I can see pictures on a circular screen all around. He is pointing at his finger at the screen. I can't see anything. This is a great disappointment to me. Then he points to one particular section and it comes to life. What am I to see here? This is strange!

There are galloping horsemen of the desert. They are galloping like mad towards us. It is a bit like being at an Imax cinema for they don't actually leave the screen. I don't understand this at all. They are escaping from something, running away from something that is threatening to overtake them. I don't understand this.

He moves his hand round to another screen, and that too comes to life. What has overtaken them is water. A wall of water, they were attempting to escape but there was no escape. The water came too fast and has covered everything. The water has covered everything. It settles and the agitation in the waters settles down and becomes tranquil as if it has always been there. There is a quiet scene of water now with no trace of the galloping men trying to escape. No sign that they ever were. It is a sombre picture but peaceful and I don't feel bad about it as one might expect.

The finger moves on to the next part. I slowly turn to watch. Pushing up from the waters now is land. Just pushing up from the bottom with waters running off. New land. Birds start to fly for they have not been destroyed. Birds find this land and they come carrying their seeds, making their nests and beginning the growth all over again. As I watch I see a speeded up growth process in front of me. New shoots, new creatures, all kinds, vegetation, life in the full, enriched life. Very much enriched.

Now there is a picture of ships and people, habitation, buildings, transport, industry, all growing, all beginning. A lot of movement, a lot of activity.

The finger moves on. Now there are children playing, dancing and playing children's games, and studying books. They are studying the ground, they are studying the plants and the skies. They are studying things with seriousness and really enjoying what they are learning. Many children with maturity, mature in mind, if not in years. Impressive to me, most unusual. They make one think and wonder. Wondrous.

The finger moves on. Now I ask what this is all about because it is all very nice but I like to understand why I am being shown this. Why am I being given this and to what area and era are we referring?

"We are looking from the past to the future. The children you see are the horsemen who attempted to escape from the waters. The children are the product of the generations that felt they were vanquished from the land. There is never to be complete obliteration. Those who perish will return yet again to a more refreshing period with the wisdoms and understanding of the follies of past times. The children you see are the descendants of earlier generations. They are generations now with knowledge and a maturity that is born of experience."

I ask, "What time?"

"It is clear. When the waters overtake your land, when the waters come from which there is no escape, when the land is in upheaval. We are aware that you ask when this is. We say, that we are not to advise you of the time precisely, for actions of an adverse nature would then begin. There would be confusion, panic and misdeeds. We require only that the behaviour and attitude towards each other be enriched in preparation for forming a firm character and personality base for the generations to come. We give this to you so that you may pass on knowledge that there is to be continuation of the generations of mankind. There is to be a progression and not finality."

I ask him to tell me clearly what his name is, as I really want to know.

"I am Set(h)."

My mind starts to dart around. I am becoming confused. Things are not holding together for me. I can't seem to form any clarity of mind. It is breaking up around me. He is wavering in and out. Here one minute and not the next. I am feeling confusion, totally mixed now. Everything is breaking away and I feel I must come back. The energies are building very strongly. I thank them for the pictures, though I feel it is incomplete. There must be something in me that is stopping this or something from them that is stopping this because they are still here. I don't feel I can carry on. Perhaps another time, though I know they never repeat the same scenario. I allow myself to come back fully.

138

FEBRUARY 5th 1995

HEALING MANKIND [in trance]

I have been given green, a jade watery green like the sea. The clothes are heavily weighted. I am in a bewildered state and am not functioning mentally at all. I can't decide where to go. Two pairs of hands have steered me and turned me very caringly and gently in the way I must go. I am in a confused, almost drugged state. The walls are leaves, big broad leaves and are covering the walls completely. I walk along uncertainly, not knowing if I am going to trip over anything. It is a very unsteady state. I must go down a few steps, not many, just three. I hold on to the walls, a hand on each wall to guide myself down, down, now the last one. There is a slight gentle slope like a ramp. It is carpeted in rough matting so I don't slip. I am still holding on to the walls for support. I don't know why I should feel like this. I feel alright, just a little disorientated. I follow the slope round to the left. There is an opening on the right like an archway. I go through. It leads me outside to the fresh air. The cough sets up a reaction and where I should be breathing more freely I am not. My chest is restricted, it is difficult to breathe. I breathe deeply. That is better.

My mind flashes back to when I had operations as a child. I feel there may be connections here. Yes. There is a connection here between those two operations and the breathing difficulty. I am outside and there is a house opposite. I feel stronger. I stride towards an ordinary looking house, standing all by itself. I go straight in the doorway. My chest is hurting. What is in the house?

There is a man at a table with his back to me. Of course he would have his back to me. He doesn't want his identity known for he maintains his back towards me. If I move round he turns. He is a little bowed over, hunched up. He is in brown, well bent over so I will not see who he is. I go up to him and put my hands on his shoulders and pull his shoulders back to straighten him. My two thumbs on his spine. I pull backward so that he sits upright. I pull his shoulders back so that he can breathe. He still doesn't turn round but it doesn't matter. I make sure that he is sitting straight now. He is quite compliant and doesn't think it odd. I put

139

my arms around his shoulders and heave his shoulders back using my full arm so that he doesn't spring back into the slouched position again. I can feel the roughness of his cloak, it is clean and I don't feel bad about it. It is a nice russet colour brown, a good colour. I get the urge to put my knee in his back as well, that's odd. I do this and straighten him even more. He has to sit down for he would be too tall for me if he stood up. I am still in green, heavy, full length clothes.

What else? There is something more. I reach behind him, kneel on the floor and from behind take his hands. From the back I put my arms around his waist and hold his hands so that I am pressed close to him and touching his back to my front. It is merging the auras and the contact is making this complete. I have to hold his hands and straighten his fingers which are all clenched. With my fingers I am making sure his uncurl by placing mine over the top of his and making sure they are straight. Both hands, so that they relax. I spread his fingers and thumbs out over his knees so that they are resting but spread instead of being tightly curled.

Now he is sitting straight. He has no alternative. His hands are unclenched. I don't know who he is or why I must do this, but already the positioning of his body gives him more self worth, more confidence and ability to go forward. Is he ready to show me his face so that I may know who he is? May I see his face?

I stand up and he stands. He is large and tall and big. Much bigger than I. He turns round but where his face should be is the globe of the world. That is all it is, the planet. I am taken aback for he has a man's body and the planet's face revolves in the space where his face should be. This is very odd. I still feel as if he is a man and that this is an illusion, a trick that behind that revolving globe must be a face.

I hear a voice: "It is still a man, mankind. You are looking at the face of mankind upon your planet and you are effective in healing the attitudes upon the planet. You are to effect a change in the attitudes. The body of those who dwell upon your world will stand more erect and be more relaxed and confident about their future. It is your moulding and melding and authority that will assist in this process."

I ask, "Why was I so unsteady and disorientated in arriving here?"

"The work that you carry out will be in a state of disorientation, will be in a state of not knowing where you are going or who you really are for the execution of this process. You will be in a daze, but that condition will only exist at the first stage of your journey. The strength will come through you when faced with the duties before you."

I feel that I know what they are saying though they are going about it the long way. That is strange, this great big figure has picked me up, for I am quite a lot smaller. He has picked me up in a hug. I am now being embraced. I have never been hugged by the world before. It is not bad. In fact I kiss the spinning globe and that is not bad either, for it is spinning slowly. I am put down again. I get down on my knees and put my hands together and pray in front of this figure that represents mankind. It is much more than humanity for the figure before me is the Creator of mankind that is represented in each one of us. It is a great figure. It turns into a shining light before my eyes, it begins to glow. It is beautiful, beautiful. I feel all tingly. There are shivers all over me. Dear God. I weep and weep.

MERGING INTO THE LIGHT

The colour is silver green. Healing by truth, I feel. The walls are rough, the sort that if you rubbed against it you would hurt yourself. Very rough stipple. The stairs are covered in worn patterned lino. Very old fashioned. I fail to see how this lino would bend over the treads but it does. It is held into place by metal stair rods. This is an old fashioned setting. I go down and although the walls are rough there are no banisters. I am holding on, being careful not to graze my skin. The stairs are quite steep as if I am going down into a cellar, not the normal household stairs. Steep.

We are going down deep. It is a long way down too. We are going to an underground passage. The passage is going to lead somewhere else. I am at the bottom now. It is dark and narrow. Not much light. Very gloomy. I go ahead a little bit and feel for my turning off. It is very dark. I turn off to the left. It is leading me somewhere and is going on for quite some way. The floor is a cement floor, a bit rough. The walls are rough too, brick. I come to an unpainted rough wood door. I put my shoulder to it and push hard. It takes a bit of moving but it does and I go in. I almost feel as if it would swing back on me. I get through. I look about, hoping to see something.

There is a bench over to the right. It is gloomy here. The bench is the only thing I can see so I go towards it. It has no back. It is thick solid wood, much used. It has been around for a very long time. It will last forever. I stand in front of it. It seems the obvious thing to do is to sit on it, as a bench is for sitting. But no, this bench is for standing on. I climb on to it. I can see much further even though it is gloomy. I realise the bench is against the wall. I feel the wall and feel about with my fingers, for I know I am to find something. The wall is cool, very rough. It is like feeling coal on a coal face. My fingers are feeling lots of things and I can't tell what is important and what is not. There are knobs and cracks, rough edges. What am I to feel?

My fingers have found a definite ledge. I stand on tiptoe to feel into the ledge. There is a box in there. I am really stretching now. It is not that easy. I am trying to get a grip on it so that I can pull it nearer and pull it out. I have just about got it. It feels like a brass box. I pull it nearer to the edge until I have a good grasp on it. I pull it off the ledge and get down and sit with the box beside me. It is a little bigger than my hand, about twice the size of my hand. I can just about see. It is studded with jewels of some sort. I don't feel they are very precious jewels for the box is in brass and my logic tells me that very precious jewels wouldn't be set in brass. It is more for the effect to make it look pretty.

I obviously must open it but while I think about this I know I am not by myself. I feel that I have company and that this company, whether it is one or many, is waiting for me to open the little box. That makes me a bit apprehensive. I feel as if I am opening Pandora's Box. What is inside this apparently innocuous thing? I take my time and think about it. It is not locked and I know I don't need any effort to open it. It is a question of just opening the lid. Why am I hesitating to do this? I can feel it with my fingers. My hands are running over it. It feels quite nice. Why the hesitation?

Suddenly I open it. I can't sit there and not do anything. There is light coming from it as I knew there would be. I knew there would be light. The light is casting a glow. It spreads far. It is all coming from the box, like turning on a switch. The light inside is so bright, I can't see the contents. So I must put my hands in now. I am almost afraid to do that too. Is it hot? It must be special, this light. But I don't need to put my hand in after all for the light moves out and the source of the light lifts itself out of the box. I feel very emotional.

It moves gently, the source of the light moves about in front of me so gently – oh – it is like a floating fairy – it is so very gentle that I get a lot of emotion from it. I am moved by the love and gentleness that is coming from the light that was contained in the box. It is almost overwhelming. It floats down and places itself in front of me, a little distance off. I am looking down at it on the floor. It is just beautiful. As I watch it grows and gets larger. It grows and grows until I realise it is a glowing figure in front. I can't see detail; just that it is a glowing figure, a Being of some sort. There is something inside the centre of the light which is very gentle and loving. What am I to do? I don't know what I am to do. What am I to learn from this?

"Step forward."

I step closer, nearer. I am almost afraid, not real fear. I am close now. I kneel down. The light from the Being is all over me. I feel as if I don't exist anymore. I am in the light and have disappeared in the light. I am not me anymore. I can't see me, I can't feel me, and I have melted into the light. I am in and part of that Being. I am not a separate thing. I have been merged, ingested into the light. I can't be separate anymore. I have lost the Me that was. It is no longer, it doesn't exist anymore. I don't feel bad, just strange.

"You are no longer separate, no longer what you were."

The logical part of my brain tells me that I still operate as a physical being. The brain is still working. It is as if the brain is separate and functions apart from the Me that is absorbed. Weird! I feel I rock and waver like this light. We walk together. No, we glide. We move gently. As we move, my physical body brings me back.

FEBRUARY 26th 1995

ISOLATED SPOTS TO BE INCLUDED TOO

I have a picture of climbing, by the sea but up high. I feel it is an island. I am climbing up rocks with somebody else. It is very rough climbing over the rocks. We don't seem to be climbing up, though we are high. Climbing over is more the way of it. The rocks are very grey and black, no grass on them. They are very wet too. I have a clear picture of it in my mind. The weather is not very good either. Mist, wind and fresh air. I don't know why we are climbing or who the other person is.

We are making our way to a very isolated cottage. It is lonely countryside, Ireland or Scotland where it is wild and isolated. It is not one of those pretty cottages, but functional. The yard is very practical looking. No roses round the door. We open the gate and walk up to the front door. There is a little porch. We go straight in. There are no locks or anything like that, just straight in. A woman is sitting by the fire.

We appear to be two men. I am a man. We take our wet coats off, boots, hats. We stand by the fire warming ourselves and the woman gets up to make some tea or something. It is all very ordinary and comfortable. I don't know why we were climbing over the rocks or what this is telling me.

We are here to talk and there are more people coming in. They have come from afar – they are filling the room. They are all coming in wet. It is odd because this is an isolated spot and yet there are many arriving. Coming in and all sat round the table for a discussion. It is a meeting of sorts. The woman is there to make the tea, to keep the fire going. It is men's work. They have taken the role of leadership.

They are the leaders. They are talking about education for the children. Proper living for the families and the need to be included in all the other activities that go on in the towns and not to be excluded, not to be set apart.

"We have come to make our opinions known and plan a campaign to ensure our acceptance into other things so that we have a say and are no longer on the fringe. We are putting up our viewpoint, putting our case forward."

I understand.

145

MARCH 5th 1995

STUDENTS AND TEACHER AT SCHOOL

I have asked White Owl to take me where I need to be, as I need help. He has come. He is with me. Dr.Po is here too. I am shown a few little steps going down. Not a great stairway. The little passage at the bottom twists and turns, never going in a straight line. It is a zig-zag, almost deliberate change of direction so that one loses one's sense of direction. Like in blind man's bluff when one is turned round and has to find one's own way. I can only stay on this one zig-zag passage because there are no alternatives. I weave my way through, turning sharp corners all the time. It is very narrow and my shoulders are brushing each side. Eventually it comes out into an opening like the end of a tube, fanning out like a trumpet. *Laughing* A musical note has come out at the end, blown by my friend.

As I come out there is a row of school desks, which are all facing me so I don't know if I am the student or the teacher. Waiting, there is nobody else there. I feel compelled to go and sit in one of the seats so that I can face the front. I decide to sit at one side and wait. There are no other students and there is no teacher, no books, no pens. Just seats and the desks. After a while I get fed up with this. It seems like a waste of time. Perhaps I am in the wrong classroom. That can't be because this is where the passage comes out. I get up and start wandering round the room, looking for some clues as to what this is all about. No windows, just a room.

There is a door. It is obvious there is nothing going on here so I go to the door, turn the handle and step out into a broad passage. Very broad and clean and very quiet. I turn to my right. I am going to see what I can find now. A little dog has joined me, scampering along with its claws making a little pitter patter sound on the polished floor. I can hear it quite distinctly. It has decided to join me. It is a small dog, friendly and bouncy. The dog sniffs at a door so I think; *alright I will go into this one, this classroom.* It is a bit further along than the other. I open the door and the place is absolutely full of students. They all look up as I come in the door, as if they have been waiting. I feel much older than they. I feel as if I know more. They are all waiting so I go to the front.

The little dog follows. I don't know why I am there but it is obvious I am not one of those students. Why am I here and what am I to say?

They want to ask me questions, questions on spiritual causes and effects, questions on living and dying. Looking for answers and hoping I will tell them. They want to know more than they already do. I lift the little dog on the desk in front of me. It stands there wagging its tail, quivering with pleasure and trust. I tell them that this little creature is as they should be. They look puzzled. I explain that this little thing is full of unconditional love, full of trust and full of pleasure in its life, in its surroundings. It gives itself totally to those who are close to it in its area of being, instinctively without hesitation. It has a certain amount of intuitive feeling that tells it where it is welcome or unwelcome. It quite simply avoids those areas where it is uncomfortable.

I feel that this is something for these students to ponder upon. But *I* am looking for a teacher, I am looking for guidance and I haven't yet met it in this school. The one that I am seeking is passing through, I feel. The door opens again and in walks someone much more than I, somebody who is in authority. He walks up to me, puts his arm across my shoulders. We stand facing the students. I feel suddenly very young, as if I am another student trying out my words. He is The Master. We stand together facing the students. He motions to me to sit down and begins to demonstrate himself. He begins to speak on greater things with more authority, while we all listen with rapt attention. We are in the presence of one who knows.

THE BOOKS AND CHRISTLIKE FIGURE

I have rose pink. I am standing at the top of an escalator. It is long because I can't see the bottom. I step onto it and hold onto the rail. I can either walk down as it moves or let it carry me. I decide to stay where I am and let it carry me because I am intrigued by the pictures on the walls on either side. They are all dancing figures, clowns, dancing jesters. Oh! People doing silly antics to amuse. There are more of them on my right. I am barely registering. It has taken my attention from the length of time it is taking to go down. I am reminded of the moving escalators at airports where one seems to go on forever. The pictures are giving way now to country cottage type scenes with smoke coming out of the chimneys. I don't know what they are meant to be advertising. It is usually for advertisements. Eventually I get to the bottom. I step off and forward momentum propels me a little bit forward. There is a slight slope now. I don't know where this passage is leading but I have to follow as there is no other way. It bends to the left.

The theme of underground stations continues because there is an opening that one normally sees before going onto the platform. No doors, just walk through. As I go through there is a vast area, no trains. What can I see? A row of tables. A whole row of tables set in a semicircle. I walk towards them. In the middle of the semicircle the tables are spreading all the way around, piled high with books. I walk straight ahead, it seems the logical thing to do. They too are piled high with books all stacked up neatly, all identical. There is a man behind a table. His dress is of ancient times long before there would have been books, so he is out of place. Books are modern, modern printing and yet he comes dressed in white robes. He appears to be a Christ like figure, a biblical figure. Why biblical?

"We represent all that is good. We demonstrate this to your eyes so that you might recognise from whence we come and not be confused in searching your mind for origins. The books are yours."

I laugh, disbelieving.

He puts a book in my hand. It is heavy, a hardback. I can't see what is on it at all. I don't need to open it. I feel a tugging at my clothes. I look

148

down and there is a child who wants me to give her the book. I give it to her for her to carry. That is what she wanted. She is happy and wanted to carry it for me.

I wonder what is on the other tables. I walk around them slowly and they are all piled high with the same book. An inexhaustible supply. There is nowhere to pay so I don't know how one goes about buying them. It is a distribution centre. That is what this is.

MARCH 17th 1995

TEACHING CHILDREN IN AN AFRICAN VILLAGE

There is a silver stream with little flecks of gold in it. I merge with the stream and climb on to something which carries me down. We seem to be descending gently – no – it is a bit of a torrent really. The banks on either side are going by so quickly and whatever I am sitting on is swept to the side and bumps into the shore. I get off and climb up the steep bank. It is a hands and knees job. I hold on to tufts of grass so that I don't fall. I am definitely not in condition because I am puffing a bit. I must get back into form. I am dressed in an incongruous silver and gold speckled suit.

I come to a hut such as one would see in an African village. A round hut, rather large. As it is the only thing of interest around, I go in. Stooping to enter I see a man sitting on the floor cross-legged. He is not an African. I can't see him clearly enough. I need to know who he is. His eyes are striking, clear. They look at me to the point where his eyes are the only things I notice. Such eyes! I sit down in front of him on a little cushion. He sits looking at me. A lot of children come filing in through the door. Children of all ages, little children, big children. Lots and lots of them. They come in until they fill the hut and are all standing around filling every space they can get into. Lots and lots of them. What is this all about?

He looks at me and hands me something. This is very incongruous in an African village. I must call this a round house. He hands me a microphone, a big one, the sort you hold in your hand. I wouldn't have expected it here. He gives it to me. What am I to do with this? He points to the children. They are my responsibility now. These children have travelled some distance from all parts and I must speak to them. I must speak to them about what I have learnt, what I believe and what the responsibilities are as a result of that.

He waits for me to begin. I tell the children to sit down so that everybody can see, even the little ones. The little ones must be here too. I teach them how they can listen to their inner thoughts, how each of them has a little being inside of them that they cannot see, but can only

150

sense and hear and know it is there to help them. I go on and on and on, giving them the mysteries of life, the realities and purpose of existence. I encourage them to know that each one of them is important and has a role in how the world is and how the whole of mankind behaves. It rests on each one and they can all do something.

I can feel now a weight on my right hand. Something pressing heavily on it, I don't know what it is. It is on my hand which is on my lap. "It is in your hands now. It is up to you."

How do I do it? How do I do it? The book must be the introduction. It must be the key. There is something more but I don't know what more I can say or do. Now he takes a map from his clothing and spreads it out on the floor so that I can see. He weights it down. It is a map of the world. He turns to the children and beckons. They crowd round to have a look. He points and tells them who must go where in the world. They are to spread and the influence of what they have learnt must be spread all over. I am in the Round House. I understand.

MAY 23rd 1995

CLARITY AND HELP

There is a green disc. Somebody is with me. I am in silver green. There is no problem with this. I don't seem to be able to move along my normal path for I am rooted to one spot. Coming towards me are groups of people, figures walking towards me very slowly and deliberately. I can't distinguish who they are for they are just people of all ages, all sizes and both sexes. They are not only coming from in front, but from all sides. From above as well. They are all crowding round and leaving me standing on a little circular disc. It moves around very slowly so that they can all see me. It is like a moving circular stage. They are all waiting for something. I don't know what to say other than hello. My friend [Dr. Po] is with me. What do I say to these people?

"You ask them what it is they require."

They respond with: "We need your help. We need clarity. We need to see what we are to do. We need to feel as you do. We need to look at you so that we may emulate and observe your behaviour."

I think, *I am just like them, how can I show them anything different from what they are.* I have something in my hand, weighing heavily. I can feel a tremendous weight of energy in my hand as if something has been put into it. An enormous energy. I am feeling it hot and so powerful. It is in my right hand. My focus is taken onto this enormous energy. It is beginning in my left hand as well now. I am being given power from the Source so that I may do what I have to do. I am being provided with more than I had so that I can direct this energy for the benefit of others. I feel these are all lovely words but it doesn't tell me how I must do it.

"Give examples, an explanation of what life is all about. How you see things. Show them your love for them. Give of yourself, for you have more to give. Give of your time, your attention. Give freely of the wisdom that is given to you. That is sufficient for any soul. If that is all you do in your life then you have served well. You will be sent assistance so that you do not feel so alone."

AUGUST 22nd 1995

LITTLE ONE RETURNED TO FATHER OF ALL

The colour is yellow and the floor is yellow, but in shards. It is sharp to walk on with long grooves. I walk along the edges, on sharp ridges like flint stones on end. I don't know why they should be like this but they are. They are in yellow. I have thick sandals on to protect the feet, though it is still difficult to walk. I go forward and come to the edge of the first step down and that seems to be where the sharp ridges finish.

The steps are very worn and hollowed, as if many feet have been down here. It is natural stone which has been worn. They are put there deliberately because there is a board running in front of each one to hold it in place. My throat is tightening up now. The ache is growing and growing. I feel I want to cry but I don't know why. The ache is taking over my throat. I feel very emotional and tearful. It is difficult not to cry but I have no idea why. Perhaps my emotions are the emotions of the one who is coming in. Energy is pouring in. I keep treading down trying to keep my mind on the stairs. I reach the bottom step which is smooth stone, worn smooth. I go forward and turn off. The walls are of stone as well. Smooth and cool, no jagged edges here. My throat is still tight. I find an opening and am almost unable to think for the emotion I am feeling.

I am blinded and stumbling as I go into the opening. It is like going home. I feel safe but it is empty. I look around. There is another opening ahead of me. I feel again a little tugging on my clothes. Something wants me to take notice. There is a little person who is pointing over to the right where there is another opening. So I have a choice. There are two pathways like a Y and I must decide which way to go. I am drawn to the one on the right. The little one holds on to my clothes as I walk. He or she is coming with me. I step through into the other area. I have to lift my legs high to get over the threshold. I lift the little one over because the step is too high for it.

As soon as I step over I find we are in the open countryside. The birds are singing. It is summer. The land is flat and open. Pleasant. It tells me nothing. I decide to walk holding the hands of the little one who gets tired. I give it a piggy back riding on my shoulders. There is a figure up ahead, a man. He waits for us to come up to him. It is obvious he is waiting for us. As we come up in front of him he lifts the little one off my shoulders and puts him down in front of him. The little one belongs to him. He thanks me for bringing him home. I have no idea what this means.

The expression on his face is of compassion because I don't understand and he can't explain it to me. I have to find out for myself. He puts an arm on my shoulder, his left arm to my right shoulder. I am his child also, maybe grown up but I am still his child. He may look younger but I am his child. He is the father of everything. I cry.

AUGUST 29th 1995

MERGE WITH LIGHT TO PASS THROUGH

I have gone up asking for some guidance. I go reasonably high and am walking along. On either side of me is a little fence edging, telling me to keep off the grass. I feel this is another way of saying, keep to the path. It is quite clear. The gravel is crunching underneath my feet. All along the pathway are park benches, placed so that people can rest and look out over the scenery. Most of them are empty. I walk until I can find a bench that either feels right or where somebody is sitting. It is quite pleasant but empty. I have the old emotional feeling coming over me, a sadness because it is empty. As I feel the emotion I see placed in front of me, not sitting down, a very tall, very special, glowing person. It is a very spiritual Being, very large. He is stopping me from going any further. I walk up to him and look very tiny in front of him. I feel even more emotional now. I don't know what to do. I can't see past this Being to the rest of the pathway. He is pointing to a bench at the side as if to say, why don't I sit down on it. I do as I can't keep standing.

I am sitting on the bench now but not feeling any better for it. I feel frustrated. I suddenly notice that the other benches have people sitting on them after all. They are all sitting on the benches seemingly waiting for something, as I am. It is like musical chairs. One moves up and moves on to the next seat and they all shuffle along to the next space. It is like a queue on different benches. I am at the head of the queue here because I am nearest to the Shining One. Is he going to let anybody through? They are all waiting to go through. I get up again and go and stand in front of him. I ask him what I must do to pass through and continue.

"You must be filled with the same light so that the one light will merge into the other. There will be no resistance and in the merging will pass through to the other side."

"How do I do this?"

"You immerse yourself in goodly thoughts and goodly deeds. You become part of Spiritual Law, not merely an observer. You become Spiritual Law, with spiritual ideals and in doing this you may pass the spiritual body that is before you, for you will be one and the same. There is no barrier."

That is quite a lot to think about. I don't think they are going to tell me any more than that.

AUGUST 29th 1995

RECONNECTING WITH THE BROTHERHOOD

I have green and I seem to be enveloped in a lot of green material which is hampering my movements. It is like being covered with a green net. I am trying to get free of it so that I can move. As I pull it off my arms and hands there is still plenty of it. It is dark green, not a spring-like colour. I can't get free of it so I walk forward. As I go the material comes with me. My chest hurts. I intended to go down but I can't see where I am placing my feet because the material is over my head, covering me. I have to feel with my feet and find the edge of the first step. It is difficult going because I am scared I will trip up. Even pulling it up doesn't clear it off my feet. I am having to kick it away as I walk to give myself a certain amount of foot space. It isn't easy, not easy at all. I am holding on to a rail even though my hand is covered in the green stuff. The encumbrance seems to get a little bit less as I go because the steps themselves are pulling the material away from me. It is as if it has been caught as I am working my way through it. I come to the bottom and the last of the cloth finally clears me. I am free.

I am standing on the bottom and at last have got rid of the enveloping stuff. I step forward onto a spongy path. Not unpleasant, just not firm. It is like walking on a wad of foam rubber. I turn off. There is a wattle fitting for the door, very flimsy. I pull it towards me to open it. There is a lot of fresh air as I go in, almost a wind. It is a lot of moving fresh air similar to when there is a fan going, moving the air. I don't know what all this is leading to.

I am in blackness until I see a faint outline of a tunnel or gateway through. I go towards it as it is the only thing I can see. It gets narrower as I go along. There is a little door at the end. It is a small opening so I have to bend down and squeeze through. I find myself in a room full of men sitting on the floor. It appears to be some sort of conference, a meeting of some sort. I have broken in on their talk. They look up as I come through. They are not bothered but I feel a bit of an intruder on their business.

They make a move for me to come and sit with them. I sit down on

157

the floor with them. Why am I here? They put a hand out and place something in the centre of their little circle. As they take their hand away there is a crystal that each has put in. Now there is a little pile of crystals, all different. I don't have a crystal but I am told to put my hand in anyway. I put my left hand in, over the pile of crystals and I leave it there. I know that is what I have to do. The light from the crystals comes into my arm and travels up the arm. It is as if I am being made transparent by the light, like an x-ray or when a torch is shone through one's fingers. It is like a light being shone through my body, lighting up all parts of me internally, and right down to my toes. I feel like a human torch, lit up and plugged into a socket.

I stay with this for a bit. They simply watch. I can't keep my arm there any longer and take it away. Strangely the light stays with me and doesn't go, as if I have been charged with it. The light is still there.

One of them says: "You have been reconnected."

That is rather nice.

"You are now reconnected and joined yet again with The Brotherhood."

I have a sense of relief and contentment, and a great sense of thankfulness. The relief is overwhelming. I am no longer an intruder and am part of their gathering now. They are all standing up and talking and wandering around. The formality of it has gone. I see there are quite a few children here. I hadn't noticed them before. They are just playing around and enjoying themselves. I find my mind beginning to wander away with the sounds of things going on outside, though the energies are still there. I try to bring myself back out.

SEPTEMBER 27th 1995

MAN LIT BY FLAME

I have an enormous flame shooting up like a geyser. As I watch the glowing flame of light, I see a shadowy figure of Man alongside it, looking rather small. The flame gets higher and higher and Man appears smaller and smaller. He is insignificant in comparison to the great force. He is almost minute and is not lit by the light. He needs to stand closer but he is afraid of being burnt. The flame is not all consuming. It is embracing. Man does not trust this. He needs to trust.

I walk up to Man and take his hand. I walk him directly into the flame to show him that it is wonderful to be in this. It does not burn and it does not destroy. I see our outline standing in the flame, still intact and with light all around us. Now I lead him out and he is glowing. The light has been given to him. This is the message.

LEARN FROM HISTORY

I have red. The carpet is deep red and everything is glowing red. It is hushed; I am padding my way down the stairs. All is soft and quiet, secretive. The stairs are wide with rich mahogany banisters on both sides. I go down quickly as there is no need to be slow. I am confident here as if I am at home and used to going down these stairs. It is my own place. I go forward at the bottom, there is a homely feeling. I am not a stranger. I turn off, everywhere the same comfort. I am at ease. I come to the door which is studded leather, buttoned in dark green with a brass/golden lever handle. I push down on the lever and go in. It is very dark in here. There must be a light switch somewhere but I don't need light for there is a window. Coming through the window is a shaft of light which is shining on a table. I go towards it to see what is on it.

There is a book and a jumble of other things. Before I open the book I must look at the jumble to see what is there. There are two rings, almost identical but one larger than the other. Plain wedding rings. There is a feather, one long large feather. There is a leather thong, soft brown hide. Soft, not hard. There is a little round box, reminds me of a pill box or snuff box, quite fancy. I don't know what use that might have for me. It is ornate. And there is the heavy book with a solid stiff cover. Old fashioned with metal edges, fancy work. I open it and it has very thin Bible paper in it. It is an old book with a tape marker. I turn to where the ribbon is marking it. I want to see what is on it.

As I go to look a big hand comes down over mine, as if to say, you can't; don't read it yet. The large male hand is over mine. I turn to see whose hand it is. Standing there is a large man with a beautiful figure, a fatherly strong figure. He is definitely in charge and used to being in a commanding position. He is no sop, this one. I look at him, he looks back. There is a bonding and an understanding, recognition between us. It is as if I am one of the family, his family. He is no stranger to me and I don't feel uncomfortable or difficult with him. I do not take his hand on mine amiss in any way and just accept it. It doesn't concern me that I can't read what is in the book. I stand up straight.

He takes me and guides me to the far end of the room. We go

together to another much smaller door. I pass through easily but he has to bend down to go through. It is not as fancy as the first one but is still leather clad. It is soft. Everything is soft here. I go through first and opening out on the other side is a very large hall. It is a great big hall such as one would see in a country house. It is a gallery rather than a hall. I don't know why I am here.

"Why am I here?"

"The Halls of History. The Halls of Knowledge. Knowledge that comes as a result of historical events. Each event that happens should teach those who experience those events. They should learn from their mistakes, from their triumphs and from their strivings. When understanding has taken place then future actions should reflect this understanding. Advancement and development should be as a result of past experiences, as a result of having not acted wisely in the past, leaving you with determination not to repeat the same mistakes."

"What has this got to do with me?"

"Have you never made mistakes? Have you not experienced things in your life? Have you learnt from them?"

"Yes. I hope so."

"You too would do well to reflect back and place in your mind what you have learnt. Clarify what life has taught you. This urging is true also for the whole of mankind, for each nation, for each race. This rule operates on all scales, at all levels, whether it be large and wide or small and personal. Learn from the past and look forward to the future with determination and courage."

I look at him and thank him in my mind. We don't need to speak for we understand each other. I know he knows what I think and the feeling I have for him. I know that he knows. Although we don't embrace, I can feel an embrace even though we don't touch. I can feel it with his mind and with his heart. I am very comforted and warm and content. Protected is the word. I feel very secure. Now I must come back.

PREPARE WELL FOR FUTURE WORK

Yellow is the colour. I ask for meaning of the dreams I had last night. I am on a sandy slope. The sand makes it slippery. I slither sideways down, trying to keep my balance with arms outstretched. I can hear the seagulls crying and the waves crashing on a sandy beach. I am on the sand now and go down to the edge of the sea. There the sand is firm, solid and hard. I come across an old boat, beached and dried out. I climb into the boat as a child would. It hasn't been to sea for a long time. I sit across the seat and imagine myself at sea with the motion of the boat and the waves. Andreas arrives and takes my fingers in his hand. He doesn't say anything but I feel happy he is here.

He has come from the past, has escaped from the past. He has come to witness events, memories which are best left. He climbs out of the boat and holds my hand to help me out. We are to go from the beach together. Where is he taking me? He is taking me to see an old man in an old beach hut with a wooden veranda. It is old wood with gritty sandy steps. The old man is waiting for us. We go in and sit down on bench seats across the table to him. He takes my hands across the table and looks into my eyes. I feel he is reading my mind.

He is seeing the future for me. "You have a way to go yet. Study, practice and application. It is not time to sit back and let things go each day without change. It is time to push forward for new knowledge and get into action. There will be time for relaxation and time for what you are currently doing. Do as much as you can and put into practice what you learn so that you are ready when the opportunities are presented. All that we are asking is that you prepare yourself to meet challenges with confidence. We know that you have already prepared yourself in your heart and inclination. Do not sit back and take things easy. There will be yet more work to fill your days. Absorb newcomers who will come and demand great things and who expect a positive response to the suggestions put to you."

I go out of the hut into the fresh air.

OCTOBER 28th 1995

THE AGREEMENT

There is a walkway that is closed in on all sides and is high. I am seeing it as a cross walkway between two very high buildings. As I reach the other side I go down a few steps. It is very green. I go down to a pool and know that I am going to have a swim. The water is green also. I get in, it is quiet and gentle. It is easy to swim. I get out of the other side of the pool, dripping a bit. I pick up a towel from the side and put it round me. Keep going forward. I am not cold at all. In front of me is a door. As there is nowhere else to go I go through. On the other side are several men. I have come to talk to them. I feel a bit silly in the towel but they don't seem to be worried about it. I sit down and face them. They are seven.

The one in the middle pushes something across the table towards me. It is a book with a pen in it. I know I am to sign with this. I simply write my name in the book and push it back to him. He passes the book to the others and they all have a look, passing it along. Each of them signs it so their signatures are with mine. It is a pledge, an agreement. It is an agreement to work together. I know quite well that these men are Masters, Helpers, Guides or whatever you would like to call them. We have entered into an agreement. I have agreed to work with them and it seems they have also agreed to work with me, always for the benefit of others. Nobody has spoken yet.

Then the middle one passes a telephone across to me. It is a telephone line, a communication link which I am to take. On the dial is 7 7 7 . I am to dial this number to receive their advice, their help and their communication. It is a number I shall remember easily. I must dial this number whenever I need them. I shall not be left alone to flounder.

VISIT TO LIGHT BEINGS.

I am on a ledge high up. A narrow ledge and I can't go down. I walk along until I find some steps. I climb, though I am already high. I get to the top. I am so high it is a little scary. I go carefully along a narrow stretch until I reach a wider area to stand on. It is a bit more secure. This is all manmade, not natural. There is a big entrance, all lit up inside. It is polished, comforting, inviting. I go up into the light, very broad, like walking into a very well lit hall. It is busy with moving shapes, moving beings, all Beings of light. I can't pick out precise shapes. It is as if everybody has a light which blots out physical form. I am moving among them, very dark by comparison. It is beautiful to be here, pleasurable, happy. Happiness! I don't want to stand still. I want to move until I meet someone special. There is one who is larger and set apart from the others, waiting. He is standing and waiting. I am overwhelmed, deeply moved by this.

It has been my practice to hold development circles on a regular basis. I have been doing this since 1992. The section below is one such occasion when I channelled Abraham. A member, Yvonne was present to ask questions.

NOVEMBER 7th 1995

ABRAHAM SPEAKS OF THE ARKS AS ENTRY POINTS

I have a very strong spirit with me – like a Michelangelo figure, very powerful and muscular. I think it is Abraham. He is the father of the Jewish faith. He says: "You are all my peoples."

We are now going back even further, beyond him. We are going back to the time of giants, very large tall men, perhaps 7- 8 ft. Not more than that I think. I have asked and said: "This is all very nice but what help is it to us in our present time to know this?"

He says: "Remember Noah's Ark." Preparation! He has an indulgent smile and says: "There are many Arks. There isn't just one. There is preparation all over going on now. People *do* know what to do."

Me: "I feel the Ark is a symbolic message."

He says, "Mind and Intelligence. When you 'get it' it will feel Eureka. If I tell you now you will file it away with all the other bits we have told you. You will put it away in your mind and do nothing about it. So you will need to have it hit you inside and you will know. That is when you will act on what is given you. Words [from us] alone will not do it. You would say, 'that is interesting' and forget it." He is smiling indulgently as he says this.

Yvonne: "He will make sure it hits us when it needs to, won't he?"

Me: "There is more than one kind of Ark and we are now talking Extraterrestrial. I see something opening and closing rather as some flowers do or sea plants. He is getting more modern now."

"There are entries and exits to do with timing." Laughing, he shows me a supermarket automatic door. "Sometimes you do have to wait that fraction of time. If you try to go through it when it is shut you could bang into it. You might have to wait that second. You have to position

165

yourself in front of the door but if you rush at it you are just going to hurt yourself. It will always close behind you."

Me: What does this all mean for heaven's sake?"

"It is to do with space and we are talking of entry points here. Timing! And we are not talking of a limited or selected few either." He is making that quite clear. "Those who wish to make an entry or exit need to know the door is there. So awareness is necessary. Anybody who arrives at the supermarket goes there because they know it is there, else they wouldn't be there, would they? It is the same with these entry and exit points. You need to know they exist and to be aware that you can pass through. Otherwise you will just remain in ignorance."

Yvonne: "Are these real places?"

"They exist as a reality. We are not talking of places. Just as you speak of spirit world as 'upstairs' and 'up there', it isn't any more up there as it is down below. It is everywhere and in that way, it exists. Forget place and think of space. Forget area, forget time."

Yvonne: "Will we be in the right place?"

"Go where your mind is. Your mind will be where you are."

Me: "He is reminding me that although he is here, he is not of our time, and he is not of our place, but he is here. He is holding a lot of reigns/strings. On the other end of the reigns are all the different races and religions. He is holding on to them all. They are all attached to him and are all a part of him. He is trying to keep them in hand."

166

NOVEMBER 11th 1995

CHRIST FIGURE

I am in sea green, blue and the green together and not merging. At the bottom there is a very dark tunnel, no lights. I feel my way along to the opening in the complete darkness. I feel to find the door with both hands because I simply can't see anything. I come to the door and fumble with the knob. As I open it all the lights go on. There is a big crowd and they all shout, "Surprise, surprise!" It has been a prepared surprise and the lights were out deliberately. Everybody is happy and smiling but I am a bit bewildered by it all for I don't know what they are celebrating.

There are quite a few people here, all my friends, all my helpers. I see standing at the back one rather wonderful Being, calm and smiling gently at all the excitement. I walk through the crowd up to him and I kneel before him. He lifts me up and I kiss his hand. He puts his arm round my shoulders and guides me away. We go through a door at the back, just he and I together. We are now outside in the open countryside. The world. It is peaceful and green. We are looking down over villages, looking at the scene from a distance.

He says: "This is your world. Go out there, do what you have been taught to do. All you need is yourself. You do not need the tools of the trade. Take your own being, that should be sufficient. Your book is your passport, your entry ticket."

RESTORING THE ORB TO SPIRITUAL REALMS

I have clear jade green. I am wearing a heavy brocaded green gown right down to the feet. The steps are in beautiful clean jade colour but in highly polished marble. I go down. Everywhere is beautifully clean and shiny. I go carefully, feeling the edges of the steps with my toes. There are no jagged areas. At the bottom there are great corridors of smooth jade crystal, cut and highly polished. Glorious! I turn off into the same kind of tall corridor in deep jade. I can't think of the name of the actual stone, just that it is in this glorious colour. I come to a cut opening, no door just an opening. I walk through.

I see something on a ledge slightly to the left of me and ahead. I look upwards because it is above my head. I reach up and feel around because I can't actually see it from down here. I feel for it. It has been placed here and is rolled up in some kind of cloth. I manage to grab hold of it and bring it down off the ledge. It is quite heavy so I need both arms to take the weight. I lower myself down with it in my arms and unravel the cloth on the floor. Inside is a rod or staff with a globe on the end. I don't know what you would call it, a sceptre or orb or what. It is a ceremonial rod, but what is it supposed to be telling me? I have to hold it near the top because it is weighty and would unbalance if I didn't. I lift it upright and stand it on its end. The golden ball on the end is higher than my shoulder. I don't know what I am to do with it. Being left handed I hold it in my left hand. I am being told not to hold it that way but to rest it across my arms.

I hold it across my two arms which takes a bit of doing as it is top-heavy. I carry it in the crook of my elbows so that it is safe and doesn't roll off. I have to take it somewhere. Everywhere is still in beautiful green. I wish I knew what this was all about. There is a long rectangular deeply padded stool in purple before me. I am to put the orb on the stool. It is a ceremony of some sort. I go up to it and kneel down and place the orb lengthwise on the padded stool. There must be another name for it but I don't know what it is. I step back. I still have no idea why I am doing this or what it is for. I am asking them now.

A host of Heavenly Beings are arriving. A great throng of them.

They are what one might term Angels, I suppose. Heavenly Beings. They are crowding round to look at this rod. They are all very pleased. I feel they couldn't have got it for themselves and needed somebody from the physical world to restore it to its place. It had been left on the shelf gathering dust, doing nothing, high up and hidden. Now it has been restored to its rightful place in the spiritual realms. I still don't know what it is but whatever it is, it is important to the spirit world. Being restored it has been brought back into action where it can be utilised, whatever that means.

I wonder what to do next as I kneel there. A little child pulls on my clothes. I turn round. It is difficult to tell if it is a boy or a girl, a cherub of some sort. Yes. I turn round and pick it up. This child is only small, angelic. It kisses me on the cheek and snuggles into my arms. It is lovely to hold it. I stand up and decide I must go somewhere. I go ahead, to the right of me. There is a sort of bed which I lay the child on and cover it up so that it is comfortable. None of this is giving me any answers. It is all very nice but I want answers.

"You are playing your part, even when you do not realise it."

I am very cold as I come back.

DECEMBER 10th 1995

LOST CHILDREN

I am standing at the top of a short flight of stairs. I am in many colours down to the ground. The steps are wide and there are no walls, just shallow steps. There is a tunnel hewn out of rock, dome shaped. I go through a rough wooden door with a latch. The door pulls outwards, not inwards. I am in a dark area, long and deep. I hear voices and feel a hand on my shoulder. I turn round and see a beautiful strong upright golden figure, much taller than I. I want to rush into his arms but don't dare do that.

He moves off. I am to follow. He looks to see if I am with him as he glides over the floor. He is not making steps but just moves – it is wonderful. I hurry after him as he goes down some stone steps cut out of the floor. I go down after him into a small chamber. The light from him fills the chamber so that it is brightly lit. There are children sitting all around, ragged children. They are waiting and hoping. They all look a little lost. I go over to them and hold their hands and hug them. I go around hugging them all, giving them the love they need. They need it, they are lost but what can I do to help them?

"You can give them what they need the most. You can give them love, you can be with them and give them the companionship and be there for them whenever they have a need."

TWO FLAMES MERGING

The steps are steps of fire, red and glowing, not solid. All around me is red like being in a fire without the burning. I am stepping down as a flame, as part of the fire and moving like a shadowy figure, not clearly defined. I feel quite calm without emotion. No emotion and no feelings about this, one way or the other. It is just happening. I arrive at the bottom. I am not going down anymore and that is the only way I know it is at the bottom. I do my usual walking ahead. Moving is more accurate than walking because I don't feel I am a figure, the normal me. I turn off and seek an opening to pass through, much as a flame would do, a living flame.

I find a way through the wall, slip through it and form on the other side again. But the flames surrounding me have been kept on the other side so I am completely alone and not engulfed any more. I am still burning and am still the flame. There is emptiness all around me and the flame, the me is seeking another way forward. I say 'it' because I don't feel it is me. IT is standing waiting to see where it must go next. I see another white flame. This is a fire that is burning in white, whereas I am in red. Two flames, myself and the other draw closer together until we eventually stand facing each other. The white flame that is alive but not moving is stationary. It is still and not seeking another avenue to go into. It is contained.

My emotions start to come for I wish to be like this white flame. I try to reach out with tongues of my being, tongues of my flame that is around me. I, the flame try to reach towards this white one. I can't quite make the connection though I reach and reach, stretching the flames as far as they will stretch. It needs more fuel, it needs more energy, it needs more. There is frustration in this. The white flame reaches out an extension of its being and touches the red, the red that is me and takes hold, though how that is possible I don't know. It pulls me closer so that I can reach, so that I can touch. I feel very moved. *crying*.

* Crying through this now)

What is happening is that the red is turning to gold. It is now a golden flame, not red. It is quieter, more still and more at peace. I am drawn into the white, ever closer so that the white is wrapping around me now. *(The emotion overwhelms and I weep, tears running down my cheeks before I can continue)*. Now I am released and am standing there as the normal me. I feel very small, very emotionally charged. I am turned to face the way I have come and now must come back. I have been sent back to do what I have to do. It has been wonderful.

CHAPTER SEVEN

JANUARY 15th 1996

FAIRIES RELEASE THE JOY

I am dressed in a long green gown. The steps have a metal bar across, edging it to stop the wear of the tread. It is very austere and derelict here. I can't see the bottom although the steps are not steep. I keep going down holding on to the unpainted wooden rail at the side. Everything has been neglected though I feel it is still used, otherwise they wouldn't have the rail or the metal strip across the steps. So some care is being taken for people who do use it. I can see the bottom now. The floor is broken tiled. I get the feeling of being in a building that has not been used for a while and has been allowed to disintegrate. I now see offices such as one would get in an old warehouse with the corridor running between them; glass panelled, windowed offices. Lots of windows running along the entire length of the corridor. I come to a door, a cheap office door. No luxury here. I push the door open. I step inside. It is quite light, plenty of space, an empty office building. One almost expects there to be squatters because the building itself is sound but is just unused and left to rot.

I look around me and see desks. There is one in particular over to the right, piled high with an odd jumble of papers and files, all piled up in a heap. No order attached to it. I walk over to it and fiddle around, trying to pull something substantial from the pile. There is a thick heavy file underneath heavy papers. It is in black. I open it. I must know what is in it. This is bizarre because as I look, I see dancing figures like in a fairy story; only these figures are alive and dancing across the pages. I don't know what this is trying to tell me but it is delightful. There is such joy in opening this book again. The spirits have been in the book all this time, waiting for someone to come along and release them. They are leaping off the pages and dancing about the room. Little fairy figures dancing about in absolute delight. Oh they are beautiful. I still don't know what this means.

"The fairies of thought, the fairies of ideas, the fairies of creation, the thoughts that have gone into these pages have been released from the dust of old time and are free now to scatter themselves wherever they feel fit to go."

They scatter around the room, stirring the dust, sweeping the dust and touching everything with a magical light, transforming the dusty office into something bright and shining. Renewed! I still don't know how this relates to me and to anything I must do.

I suddenly see a tall shining figure, standing in the corner, watching all this. A beautiful spirit Being, full size, watches with a smile. I go up to him. The fairies are still dancing around and enjoying themselves. I ask him what this means for me.

"Release the thoughts that have been buried, not only in yourself but in others. Release the trapped joy that is in everyone's life story. Release the gladness that is there waiting, so that renewed life may come. It is not that you bring gladness, for they already have it, but in so many it is trapped. They need someone from outside themselves to help them open their hearts and their memories that have lain dormant in the dust of their past. Allow this renewed joy and creation to flourish in their present time. Help them see what lies within. This goes for you too, for you are not exempt from burying what you prefer to forget or burying the goodness that lies inside you from your past."

The little fairy figures have grouped together and formed a ring. They are holding hands and dancing around clockwise, creating a continuous circle. They move faster and faster until it is just one band of coloured light that is spinning. They are creating a vortex, which as they move faster and faster, moves upwards like a column of light with the fairies at the top of the column as it pushes upwards. The column reaches up and goes through the ceiling out into the sky. It goes higher and higher until the top of it goes out of my sight. A beautiful pillar of light from the centre of the room, created by the fairy figures. As I look at the column, the glowing figure in the corner moves forward, takes me by the hand and walks me forward so that we are both standing in the column, so that we are encompassed within the circle of light. As we do so we both disappear and the room is left empty. Although I am not there I can see the empty room. And that is all.

JANUARY 19th 1996

PROGRAMME IN HAND

I am standing on what appears to be lemon slices. Most peculiar! It is
not unpleasant but refreshing. I walk down a ramp. I am reminded of
the airport ramps for the luggage carts, zigzagging down, floor by floor.
I am not pushing a trolley though I feel I ought to be as the connection
in the mind with airports is so strong. I get to the bottom and yes I have
now got a trolley. It is there with luggage on it. It is heavy. I push it
forward, still in a yellow outfit. Very smart! I ease the luggage trolley
round the corner. This is an airport. The doors open to the right, I push
the trolley through. I have no idea where I am going. I appear to have
arrived. I am not departing. I push the trolley out to where all the taxis
and buses are waiting. It is a busy scene.

A big car pulls up and it is for me. It is an official car, a stretched
limo. My goodness! The luggage is loaded in the back and I am
invited to get in. I sit there in front and get whisked away. I don't
know where to or where I am. It is a civilised country anyway. Tall
buildings, lots of traffic, very busy. I suddenly realise somebody is
sitting in the back of the car with me, quietly observing. Who is it?
He puts a hand out and touches me on the shoulder as if to reassure
me. We drive out into the country. The car pulls up onto a lay-by
overlooking the land. Beyond the land is the sea. It is a viewing point.
I get out and the man gets out too. I stand there looking over a long
view. There is a haze over the horizon which stretches as far as the
eye can see.

The man again puts his hand on my shoulder and says: "Yes, that is
the land you have to encompass and cover with words and actions."

I think, *well I don't even know where I am, let alone have a programme.*

"Do you think it has not all been arranged? Else how could the
transport have been waiting for you if we did not have a programme in
mind? We have organised it. We will ensure that you are at the correct
place at the correct time to do your work. All you need do is acquire the
knowledge and ability to do the work. You may leave the rest to us. So,
while you are waiting for this, learn, absorb and put into practice so that
when we call on you, you are ready."

I feel quite comfortable with that. It takes the pressure off me not having to worry about organising where to go and who to see. I feel much better about that. All I am left with is the work. I get back in the car and so does he. There is a child there now, sitting between us. We are all in the back seat now. The child is a little girl of about five or six. How she came here or why, I don't know. I am asking.

"The child is wise and a protection."

I don't understand that. The cold is coming over me now. Somebody is coming inside me. The cold is quite intense.

I have a Native American. A strong male. He is with me now, a man of few words. He must realise I need the words or to hear his thoughts. They must be voiced. I invite him to voice his thoughts.

"Work and you will be rewarded. Stay idle and you will receive nothing."

Oh, it is so cold!

FEBRUARY 3rd 1996

FOOTPRINTS OVER THE GLOBE

I have Raman and the nun and dear Dr.Po [my guides]. They are all here turning round and pointing to show me something. I look but I can't see. Soon I see a bowl, like a sunken bath in the ground. I go over to it. It is full of a blue steamy something. All I can see is blue misty stuff rising up from it. I am reminded of a chemical experiment when the liquid produces a vapour. It is a large bowl. I put my hand into the mist to see how it feels. It becomes a little wet. My friends come closer and stand around the rim of the bowl and look into it, as if trying to see something. I do likewise. If they think they can see something then so can I.

I ask them to show me what I need to know.

I stare into the swirling vapour. Then it clears and I see a country as if viewed from a long way up. It is the coastline of an entire country, as if I am seeing it from space. I try to see what country it is and realise it is moving. It is the entire globe underneath the vapour and is slowly spinning. Many countries, there are the two Americas, Australia, Japan, China. It is the globe. I want to know why I am being shown this. As I look I see footprints, outlined on the surface of the globe as if somebody is walking over it and leaving their mark behind. It is in a steady straight line. Large footprints, they are my footprints as I walk over the globe and leave my print behind.

I say to them, "This is all very nice but how is this going to happen?" They look at each other and they look at me and shake their heads. This doesn't help me at all. I repeat, "How is this going to happen?" They put their hands out towards me and take mine. They hold both my hands and all the hands are joined. There is no break in contact. They pull me close, still holding my hands which are now buried in theirs. I get the message that we are all involved in this and it will be done. We all work together to see that it does. I am the physical counterpart that can do what they cannot. I am the physical earthly representative. They stay at headquarters and send out their messages to me while I am the one that must deliver. I ask them, please give me the ability to relay what they have to say accurately, with conviction and no hesitation. But also with clear words that flow correctly and smoothly so that it holds the attention throughout of what they have to say. I ask that this begin immediately.

They draw me around to the other side of the circle where there is a table and chair. I am to sit at this. There is a book and pens. They have put the pen in my hand, the wrong hand. I change it over to my left hand as I am left handed. They take it out and put it back in my right hand. I am not clear what this means as I don't write with my right hand. They have put a pen in the other hand now so that I have a pen in both hands. They tell me to write. I begin to write with my left and they shake their heads and say "No, both hands."

I try to write with both hands but don't know quite how I am to do this. My right hand is writing backwards from the right side of the paper and meets with the left hand. It doesn't make sense but I clearly have to try. Perhaps it is using both sides of the brain. At this thought they nod, yes. Both sides of the brain. *Bring intellect into this as well as your intuition, apply your mind in all its facets.* They lift me up and walk me further along, further away from the bowl. We go down some steps, a little group of us. They surround me. They are even behind me making sure I don't turn round and go back. We go down quite a long way down. I can't see where we are going. Keep on going.

I begin to see little lights in the darkness and realise with a shock that there are eyes peering out of the dark at me, at all of us. I wonder why I can't see the faces.

"You would not want to see the faces. We have hidden them from you for your protection."

I am confused by that but will accept what he says. We go on down. The faces that we can't see are behind us now. We come through an opening at the bottom into brilliant sunshine. Glorious light. Everything is brilliant. It is difficult to adjust the eyes. I take a deep breath, glad to be out in the fresh air. It is a glorious, wonderful feeling.

Dr. Po speaks: "When you have gone through the darkness and have passed all the disturbed souls successfully, then you will come out into the light where you will be happy and glad to exist. You will remain with us as we will remain with you."

This moves me for there is such sincerity and kindness, and gentleness in his voice. I am deeply moved by it. I have so many good friends, though I know they are not all here. They are around.

I feel so very cold now and have to come out of this for the cold is too much.

FEBRUARY 4th 1996

CATALYST FOR NEW LIFE

I have yellow and am knee deep in pollen dust. The pollen is prolific.

"It is before the seed of new life, there and available; ready for fertilising, ready for the catalyst that will start new life in the form of new seeds of growth. The specks of pollen are uncountable, as are the specks and numbers of man each waiting for a catalyst to start afresh and unsullied into new life."

I don't understand why I am being given this.

"You are wading through the pollen, stirring it into movement, spreading it far and wide so that a catalyst will chance upon this and will act according to the laws of nature and the laws of God, which are one and the same. For a catalyst there will be. From this stirring, which is your purpose at this time, there will be fertilisation starting into new life. It is time you began again to work in earnest, to rise early when the waves of the air will be quiet and there will be no disturbance. It is time to begin this process once more so that you may leave your day free for other things. It is time to begin. No longer is there time to sit around. There is work to do and we ask you to do it."

Apparently I am to be pushed a little harder.

179

DETACH FROM THOSE WHO WILL
NOT HELP THEMSELVES

I am in pink. The stairs are very steep, almost vertical. I can't see the bottom. At the bottom it is very enclosed, just like a well. There is not much room to turn around, very confined. There must be a way out. At last I see a passage. I go along it. It is dark and dismal. It is quite high here but narrow. There must be a way out of this. It is so narrow. I find another passage which I go into. This one widens out a little into a great open area. It is still dark but at least it is open and I can move about. My pink colour seems to be out of place as it is the only colour here. It is dark and dismal. I ask for a meaning of the dream last night.

I see a lone figure at a table, a dejected figure. Sad and sorrowful, isolated and with nothing on the table. I go up to him. He looks at me miserably. He is not there for me, I am there for him. He needs cheering up. I get the feeling now that this is an act and if I lift him out of his depression he will not be grateful. He will have caught me and dragged me into his misery, so I must help but not become caught up. I don't do this in words but with feelings in my heart of compassion and pity. I ask for help for him to be lifted out of this dark and dreary place in whatever way is required. I surround him in my mind with a bright light of many colours. He is surrounded with this light so that he may be warmed by it.

He looks at me with a sad face, trying to evoke pity. It is a deliberate thing. He must help himself. He must look at himself, he can't run away from himself. The bright light continues to shine about him. Sooner or later he will notice it and feel it. I tentatively put my hand out to touch the light. As I do this it becomes charged, like giving it a shock. I know he felt that because it completely surrounds him. It is charging him like a battery. I withdraw my hand and walk on past, leaving him there. That is all I must do for him. I must not stay. I keep walking and gradually come out of this dark place into a lighter area, green and pleasant. There are other people here generally enjoying themselves. This doesn't really explain the dream.

"You must detach yourself from those who will not help themselves and do not see that they can help themselves, who wish to repeat old familiar patterns. You must detach yourself and not become ensnared."

FEBRUARY 12th 1996

WHITE BROTHERHOOD PROTECTING ME

I am again in pink and walking on eggshells. Very peculiar! Some of them are quite whole and some are broken. As I walk I hear them crack. There is no way I can avoid them for they are all over the surface. I must go as lightly as I can. Everywhere is thin and fragile and easily broken. I go through carefully and down a slope with eggshells all around. I don't understand this. It is not far to go and am soon at the bottom. The shells have been pounded smooth now and are not so difficult to walk on. They are forming a solid floor. I still don't understand the meaning. I walk forward and turn off as usual. I come to an opening which is covered with a shell. I will have to punch my way through. This is not too difficult. I put my fist out and punch a hole until it is big enough to get through. When I get through I find it is cosy and warm. I swear it is downy as well. This is a chicken theme; soft, comfortable and protective. What has happened is that I am returning to the shell. I haven't broken out of it, I have broken into it. That's what it is. I have gone back into protection and nourishment.

I find I am not alone. There are a lot of special Beings here, sitting at a long table. I have come to see them. They wave me forward as they have done before. I recognise them. They are The Brotherhood. I go up and stand before them. The middle one stands up and takes both my hands. He pulls me closer and kisses me on both cheeks, that is lovely. I don't know what to do now. He waves his arm indicating to the others sitting at the table.

He draws them all in saying: "We are all here and we are behind you, supporting you. We are listening to your requests and taking note that you wish to work in service for others. We will do what we can to help. As long as you keep your intent firmly fixed in the right direction, assistance for your goals will be given. We will not let you flounder. Help will be given in your striving just so long as you maintain your resolve, just so long as you do not sit back and give up the struggle."

There is an almighty storm going on outside. It is very strange at this time of year [February]. It takes my attention away from the men who are still here. They are listening as well to the storm that is going on.

"We are very well aware of all the events in your life. We are not some distant grouping that you meet with every so often. We are with you all the time in our thoughts and considerations. Carry on with the work, carry on with your resolve and keep it firm."

I am having difficulty to maintain contact because of the storm outside, so I leave it there.

FEBRUARY 21ˢᵗ 1996

DIRECTION ON CHOICES

I ask for my soul self to speak to me. I ask for a picture to show me what I am to do. I have a picture of me wading through people. I am knee deep in people all reaching their hands out. I am literally pushing my way through. It is like being in a sea of them. This could be healing or it could be teaching. I must know what.

"Make it clearer please."

"Healing comes about as a matter of course. You do not need to focus on it as it will happen anyway. The crowds are just that, they are the public not groups specifically coming together for teaching in select groups. It is the masses who have come to hear, who need help. They have come because they believe you can help. Use your words wisely and for the general public, not only the special few."

In my mind that means lecturing. Three things.

"To receive the wisdoms, to bring forth the words that these people wish to hear, you must delve into the spirit world, your own included."

That is telling me, trance work, channeling. That is two.

"How will you draw the public to you in the first place? How will they know of you?"

I know they are referring to the book, so I must write. There I have it. Healing, writing and channeling. Three things.

"May I receive some confirmation that these choices are the correct ones? Some sign, something."

183

ADJUST TO LIGHT OF THE MASTERS

I have a really alive fresh vibrant green. A green of light. I am going down very steep stairs, so steep I have to go down backwards as if on a ladder. I can't see where I am going and am taking care not to look down. I keep going until my feet touch the bottom. The green of me is fluorescent so that I am my own light. I wonder where this is taking me. I turn around. It is dark apart from the glow around me from my own light. I move ahead not being able to see where I am moving to. I feel with my hands for the opening to the side. I just about make it out in the line of the walls. My hands touch the crack which I assume is the door. I fumble for the knob, turn it and go inside.

There is a hushed still feeling here. It is hushed and expectant, as if waiting for something to happen. There is a man sat at a desk with his head in his hands, not in despair but in contemplation. I know his mind is somewhere else, thinking. He does not seem to be aware of me, but as he is the only one I can see I must go to him. He is a very old man, very bony. I walk up to him and touch him very gently on the shoulder. He looks up and straightens. His eyes are blazing, full of light. Clear blue, brilliant light, almost unreal. Like two laser beams. I am not bothered by this but rather pleased. He continues to look at me. He is not so old after all. I cannot see or decide on his age for his eyes are the whole of him. It is the eyes not the body that I must focus on.

I try to read what is in the eyes but I can't for I am transfixed by them. They soften and a feeling of kindness and gentleness comes to me. The power of those beams are tempered and lessened so that I can absorb it. I wonder what this is telling me.

"If you would look into the souls of The Masters you need to be adjusted to receive the strength that is in them. By this we mean the full force. We may temper our power, our energy so that it is comfortable for you. To receive the fullness you need to make your adjustment to that of a higher vibration."

"How can I do this?"

"Bathe yourself in the light each day. Bathe yourself in full brilliance, feel its penetration into your being, into the cells of your body until the cells of your body disintegrate and become one with the brilliance. Do this each day and you will become adjusted and able to absorb the fullness of our strength.

"When you achieve fullness you will have the communication that you seek, for it will be present with you at all times. There will be no need to ask for it because it is with you. With your adjustment you will have instant access at any moment, at any time that you call on it. Adjust yourself to the light in its fullest power. There are those around you who have yet to do this. You ask to serve. When you have adjusted then may you serve to your full capacity."

I ask if I can do this now. The light is turned on from his eyes more fully. It is directed at me.

TRUST IN PROGRESSION

I am all in blue. As I walk forward I am swishing through water. I am paddling in water that runs down the stairs. It reminds me of an overflowing bath. We are not outside. I am going down the stairs with the overflow brushing my ankles, washing my feet on the steps as I go. It is not uncomfortable just odd. I ask for help. I am feeling a little lost. At the bottom there is a pool where the water has accumulated. It is almost up to my knees. I wade through and find the usual way with walls on either side. They appear to be brick walls, crumbly old porous brick. I go along and come to where there used to be a door. There is just the framework. It is all in poor condition. It is not surprising really with all this water. I go through with water still pouring in. I look to see what I can find.

All around the walls is shelving, like in a warehouse. Metal shelving with things stacked on them. Not posh, just a storage place. I need another doorway, a passage or something out of here. Between the shelving there is a way through. I work my way between all the storage. I have no idea where I am going and have asked for help of some kind. I need help.

There is a man sitting at a desk writing. He is writing out orders and invoices. He takes no notice of me though he knows I am there. He puts his pen down and looks up and hands me a bit of paper. It is what he has been writing. It is an order form, a requisition slip. That's the word. I am to take the slip down the passage behind him. I am not to look at it but take it and walk past him. It is as if I couldn't go any further without the slip of paper. The man is not important. He is just doing his job.

The floor is now dry. I can't see or feel the water any more. Bare boards. I walk down looking at the shelves as I go, wondering what I am doing here. I have no ideas, no feelings, just carrying out my orders, doing what is expected of me without question. As I come to the end there is a blank wall and I have to turn off. I mustn't go back. I can go left or I can go right, it doesn't matter. I look in both directions. To the right somebody is standing there. There is nobody the other way so I go towards him. He is a large figure and looks out of place.

He is special and is the one I have come to see. He is a glowing figure who has come especially for me. As I get to him I put my hand out to see if he is physical or solid. I wonder how I am going to give him this slip if he is not solid. I hold it out to him and he takes it anyway. He reads it. I still don't know what is on it. I have no idea and am just carrying out my duties. He turns with the paper in his hand and begins to walk away. I follow. It is an order\requisition slip after all, so I must be given something. I am here to collect something. I trot along behind him. He doesn't appear to walk not being physical, he is spirit.

We reach a shelf and there is a book which is glowing the way he is. I can't read it because the light covers it. He takes it off the shelf and puts it in my arms. None of this means much to me at the moment. How can I read a book that is not visible? Yet I feel it in my arms. It is big and I need both arms to hold it. I can't hold it in only one arm as it is too big for that. It is edged in gold as if the pages themselves are golden. The cover is silver, all glowing and shining.

The figure before me points for me to open it. I open it at random. There are two words, one on each page in big capital letters filling the page 'TRUST' and 'PROGRESSION'. He points to me. It is a message to me. I take it to mean that if I trust, there will be progression. Just take each day and not push. Just handle what I have at the moment. Deal with what I have at the moment and the rest will be placed before me, all in its time.

"How can you go on and take on more understanding if you haven't dealt with what is around you right now? Sort that out, deal with that then there will be space for the rest. You are trying to fill a cup that is already overflowing. If you do this it will fall and go to waste on the floor where you stand. Absorb what you have into your being and there will be room for more. Be calm and trust in your friends who care for you, who assist you and watch over you while you struggle."

I thank him and ask him if I can keep the book.

He says: "Yes. Open it at random in your quiet moments, whenever you feel the need for direction and guidance. The words will be on the page that will help you."

MARCH 15ᵗʰ 1996

JOINING WITH SPIRIT; *enjoy this meditation for yourself.*

"There is a tree in front, an old tree that has been there for a very long time. Study it and turn your back to it and lean against the trunk. Feel with your fingers, the bark, the roughness. Lean your head against it. Feel it against your body, through your clothing. Feel the strength and the solidness of this big tree. As you stand there resting, feel yourself gradually merging into it. Your spirit is being drawn inside the tree, mixing with the fibres and permeating into it as if it is nothing. Your spirit is now inside the tree. Your spirit spreads its arms, stretching itself up in great joy and freedom. It spreads and spreads up through the trunk out into all the branches. The spirit essence permeates every branch, every twig and every leaf. As it spreads further upwards to the top of the tree it cries with absolute joy, abandonment, ecstasy. It reaches up in great happiness.

"Your spirit can now hear those cries of other spirits, other celestial beings. As you reach up those celestial ones reach down to you. Their spirit forms reach and take hold of you and gather you to them and pull you up with them so that you are joined. Your spirit essence and theirs united. You can ask any question you like of them for you have become one with their minds."

"What am I to do on this Earth?"

"You are to become as you feel yourself to be now in the spirit. You are to feel and experience the joy of being spirit. You are to reach out your fingers, your essence so that it touches others, so that they may experience the joy that you feel when you join with us."

"How is this to be done?"

"Be what you feel. It is simple. Be what you feel to be and let this be felt by others. It is simple. The joy you receive, you give. It is simple. It is not difficult or complicated. When you reach to us, we will guide your thoughts. We will guide your actions and we will protect you also. You are to do our work."

I ask about the book.

"Pour yourself into the pages. Pour your joy into the pages. Pour the hope, the aspirations and the challenges into the pages. We will guide your words as we guide your actions."

188

I ask about getting it published.

"If the work is found to be of value in the eyes of spirit then a way will be found. If however it does not reach the value required through interaction with the human mind, then it will need to be re-adjusted and cleansed. First you must feel the spirit, be the spirit and share the spirit and all that that spirit encompasses, including the wisdoms. Challenges are necessary in life as challenges are necessary in the book so that they may be overcome. Yes my child, you are to show people how they are to overcome their challenges. There you have your answer. Present the challenges and show them how they may be overcome. In this way you present a pathway for them so that they may reach the joy of the spirit. Have patience. It will all fall into place, even setbacks have their purpose."

I know I must come to an end here, very quickly now.

MARCH 18ᵗʰ 1996

PASSAGE TO NORTH WEST AMERICA

I am in slippers and am padding softly along. Everywhere is soft and padded. It is a corridor, a passage. Soft, comfortable and hushed. Silence is the thing. I keep walking. There are no stairs, no windows, just an endless passage. I am reminded of the airport where the corridors go on and on, never seeming to come to an end. At last, ahead of me are open swing doors. They open ahead of me as I approach. I don't have to put my hand out or push as they open for me. I walk through. No carpeting here, shiny floor. Clean hard walls, no carpeting or padding. Clear, clean and pure. It is still a corridor. I keep walking. It gets narrower as I go until I reach a narrow single door. This I must slide sideways through. It is a gap, not a door but an opening. I squeeze myself through sideways. Entry is not so simple or so easy this time. It is inviting because I am going to the heart, to the treasures.

There is a little circle of people sitting on the floor cross-legged, quite comfortably. I feel they are Native Americans, though I can't see them clearly. I can just see them. Yes. They are Native Americans in a circle having a meeting. That is interesting! *What is the meeting about?* I ask myself.

"We are talking about you. You are the subject of our discussion. We are trying to decide for you and put things into place so that you may see more clearly, so that you may continue to work with more peace in your heart. We wish you to sit back and relax over outcomes. Continue as you are doing and we will deal with the outcome. We do not intend that your objectives not be realised for they are also our objectives. We know what we intend and we are able to arrange matters that you are not. Continue as you are doing and do not lose heart. Your objectives are also ours. We will unite the forces together. Stay firm in your resolve. Continue in your studies and the rest will take place quite naturally."

I ask: "Why the long corridor? The long passage?"

"Your first thought of airport was correct. Your passage leads to our lands. You are to go to our lands. This is self explanatory. We want you to go to our lands."

"That's not very helpful. Your lands are all over America. You'll have to be more specific."

"North West," one said.

"That's still not precise enough," I said.

He pointed to a large map and placed a bony finger on Calgary. "This is a thank you for a good deed you did for one of our kind." I wracked my brains to remember. Yes, I had helped a full blood Native American Indian woman and her children in Italy some years before, when she was without friends or money.

"I want to know why I can't be told why. It would make life so much easier."

"We will show you before you arrange your passage. We will indicate to you in our way. We do not wish your mind to leap too far ahead. We are aware of your thoughts."

One of them has got up and put one of their skins round my shoulders so that I may be fully dressed for the occasion. I don't understand that either.

"Attend the ceremonies and you will observe. We remind you of the girl that you assisted who was of our blood. You will be assisted in like manner."

*I went to Calgary and they kept their word. Although I did not know a soul when I arrived, on my very first day I met many people who arranged for me to conduct readings, talks, workshops and gave me accommodation. It was marvellous indeed.

MARCH 19th 1996

THE LITTLE OWL CARDS BEGIN

"How much do you value the communications? How much do you value what we give you?"

"I value it very much."

"Do you? What are you doing with it?"

"I take note. It gives me courage, confidence and clarity whenever I need it. I value it.

"Do you keep this assistance to yourself?"

"No. I find that when I am sharing what you have given me, it has helped others also. It always seems to be just what they need at the time of asking."

"Well, don't you think it would be nice to share it with more people and help even more people? Isn't this what you wished to do?"

"Yes."

"Well. Think about how you can do this."

*

So I thought about it, and as I have many scraps of information, I have now put them on separate cards and have produced them giving them the name 'Little Owl Cards'. Seventy two messages. I have had to limit the numbers, though I do have more. This was an act of faith for I invested quite a large sum of money to do this. Living on state pension, this really is an act of faith.

"Well done. You will see how many will be helped with your trust."

Now in 2012, packs of these Little Owl Cards have had their third printing and have gone all over the world.

MARCH 20ᵗʰ 1996

ANDREAS

I have pink which is for me. I need it apparently. I am wrapped in cotton wool and am being gently guided along by many hands. They are very tenderly walking me along as if I am recovering from something. They are making sure I don't fall down. They guide me down a slope, making sure I don't slip. They really are looking after me. They have taken me into a room, just an ordinary room. Chairs, desks, not a home room but official. I am in a centre of some sort. A hospital, clinic, something like that for it has that smell about it. Many chairs and people who wait. I am sat down in one of the chairs. I have to wait. It is a healing place.

Somebody comes out. He is in white as I would expect but there is a pink glow about him. His aura is pink, all of it. The aura around him fudges the outline of him so that he is not as clear as he might be. His form is just about peeking through. He comes over to me and takes both my hands and looks at the backs of my hands. He turns them over as if checking out the state of me. I must follow him.

So I do. I trot after him. I can feel all these people who have helped me following me so that we are a little procession. I follow the man in pink and white and they follow me, tripping along behind. We go through into another room. In here are many people who are going to watch. They are to observe. I climb on to a therapy couch.

I don't know what all this is for. Nobody is telling me anything. The man puts his hands on my head … I begin to get extremely emotional. He puts his hands on my head and holds them there. The feeling goes right through me, giving me deep emotion. It is very deep. I can't describe the feeling. I am quite happy just to lie here. My head is very tense, tremendous energy coming through. He is doing something to my head. I don't know what it is but I feel the pink from him growing like a mist over me. It flows down over my body all the way down, covering me with a pink mist. I feel cocooned. Everybody is watching. I have no idea why but I am very accepting. I don't mind.

"Strengthening you with love as that is your greatest need. We are showering you and covering you with our love."

I have gone all cold and chilly. It is all over.

Over the months ahead many changes were made to my physical form during meditation journeys. One preparation I remember went on for a week, morning and evening. The sessions were conducted by Serapis Bey and Extraterrestrial beings.

This is an account of a week long meditation, if that was what it was. It gives validity to my belief that meditation is the key to opening other doors to other realities.

As this was not recorded I cannot now remember the date. The memory of what happened is as clear as if it were yesterday.

I was in meditation 'tune in' when I found myself in a large oval room. The walls were not high since the ceiling sloped down to meet them rather like an oval shaped dome. Benches or slabs acting as beds were set all around the walls of the room. In a dream state I lay down on one of them and became aware of a figure standing at the doorway, watching. I knew immediately who he was and that he was overseeing. Serapis Bey was with me. Waves of coloured light began to stream up my body, wave after wave.

Time passed and I said; "I have to go because I have an appointment which I have to keep."

His reply was: "We will continue this evening."

I faded in and out until at last I came back to my home and got ready for my appointment.

True to his word he returned me to the room that evening which amazingly became smaller each time and held fewer beds. This continued for an entire week, morning and evening until there was just one bed left. Colours streamed over me each time. I knew that what was going on was a preparation on my form. I had no need or desire to know any more than that.

My next meeting with Serapis Bey was when I was taken into a room with one solitary bed, such as you would get in an operating theatre. As I lay down a stream of extraterrestrials surrounded me. What I noticed and surprised me most was that each of them had different coloured eyes. They were striking since our general expectation is that the eyes are usually black.

I have seen Serapis Bey a few times since then but this book is not the place for those accounts, especially as they were not recorded.

CHAPTER EIGHT

THE JOURNEYS CONTINUE

MARCH 21st 1996

PYRAMID OF LIGHT

I descend my stairs to see a little girl out in the countryside who is skipping, jumping and laughing. Every so often she stops, listens and then carries on. She is happy and enjoying herself in the open air. She comes to a hole in the ground. The little girl is me. I see the hole and am curious and want to know what is going on everywhere. I lower myself and slide into it. Underneath, below ground is a passageway. I bend down even though I am a little girl here and not tall. I follow the passage and as one would expect there is earth, bits of tree root. It is underground but not deep. I come to a cave. All around is rock, glistening and reflecting back. It is not dark in here. I don't know why or how but it is quite light. I can stand upright now. I look around to see what I can see.

Standing over to one side are two figures. Two human shapes, though I can't see them clearly. They are holding hands. I can see they are humans though I can't see features. Because I can't see features I don't know if they are looking at me or not. I go up to them and being a little girl I am not afraid. I put my hand out and touch them. As soon as I do this they become clear, light and bright. Beautiful! They are bright and shining and have faces now. They look at me and smile, still holding hands. They put their hands out to me and take mine so that we form a little ring. They are very much taller than I am.

I wonder why these two people under the ground are standing here. I am thinking as a child, not as an adult. They sit down on the ground still holding my hands so that I am obliged to sit down with them. I don't mind this at all. They bring out some objects from somewhere on them. One is a very large crystal, multi faceted like an enormous diamond, huge. It is reflecting light and shining in the most beautiful colours. The other one fetches out a clear glass-like pyramid and places it over the top of the crystal, covering it completely. The light from the crystal fills the pyramid with light. The whole thing becomes a mass of light. It is like a generator, contained and glowing white hot. It is so bright I can hardly look at it. I just stare at it.

These two people, still holding my hands, put them on either side of the pyramid so that they touch it. I lean forward and touch. As I do that the light from it shoots up my arms and shoots through my body. I am lit up completely by the charge, like being connected to electricity and receiving a shock, but it doesn't hurt. It doesn't hurt at all. I look and watch myself glow as these two people are doing. I have the same form as they and I know that anybody looking at me would not see anything but the glow. They wouldn't know if I was wearing clothes or not.

"The light is in the earth and in products of the earth. The light is in all things. To see it clearly you must go below the surface of your being. You must go in to the deeper recesses of your mind and heart. It is necessary to look within for the source of the light. Your outer covering throws a blanket over this, smothering it so that it is not easily seen. When all that is within you is disclosed then may the light shine out for others to see. So my dear child, show what is within. Bring out, allow yourself to be seen, throw off the outer covering, throw off the veneer that you have plastered on yourself and stand free and naked before all humanity."

I, the child, don't know how to do this. "How does one throw off the outer casing? How is this done?"

"Discover yourself and when you have done that you will have no difficulty."

"I need you to show me how to do this."

"You keep that objective in mind and request with all your heart that you be revealed so that the light within may come forth. The way will be shown to you."

My hands are still held against the pyramid. I know I can't stay like this. As if picking up my thought they release their hands from mine. I remove mine from the pyramid but still they glow. I am beginning to feel the cold around me now which is making me come back here. I thank them and thank all my friends for what they give me and for the love they show me each time.

APRIL 15th 1996

SPEAK FOR ALL

I am all in red, bright red. It is a flame. My surroundings are in red, thickly carpeted. The walls are red and covered in a soft material. There is a golden rail, a soft cord threaded through loops. I am reminded of a theatre. I walk down wide stairs, soft and luxurious. They sweep around, very grand. It keeps on going. It is a long way down. I am the only one on the stairs. The energy is building up in me so I ask to be shown what I need to see, in all senses of the word. The wall at the side of me is soft to the touch, like velvet. Relaxed I go down to the bottom into a big hall. It is like a theatre. I look for an exit or an entrance. I see one passage which I go along. Eventually I come to a door. Again it has a theatre feel. I push the double doors open with both hands and walk through.

It is very quiet and dim. I feel there are others here with me though I can't see them. I tread softly over the carpet, feeling soft pile beneath my feet. This is an aisle between seats. I move down the aisle. People are in their seats waiting. There is a man on the stage. He sees me coming. I am a latecomer for everybody else is seated. He beckons me on and I keep walking until I reach the stage. He invites me up. I go to the side and up the steps. I can't quite distinguish him. I can't fix what he is like for he keeps changing. Different costumes, different nationalities. He doesn't hold still. The minute I think I have got him he is something else. He is a kaleidoscope of people, all in the one. I am a little confused.

He continues to beckon me on. I go up to him. He puts his hand on my shoulder. There is heaviness and warmth at the same time. I can feel the weight. He tells me to face the audience. With the weight of his arm across my shoulder I feel quite secure. I am to speak.

I am to speak to all these people, on the behalf of all nationalities that this man represents, of all that he is and all that he has been. I am to speak for him now as one personality. A spokesman for many lifetimes.

I ask him, "What am I to say?"

"For as long as we maintain contact with you, you will speak our words. For as long as you retain the connection, you will speak what it is we wish to say. As a whole we will speak as one although our knowledge

197

comes from many areas of existence and parts of the world and covers many lifetimes of varying nationalities. You will speak as one voice that is able to be heard for as long as you maintain contact. Maintain the connection."

I ask whether I am to be in trance or conscious.

"You will be conscious of our presence for you will feel the weight upon your shoulders. You will be aware of the collective mind and with this awareness will speak what flows from us to you."

"That is not an answer."

"We do not wish you to join us. We wish to join with you through the voice and the connecting line. We will unite with you in a totality. You will be present at all times for we unite with you and pass through you. So in that sense you do not remove yourself from us but become one with us."

I ask again: "Should I not try for deep trance?"

"You will speak from a greater depth of your being. You will subordinate your conscious mind. You will submit your conscious mind to the greater expression that will flow through you from us. You will submit and allow us access."

I tell them I am happy to do this. But will they train me how?

"We wish this to be and having your permission we will arrange for it to be so. Do you understand us?"

"Yes, I feel I understand you and am happy to have you speak through me in order to help the understanding of others."

I had been asking for deep trance abilities but it appears from their answer that this is not to be.

APRIL 23rd 1996

RECORDS KEPT

I have green. While everything is a nice, deep, restful spring green, soothing. I wear draping heavy material. I can't see where I am going. I move forward. There are stone steps and I feel the influence of a monk. We are in some kind of monastery. The steps are cool and curve round to the left in a broad sweep. I am in the centre of the steps. There is no need to hold onto anything. I am confident as I go down deeper. I am going to where the records are kept. This I know. I am going to where all books and manuscripts are kept away from the light of day to preserve them so that they will endure. I come to a flag floor at the bottom now. Cool and restful. I look to see which direction I should go. I should know. I should know. Yes. There is a door leading into the first passage. It is the first time I have had a door leading into a passage. I open it.

This is an Abbey. I go along and turn into a little passage leading into a room. There are small steps going into it. I must be on a hill, for although I have been going down I see through a window which looks out on to the countryside. We must be high up, set into a hill to be able to look out onto scenery in spite of going down. There are wooden benches round the room. The sunlight is streaming through the window lighting a patch on the floor. The whole of the right wall is faced with books, dusty but well ordered. Like archives. There is a table and chair in the middle of the room, so it is a reading room.

This is odd. Which one shall I take? That is interesting! There is one marked 1938. I didn't expect that. I take 1938 down. I was four years old then. Odd! Why? I put it on the table in the middle and undo the ties on the side. I open it and it is a pop-up book. How weird! I open the pages and figures pop up. What is this telling me?

"The figures are of a family. Parents, family, even a dog. Even your present life is contained within records from beginning to end. The records will be there for any to see, those who venture down to the past. You are making your past as you proceed and it will be there for all to see. It is not only of value to go back to ancient times to learn what you can but those ahead will also go back to your time to learn what they can. We point this out to make it known to you that your current life, method of thinking, believing and your deeds will be looked to by others who wish to gain wisdom and something of value. Do not discount this time. Put into it all you would wish to pass on. Indeed what you learn from your seeking of the past, you may take forward with you to make it more accessible to those ahead."

"Why four years old? Why 1938?"

"Up to the age of four you had no knowledge of who you were. From the age of four, even though you were unaware, the awakening had begun and was already started into action."

"It has taken me a long time to bring it to my consciousness."

"Work goes on within your soul being, your higher self even though you were unaware of this. Instruction was given, journeys were made, and communication was frequent, even though as a child you did not know this. We watched to see how events surrounding you were dealt with in a conscious state as a direct result of our guidance. We were not disappointed."

"I am thinking that over."

"You may retreat here at any time when you feel the need for reflection. Sit down quietly at the window and look over the sunny plain below. Take peace and know that all will be well. You have surmounted many obstacles, gone to great lengths and placed yourself in difficult situations to enter, and now we say there is no need to overcome the obstacles, for you may enter freely though the door with ease."

OCTOBER 9th 1996

FATHER IN HEAVEN *a very special experience.*

I am in green. I am walking along a path covered in green leaves. Not autumn leaves but fresh, young, spring green leaves. But they are not on the trees and they don't rustle as I walk. They are soft and tender, juicy with the sap, yet I am not bruising them. I walk over them lightly with bare feet. They are not damaged at all. It is as if I am not physical any more, the weight of me doesn't make any impression. You might say I am passing along this way rather than treading heavily. The path divides both ways covered in green leaves and I don't know which one to take. So I stand at the fork and hold my arms out like a Y figure.

I know I must go to the right and follow the path upwards. I see myself, as if from a distance, walking up, as if I am viewing me detached from a part of me. I come very quickly to an archway which is all green, plants, flowers, like an arbour in a garden. I walk under this and as I do, a shower of petals falls over me, on my head. A bird begins to sing somewhere. I can't see the bird but I can hear it. It is sweet, sweet.

As I walk along the arbour, the archway of plants, leaves and flowers, I come across a seat at the side. There are two children sitting there and there is a space in between them. I sit down in the space with a child on either side. They take my hands, one each. They hold my hands as a child would hold the hand of an adult, trusting. It feels good to hold them. It feels good.

We sit there a little while not speaking, simply trusting. Then they jump off the seat, still holding my hands and pull me with them. They pull me off into the greenery at the side from where they have come, into the bushes and the greenery. They are smaller than I, but they know the way. I go with them for I can't do anything else because they have hold of my hands. I am pulled along quite willingly.

We come to a very old man. I know that he has sent these children to fetch me. He is a very dear old man and I feel a great, great love for him. I have an enormous love for him, almost overwhelming. I get down on my knees and bury my head in his lap. The love and feeling and emotion between us is strong. It is as if I have been waiting all my life to meet this man. He bends his head over mine and puts his arms round my shoulders, comforting me. We sit there, held in each other, still not saying a word. I feel as if I have come home. I feel I have been reunited with somebody very special to me, yet I don't know his face. I don't know him. I know him as an emotion, as a feeling of great love. He feels the love in the same way back. It is a joint thing. Eventually he and I stand up. He is not as old as I thought. He stands straight, not bent. He is strong, not frail. He holds my hand and we walk together. He the elder and I the younger, with the two children trailing behind, following us.

I ask: "What I am doing here and who are you?"

He says, and I can hardly believe it: "I am your Father in Heaven. I represent all that you aim for. I represent your striving. You might say I represent mankind. You might ask how this can be. How can one person represent mankind? I say that one person does represent mankind. The love between you and mankind is strong. I am the Father in Heaven representing mankind for you."

I know what He says is true, even though He is not anybody's idea of the Father in Heaven. He is representing. Now I can understand the feeling between us. The children are His messengers. We walk on until we come to a large gathering of bright souls. I say bright because they are all bright, all glowing, all merging with each other's light, hardly distinguishable one from the other. They are all standing there, glowing in a mass. We walk up to them and into them so that we are both of us surrounded with the light from these Beings.

In answer to the question in my mind he says: "These too are all my children. I am their Father in Heaven too. These Great Ones are all my children. These Great Ones do my bidding out of love and with the love that I give them. These Great Ones journey wherever they feel it is necessary, wherever they feel that love is necessary, wherever they can shed their light. They do this out of love for me who represents the whole of mankind. You are now part of them for you too will do my bidding for mankind whom I represent. For I am the Father."

I feel very tiny and insignificant in the middle of all these Great Beings. I know I have a long way to go and I have a lot to learn and there is a lot of growth to be made. Yet I am in the presence of these Great Ones and I know they will sustain me. I know that my own guides and personal helpers who have been with me are among this number. I know they are there, merging with the others, for they are part of the whole. They are all doing the bidding of the Father. I know this too. I feel overwhelmed but inspired at the same time. I know I can come to no harm. I feel uplifted.

I find myself standing alone once more as I come back to this life. Thank you, God.

Even fifteen years later the memory of this journey still moves me greatly.

NOVEMBER 10th 1996

PATIENCE

"Be easy Little One, over the minor irritants of your day, over the little matters that cause you so much concern. Take a larger view and rest easy in your mind for it is only your own conduct that has any importance, your own state of belief, your own state of serenity. That is what has importance for you. All other things are merely testing. Do not concern yourself so greatly. They are not even major obstacles, but minor ones. All things will even themselves out. They may appear important to you, but in truth they have no importance, none at all.

"You know dear one, we are safeguarding you by not allowing you those things which you desire so greatly, for these things, were they to be given to you now, would cause you stress and anxiety. You are not yet strong enough to take the pressures that having those things would bring to you. Allow yourself a little longer. Do not be in a hurry."

INTO NEW LANDS

The colour is green. I am standing in a tunnel of leaves, in a wood. I can feel the leaves. Some are leathery and some are fine, delicate ones. I am surrounded on either side by a tunnel of greenery. There is just enough room for me to stand. I begin to walk along and can feel the scrunch of undergrowth and the snap of a twig as I step on it. I feel the crunch of an acorn as I go. It is obviously well trodden, so it is a path that is well used, probably by animals because it is well cleared but with the undergrowth on either side pressing in. I keep walking. The path goes up slightly and winds round. I am going gently upwards. I wonder where it leads because all I can see is the tunnel. It is very secluded and safe.

The tunnel winds round to the right, like turning a corner. I follow the direction and come up against a high constructed wooden – I can't see if it is a gate or a fence. It is old, heavy and right across the path. This doesn't make sense, because the path leads to it and has been well trodden before, it must lead somewhere, or people wouldn't use it. I ask why the path stops here? I know the path doesn't stop here and carries on the other side of the fence.

I push it to see what happens, not hard but just to see if it will give way. It does. I can see the hinges now that you can't see when it is shut, but only when it is open. It is a very big gate. You could get a wagon through it. I walk through and pull the gate shut after me. I know it is not intended to be known, that it is not a gate for all and sundry. It is only for those who would persevere. On the other side it is much smoother. The undergrowth has been cut back as if to allow for a greater passage. The path is firmer to the feet. I am on a gravel path which crunches as I walk along. I have no idea where this is leading. It's still upwards. The undergrowth starts to thin out until eventually I am standing on open land.

The path goes up over a rise. As I stand at the top of the rise I can see a vista of countryside. It is a vast horizon. It is so vast I can see the curve of the earth. It takes me by surprise and I still don't know what I am to do. Everything is open to me, no doors to go through. I can go in any direction.

I ask again. "What am I to do? Why am I here?"

"Go down into the world. Go down into the vastness. Whichever way you go will be surprising. New people, new ideas, new challenges. Don't limit yourself by remaining on the known path. Venture outwards now."

"I thought that was what I have been doing over this year, this last year."

"It isn't to stop there. You have a tendency to return to the land of known adventure. We say go on to yet new lands. Continue the process. Do not return."

"I don't know how I can do that. I need to be told where to go, the same as before."

"When the time is right we will tell you which land. Maintain your contact with us and we will advise you which land to go to and will set your direction."

"It is all very vague. What have I got to offer anyone? I still don't have the clairvoyance for platform work."

"You have healing and you have the ability to speak. Wait for the openings. They will be there."

"I haven't seen Andreas [my guide] lately."

"He is with you at all times."

He takes my hand and we walk down steps, down the hillside towards the vast horizon together. He is starting me off on the journey. We keep on going down and down and down. It seems as if we are never going to get to the bottom. I feel like a pioneer going into the unknown, it is so big.

CHAPTER NINE

1997

October 8th 1997

I am at the top of my stairs in thick warm clothes, thick trousers. I am really padded up. Everything is cold, like ice on the way down. I have thick gloves, thick mittens on. I feel as if I have been transported to arctic regions. Thick studded boots. I feel very clumsy going down the stairs. I clump my way down knowing I must go on this particular type of journey.

I get to the bottom feeling very heavy with all the gear on. It is like an underground cave. It is a little warmer down here but I'm not taking my outer gear off. It is not warm enough for that. I go along and turn off. It is like going through an ice tunnel, just big enough to get through. I can stand up. The passage is just wide enough for me. If I come to an opening I will surely find it because I am hemmed in so tightly here. I do come to an opening, cut into the ice.

I turn into it and once inside it is different. It is warm, it is light. There are colours, it is another world. I begin to take my things off. They are out of place here. There are tinkling little sounds, and little lights. It is like fairy land. I see people sitting at tables, talking, laughing, chattering. They are really quietly enjoying themselves. I wonder why I am here.

I see a man beckoning me from the other side. I go to him. I thread my way through the others. They are not too tightly packed. They give me an occasional glance. They are not interested in me. But he has seen me. He seems out of place because he is what we would call a spiritual master. I'm not even sure the others can see him. He reminds me of Jesus though I don't think it is him, for I would know. This figure is a biblical figure.

"I want to know why I am here, what am I going to learn? Will you tell me?"

"There are so many different worlds, so many and so vast. While you have to focus on the one you are living now, it is only a minute portion of what there is. Do not place so much importance upon it that you cannot see the overall picture. The little things you have been worrying about are so insignificant as to be almost laughable if you were to look at them with a wider view. Take the grander view and see how you personally can affect the life and environment in which you live. Look to see how you and your actions can improve life for others, without being overly concerned about insignificant matters that do not make a difference one way or the other to anybody else, including yourself.

"Focus on those things that do make a difference. Focus on those things which will be lasting in effect. If you do this then all the other little irritants will fade into insignificance where they belong. In all your actions and all your work applications, consider first, will this have an impact and beneficial effect on the life and the lives of those who share your time? Or will it have no bearing on the matter at all? Then your way will be easy. Then you will know the direction to follow. It requires but this question. You must think long and hard and think ahead to where the consequences of actions taken come in, and what they might be.

"Much work is involved. It is not easy. It is not easy to work in this way. We do not promise ease. We promise work. We promise results following dedicated application that will benefit not only your own soul but others also. It does not come about without your effort. It does not come of itself. It does not lie in complacency or giving up your energies. Remember to contain your energies for this work and not for other insignificant matters."

"Why was I dressed in all that ice gear?"

"You have travelled from the cold, unfeeling areas of your life, the elements that freeze into inaction. We wish you to emerge from inaction into a more fluid, warmer, more encouraging environment. Whenever you feel you are frozen in time, in inactivity, visualise your presence in this room where there is warmth, laughter and chatter. Where active minds dwell, and indeed where I dwell. You will see there is light and there is laughter. There is interchange between minds. Come out of the cold; come out of frozen time where nothing can be achieved."

"It is not quite clear, for I am doing things."

"Yes, my dear but you are doing things and getting nowhere. Put your mind to what you must do to have an effect."

"Interaction with others will help me to achieve. I feel I am very much doing everything on my own. The others in this are interacting with each other. I am on my own."

The figure pats me on the head. "You know you are not alone, even though you cannot see us. We move the chess players on the board."

"I would like to feel more than I have been lately, except when conducting a circle or development evening. I'd like to feel more in my daily life."

"Use your visualisation my dear. Use your mind to call them."

I must close now.

I have the colour apricot. I am going down on a very flimsy staircase. It is so flimsy as to be almost non-existent. It is as if each tread are just wires and the handrail is just a wire. It could break at any moment. It is like a swing bridge but going downhill. It is very precarious but I know I am alright. I get near the bottom. It doesn't actually touch bottom and I have to jump off the last step. Presumably this is why it was swinging as it is not fixed to the ground.

I move very cautiously forward. It is an odd passage. There are very rough walls. I must be careful not to bump into sharp protrusions on either side. You couldn't rush through here for you would hurt yourself. I turn off as usual. One has to turn off from the main entrance. There must be a reason for that. The ground is almost untrodden, fresh. It hasn't been used much, if at all. It is like a scoop through the earth. I keep going through. It is quite dark. I come to a door which is boarded up. But it does open. I think of a garden shed. Nobody has been down here for a long time. I have to pull the door open, not push it. It fills the gap I've been walking along. Nobody could continue to walk along the passage for it has effectively made a door in the tunnel as well.

I step inside over a piece of wood. I feel there is a lot of activity in here. It is just a feeling for I can't see much at all. Then I see a lone candle, very tall, very straight. I can see the candle itself as well as the flame. I go towards it keeping my eyes fixed on it so that I know where to go. I can't see if this is a big place or what. I can just see what is in front of me. I am pleased to be with the candle because it is light. It has been lit so somebody must have lit it. So I'm not on my own down here.

As I look into the candle I see a face, the face of an angel. Just a face in the candle flame. The beautiful face smiles at me. I wish it would appear totally. Immediately it turns into a light being, an angel, without wings. It is a Being all lit up. It is bigger than I. He puts his hands out and takes mine. His hands are warm and real. Earthy hands, I can feel the warmth. There is nothing of vapour about this. It is solid; I can feel the warmth of skin and flesh. The angel looks into my eyes as he takes my hands. He looks steadily into them with great understanding. I ask what I can do to do my spiritual work, to pass on what I know. He continues to look at me.

"If you would know more than you do at present, then you must maintain your contact with us. You must continue to communicate. The communication must be passed on. We will be with you this evening. We will communicate with you, even at times when you are unaware of this."

I feel much better. I know I must close for there is a noise outside. I must end here. I thank them.

I have been praying in this meditation. I see a biblical figure standing three quarters facing me. That figure is me from another time, a man. I am alongside him, as myself now. We are one and the same in different times. I know this and he knows this. He is like a double, a shadow figure, a ghost figure such as you see on the television when the picture is not clear. We walk side by side. I say that I wish to make a difference to people. I don't wish just to be a housewife. I wish to make an impact so that others may be helped, as he did. I know that he did, for his calmness and his gentleness exudes from him. I know he made a difference just by being there. I wish to be like him, not the ineffective me as I am in this life. I wish too, to exude sufficient presence that it makes a difference to others, just by being there. I ask to be given the wisdom that he must have had.

We walk together side by side. Although I know that I was he, I still view him as a separate being. I am able to detach from the me of now. I can't get inside his skin, though I would like to. I must have his memory somewhere. His qualities must still be here with me, for we are the one and the same. What can I do to tap into this? How can I reunite with my past?

OCTOBER 26th 1997

PREDICTION?

I am in red. The staircase is a peculiar one made out of planks, natural rough wood. Tree trunks, anything to hand, scavenged from the countryside, as if there were no tools there. There are all sorts of branches and boughs, scraps here and scraps there to make a way down the slope. I am holding on to bushes at the side. It has been cut through the undergrowth, not cut but bent and pushed apart, using whatever is to hand. Somebody has done this.

I keep going down into what seems to be a hole. Not a hole in the ground but a hole through undergrowth. I don't know where this is going. I am in red which means some energy for me, strength, passion too. I feel nothing. I almost feel nothing for something is welling up in my throat, a tightness. There is emotion, a great emotion of − I don't know. It is the sort of emotion when one wants to cry, but I don't feel sad. Yet this is coming so strongly. It is as if something has me by the throat, but they haven't. It is my own feelings, something very deep, very emotional is about to happen. I know that but I don't know what it is. I can hardly speak for the tightness and ache in my throat. Perhaps they are shifting something in my throat. It is all centred round my throat. The deeper I go the worse it gets. It is so hard not to cry here but I have nothing to cry about. Nothing to cry about.

I still keep going down. Eventually the tunnel opens out. I find myself on a flat piece of land. Open clear countryside. I must have been going down a hill. Where are we? I can feel the presence of spirit very strongly with me. Where am I to go? I look around, no clear path. I go forward, directly ahead of me. There begins to be more undergrowth, as if I have gone across a clearing. There is purpose in this. I can still feel spirit very strongly with me, guiding my thoughts. I turn off to the left.

I can see a whole city laid out, an entire city. It is huge such as one might look out over Birmingham, it is that big. But it is silent, nothing is happening in that city. It is like looking at the past. Only this is not the past that I am seeing. It is so quiet, no smoke anywhere, nothing, nothing; it is dead. No sound of traffic, no lights, no general hum that

213

one gets with the city. Nothing. The tightness in my throat comes again. The feeling of spirit with me is stronger than ever. Why, why, why is there no sign of life?

"This is the future that you are seeing. For that one portion of land. This is the future that you are seeing."

Where have the people gone?

"Some are still around, but not there. They have vacated themselves elsewhere. Some were too late, for they did not believe."

I am trying to take this in. They give me time to take it in. I want to know about other places. I can only see this one place. What about other areas?

"It is a pattern which is repeated elsewhere. It is a pattern in all parts of your globe."

"Why am I seeing it? I want to know why. Why are you showing it to me?" *My throat still aches.*

"You can do something about this. You can alert men's minds. You can prepare them, give them serenity before the event so that serenity carries them through. You can do this. Give them the connection with their own beings, for this is what will carry them through."

How am I to do this? How am I to do this? Nobody listens to me.

"This is where your book comes in. This is how you must angle your book. This is the bias you must follow. This is the thread that must run through it. Give serenity to men's souls so that they may not be frightened. So that the calm they receive remains with them."

It is not easy. It is not easy to reach the man in the street. How do I do this? How do I do this?

"You will receive assistance. You will receive expertise, both physical and non physical."

I am so very pleased about that, but I have been told it is alright many times and I am still struggling. How much more, how much longer do I have to struggle with this? It is interfering with my life and the work I do.

"This work is more important than all the other connections you have made in your life. This work has more importance than ever you would believe possible. Give people serenity in their hearts, not by telling them that these events will not happen but by giving them the strength to face them. Give them the strength to face even their own daily lives with calmness."

"How can I ease this throat so that I can actually stay within? This physical interference brings me back to consciousness each time?"

214

"Do you not know that your consciousness and your inner being are one now? One cannot disrupt the other for they work together. You do not lose the contact when your physical condition interferes. You have reached the point where the two are one. Do you not know this?"

"No I didn't know it. How was I to know this?"

"Please accept our word that this is so. You will find that you have the contact with your own being. When you feel our presence it is merely an addition. Not always required but there to give you comfort, to give you confidence, to reassure you that you are not acting alone. For even while you are in physical form, you are acting in spirit, with your spirit and with the spirits. Can you understand what I have said?"

"Yes. I wish I could feel more confident about this. It is so difficult, so difficult."

"Trust yourself more."

"Yes. I feel better. My throat has stopped aching. Why did it ache so much?"

"There is grief in you. There is grief in you over so many things, both in your present lifetime and in the past. When you touch spirit more closely this grief surfaces. Serves as a reminder."

I don't feel I want to delve into that. I don't think I could manage it right now. Maybe at another time. That is all I can take. I take a last look at the city that is dead. I look at its sprawling roads, motorways, buildings; absolutely silent. All in one piece but silent. I look at it and begin to hear again the sounds of my room. I bring myself back quite deliberately. I can still feel them. I thank them for being with me. I withdraw, something I don't normally do.

NOVEMBER 4th 1997

GET GOING

I am standing at the top of the stairs. I am very cold, especially around the legs. The colour is ice blue. It is very clean but there is coldness about it all. I have to go down backwards into a stairwell. It is steep, almost a ladder. It reminds me of a well because I can see a glint of dark water down there. It is obviously where I must go. But if there is water at the bottom how do I stand and how do I go from there?

In fact when I get to the bottom, it is not deep and it is not cold. It seems to be alright. I paddle through it and swish my way through. I can hear the water lapping on the sides as I push my way along. It is echoing sound, everything is echoing. I can't see where I am going, but there must be light for it is glinting on the water. I go ahead and then turn off. There is water running all along the bottom. I don't understand why this should be.

I have a feeling that I am in a ship, a ship that has … I don't know. It has water in it and has obviously been abandoned. I come to an opening. It is a ship's door with a threshold that one has to step over. It is raised to stop water coming in.

I step through the door which opens inwards. It has to because the passage is too narrow for it to open outwards. The floor is wet but it is not too bad. I look around me now to see what I can see. It is definitely a ship. I must be in the captain's cabin for there are charts. It feels like the captain's cabin for there are maps, charts and all sorts of things scattered about. It is not a seaman's cabin; it is an officer's cabin. It is a bit untidy, deserted, bits all over the place. I know before I ask, but I must ask anyway.

"What is this all about? What must I do?"

The voice comes and says: "This ship is going nowhere in this condition. You must dry it out. Raise it up and make it fast. Put things in order then set sail. Plot your course and get moving for that is what ships are for. They are not meant to be at anchor. You must take the captain's role, take command and get the whole thing moving."

I feel this is referring to the book again. I have let it go, not out of mind but certainly not moving. It is all very helpful and all very nice but it doesn't tell me how to get it moving. It is not as easy as it sounds. I need help. I need help please. Somebody has thrust a great big pen in my hand.

"The first thing is to write."

I am despondent over the task. I stand and look at the pen. Through the door comes an officer and with it come the words: "The captain doesn't sail the ship by himself. He has a team, a crew and he gives them orders. He merely does the planning, sets the sails, but his men do the work of moving the whole thing. He cannot do it all on his own."

"I need a crew then. I don't have a crew."

"What does the captain do when he needs a crew? He goes out and recruits one."

Easier said than done.

DIFFERENT LIFETIMES

I am going upstairs. It is a steep climb. It is quite hard work for the steps are high. Huge steps as if they are made for a giant and not for somebody like me at all. I keep going up. They don't appear to be attached to anything. What a climb!

I have been going for a while now and am at the top, the top for me anyway. I am helped off the step for I am quite worn out by this time. There is an air of jubilation that I have managed to climb so far without giving up and going back, which I could have done. There is a feeling of celebration that I have managed it. I am being carted off now to somewhere else. I don't know where. I am sat down in an amphitheatre. There are lots of other people here.

I am told that I have merely come to join myself in all these other times. I have come to join with the other experiences I have had as other people. If I saw them in the street I wouldn't recognise them but they are all me in different times, in different guises and both sexes. They are all me, it is strange.

"We are trying to put things into perspective for you so that you don't get too worked up over your present life and its difficulties. We are trying to give you a more balanced view so that you work through this one more calmly. While it is important, don't attach too much importance to it so that you throw out of balance the equilibrium. In having lived all these lives, we would expect that you would have learned much, that you will have the wisdom of retaining your sense of balance, your sense of purpose without being flummoxed by the experience. You would say, without being thrown into dismay.

"There should be no dismay for much has been achieved. While your time has not yet finished and there is yet more to learn, were you to leave the earth plane at this point you would be contented with what has passed. So do not spoil this now, no matter what events occur around you or how they touch your heart strings. They are really of such small consequence in the overall plan. You have endured far worse things than this. What is now required is a stronger sense of purpose and a stronger application to the deeds in front of you yet to be accomplished.

You require yet more discipline and dedication for your purpose."
Whew! That is telling me.

219

AS A CHINESE

I have red. Do I need red? The carpet is like a living flame, deep red. It is soft and comfortable. I am wearing slippers, not sloppy slippers but rather smart, stylish for occasion type slippers. One might call them soft shoes. I am wearing heavy clad, brocade clothes right down to the ankles. I am reminded of the Chinese heavy brocaded coats. It is heavy with the brocade and the silks and embroideries in it. It is Chinese.

I walk. I am not sure if I am me. I feel as if I am a Chinese man, an older man. I am not me as Shirley, yet I am just starting on this journey. It is odd. I have a moustache. It is difficult to know how old I am. It is always difficult to feel your own age. Possibly I'm early forties. I'm not sure. I go down the soft red carpet. I am very much a man and very sure of myself also. I belong here. This is my place. This is my home, my domain. As I go down there appear to be servants on either side of the staircase. They bow their heads to me as I go. I seem to be somebody of importance though I don't know my name. The stairs sweep round to the left. It is very grand, like a palace. I don't know where this is taking me or why this has happened. I have no idea.

At the bottom it is difficult to make out the covering of the floor, not that it matters too much. It is smooth, marble like. I had half expected carpet. It is very wide, very open. I don't know where this is taking me. I walk straight ahead where there is a door. It is typically old Chinese style, mandarin style, whatever that is. I go through the door out into a courtyard. This is all very nice but what is this telling me?

"You seek for a cure for all your ills. You continuously seek and yet you have not tried the one thing that is natural to you. Why do you not try this, as it is effective in your case? From then on you will not have the disturbance that prevents you from working to your fullest capacity."

"Why all the build up just to tell me that?"

"We wish to remind you of your roots, the part of you that is strongest in you, the part of your existence that has had the greatest influence on the quality of your soul. Why do you not tap into this source, for this source is strongest in you? We say this because we are speaking of this Earth time, though we would remind you that there have been other Earth times. Here your influence and foundation of being was somewhat different. Here we are referring to your memories of Earth times."

"That's intriguing, very intriguing. There is confusion now in me."

Sighing "Let us put it this way. There have been other Earth times. We are now speaking of this Earth time's recorded memory, recorded by your historians. Does that help you?"

"Yes indeed it does."

"You see my child there have been other times which have not been recorded by your historians, of which they have only a glimmer of knowledge: an inkling of understanding and no more. No facts only intimations of memories lurking in their minds."

"If I follow this route and I feel you are referring to acupuncture here, I am against Chinese medicine where they use animals. If I use this and become fully active again, will this help me with the book? This is where I need help at this time. I need help."

I get no response to that and my nose [hay fever] is getting worse so I can't even think now so I will have to close.

I ask to be helped. I am dressed in silver, in a long, slim, silver sheath, type gown. Very glittery. I walk along a path strewn with silver shards, all pointing in one direction. I can't quite describe it. It is a bit slippery. It is all flat, not going down; a narrow pathway of silver, like a silver thread, only the thread itself is composed of many things. I step forward with very small steps because the sheath I am wearing is rather tight. It is glamorous and I must be glittering as I go because the gown is like thousands or millions of sparkles. I am quite taken up with this. It is extraordinary. I feel as if I have a lot of hair, a halo of hair. I don't know where my hair ends and the roundness begins. It is as if my hair is enveloped in a bowl, golden, silver, all sorts. It is not heavy just that it has something around it. It is not a hat. I don't think it is my hair as it is all around my head. I don't know what this is telling me. I have to give description as I go [as instructed].

I am getting near the end of this now. I know that I am and put my arms out in front of me as if to feel the end. It will be the end but I won't be able to see it, only feel it. I am right to do so because I feel an energy wall which I can pass through. There is a distinct division between where I have come from and where I am going. I walk very gently into the wall of energy so as not to damage myself. I pass through as if it isn't there, but it is.

As I get through to the other side there is a distinctly different feel. It's like being in a vacuum, though I've never been in a vacuum. It is as if there is no atmosphere. It is light as there is no influence from the Earth. It is free falling or being in space. I float onwards from here, no effort required. Free, no pressure on the limbs, totally free. I am floating all over the place. It is like being in space, though I have never experienced that either. I float my way along the tube, for that is what it appears to be. It is quite a wide tunnel, the size of a room in height and width. The length I don't know because I just keep going along it. Moving along using arm movements, like swimming though I don't do too much of that because of the tight garment I am wearing.

I come to another invisible wall. I know it is there though I can't see it. I push my way through this one as well. Soon I am standing on firm ground and am free of this free fall thing. I am back in pressure and normal atmosphere. I stand there and look around me. There are all sorts of shadowy figures moving about, very tall and very thin, and indistinct too. One of the shadowy figures, that is all I can call them, comes up to me and takes my hand. He is almost not there but he is at the same time. He pulls me forward, it is a long journey this one. He is very unreal and yet he must be real for he is pulling me forward. I feel his feelings. He is very welcoming, smiling. I am feeling his thoughts and feelings. I know what he wants to do and say. I know it.

He takes me before what I can only describe as a Jesus figure. I don't know if it is Jesus. It is the type of figure that one sees of pictures of him, sitting down with his kind, gentle face. He is very relaxed. I stand before him and don't know what to say. He puts his arm and hand out in a greeting, no it is a blessing. It is the sign of a blessing on me. I still don't know what to do. I am tongue tied. I feel as if I am frozen in time, a long period of nothing but this picture. He has to be Jesus. He looks like him. Everything is frozen and great energy comes into me. I can feel it as I speak. It enters my head and I feel the difference. A part of me wants to record this and the other part is going off … away… away.

I ask him to help me with my endeavours, to help me be a pure channel.

He says: "Hush, my child. Be still. We know of your endeavours and we are pleased to see where your heart lies. Hush and be still."

I feel very moved and very still. After a long period my thoughts come back to the builders due to arrive any moment and the need to eat something. I still feel very light headed and swimmy. These thoughts are stopping any further progress. Life continues and others don't know.

I am going down a steep grassy hillside with no path. It is steep and I skid and slide a bit, almost on my back in parts. It reminds me of the Welsh hillsides. It is exhilarating but I don't know why I am doing this. I dig my heels in so that I don't slide all the way, to have a controlled descent. At the bottom there is a stream. It is really only a little brook, sweet and gentle, not turbulent at all; a gentle, pleasant place to be. I sit down on a dry patch of grass at the side and gaze into the water. It is just nice and reflective and peaceful after the journey down the hill side.

A man on the other side of the stream comes from among some trees. He is wearing a broad brimmed hat and heavy coat, long and flowing. He reminds me of the French Bergers, the mountain men in the old days. I want to talk to him. He is waving to me trying to catch my attention as he draws nearer, as if I would go away. He draws closer so that he is within earshot. He steps across the stream using the stepping stone that is in the middle. He sits down beside me. We both sit staring at the water not rushing by, but gurgling by. We are lost in thought.

He says: "Yes, life goes on whatever we do. Everything goes on. Nature goes on whatever we do. It will find a means of expression, expressing itself into life. Whatever we do nature will express itself, it will express the joyousness of life. It will always find a way in whatever form."

I look at him because he has voiced my thoughts.

I say, "We must make an influence on our kind as we pass through as a human race. We go on no matter what happens, we find expression. We ought, shouldn't we, make that expression as good as possible?"

He nods. "You are talking about your book now, aren't you?"

"Yes. I want to make my expression so that will have an effect on the race of human. So that it will benefit. I need your help. I need everybody's help for it is a joint effort after all. I am part of the flow of humankind. It is up to me to be a good part in that flow. To add to it and not detract from it."

We both go back to being lost in thought, his thoughts and my thoughts side by side. I also sense the presence of spirits. I don't feel that either of us here are alone. The minds of spirit beings are with us too, watching.

DECEMBER 20th 1997

I am dressed in purple and there is a chute. This is like a children's playground. When I get to the bottom I land on sand. It is soft dune like sand that one gets at the seaside. Although the way is soft and comfortable it is also hard work. I plod on looking for something. I see a beach hut. There is somebody standing in the door way waving and beckoning me to come forward. I make my way laboriously across loose, deep sand and go up the steps. The door is held open for me. I go in and find it is larger inside than I expected.

There is a group of men sitting at a table. They are gathered there like an assembly, a council or something. They are all looking at me. As I pass down the line each one in turn gives me a rolled up document. By the time I reach the end I have an armful of them. The last one doesn't give me anything. He holds it in his hand but he is not giving it to me.

He says, "This one you have yet to earn. You mustn't give up now for you would not be able to complete. You would feel unfulfilled. So you must persevere with this last one for it is not more important than the others but the completion of the others, and where they have led you. You need to complete before you pass beyond these doors. You have all the other experiences behind you to help you. Do not give up."

I have gone up this time, not down. The first part was quite hard, and then I was whisked up. I have arrived and am walking on beaten earth. The earth is up here as well as down there. I come to a flight of steps up to a building. There is an ordinary door which I beat my fists on. I want to be let in. I am hammering away at the door when somebody opens it from the other side. I go through. Inside it is palatial. That is the correct word for it. Enormous, polished and clean and yet it is simple as well. Clean lines everywhere. I walk with my feet not making any noise for I am not wearing shoes. I pad across. I wouldn't want to mark this floor for anything. There is another door at the far end. I make my way to it. It is a small door. I go through.

Behind the door it is very ordinary, like a working area. Books, tables, like a big office. Lots of chairs, comfortable chairs. This is a sort of library. A man asks: "What have you come for?"

"I don't know. I have just come to see where I might end up."

"I would say, you have come to see your book."

"But my book isn't written yet."

"You have come to the future. Your book is here on the shelves. Not one but many. Which one do you want?"

"I want the one I am writing now. I want to see."

He goes up a little step ladder. I see a whole row of books. All in blue and all with my name on it. He fetches the first one in line. It is *The Communicators*. [this book has now had a name change and is **'Being Human'** and is published] It is not very thick. I want to see inside it. He hands me the book.

"You can't take it away," he says, "for this is from the future and you are in your present. You may look at it."

The words at the beginning 'We were having a picnic when the thought struck me. What would it be like if I was living in the future? A stupid thought for I was living in the present. All the same I wondered. What would things be like in a hundred years, two hundred years, three hundred years from now? What I didn't know was that thought brought to me a response, from where I do not know. A response I was to have. I was to step into the future. I didn't know all this then. It all began with a thought, a wondering. People say you should have investigative minds. Maybe we get responses to all our questions, to all our thoughts. Maybe these responses come much later, long after we have forgotten the original thought. That is how it all began. A few years later I was in Calgary. I would never have guessed that I would ever be in another country as far away from home. I still didn't make the connection. I had long since left behind that day, having a picnic.'

That is totally different to the way I have begun my book. Now what should I do?

[Wow! As I write this entry from December 1997 when I had no idea of what was to follow the beginning of the book published in 2010 is exactly as predicted way back then.]

"Just let your mind roam free my dear and it will pour out of you. Which is what you have been asking after all. This is your response. Can you not recognise a response when it is given to you? Do you not wait around for the answers to all your questions or, like a child, you ask and then run on, not waiting but impatient to ask the next question? Just like a child."

CHAPTER TEN

JANUARY 4th 1998

SOULS WAITING FOR BIRTH

I am standing at the foot of stairs all in white. I have a long flowing gown, very full. I have to go up the steps. I have to pull the skirts up because it is so full. I go up without holding on. It is quite steep but it is not an effort. I go up easily, very upright, very stately. It is strange because it is just the staircase, nothing else, no foundation to them. I am reminded of a piece of paper folded into a concertina shape and then spread out. These are just steps and nothing else. Nothing below them, nothing above them and nothing around them. As I climb, my mind is brought back to the present with hundred miles an hour gusts outside.

A tall narrow door is in front of me, double doors. I push them open, they open in the middle. Once I am inside it is quite different. There is a lot of green, a lot of laughter, a lot of life. There are many children here pulling my clothes to make me go with them. They are happy but want me to go with them. I am very tall amongst these children. They keep pulling so that I really have no choice but to go with them.

I go slowly, calmly and we come to what appears to be the edge of something. We look down, we all look down and see far far below – we seem to be looking at the world. We are not seeing it as a globe in its entirety. We see activity and what is going on down there. There's a lot of smoke and dust. It is confusing as there is a cloud over it so that you can't see clearly through the clouds, through all the white stuff. I know it is the ground, land, the cities. It is covered so that you can't see clearly. I hear the sound of gunfire. It is war. There is war going on down there. It is fighting, violence. We are far removed from that up here, but it is a hell down there. It is a hell.

The children don't want to go down there. They look at me and say, "Can you change this before we have to go? We don't want to go when it's like that. We are not looking forward to going into that."

I can understand their viewpoint but I don't know what I can do.

One of the children says: "We have free choice. We don't have to go into that, so we could wait until it improves."

Another child says: "Well, if we all do that there will be no more children. If we all do that there will not be a generation for us to follow. We have to go sooner or later."

Several of them are saying, "Well, I'm not going until it is better. I'm not getting mixed up in that stuff."

I look at the children. "It's not all war. There are a lot of lovely places down there. It's not all bad. There are some beautiful calm and happy places on the planet."

A little boy from the far corner says: "You show me then, because I haven't seen any."

At that I ask my spirit friends to find a spot that is happy and calm. The land below rolls to one side. I see the tops of hills, not high mountains, just hills, similar to what you get in Wales, the rounded hill tops. I look at the hills and it is peaceful up there. Just the sheep. It is so peaceful, too peaceful.

The children ask."Where are the people and where are the houses? There don't appear to be any. While it is peaceful there are no people. What is the good of that? Don't you know it is the people who have created disorder and war? Where there are no people it is naturally peaceful. It is the people who have created the disorder, it is not the planet, it is not the gods. It is the people themselves."

A little boy says: "How can I go there if there are no people. I can't be born where there are no parents."

"It is a problem, isn't it?" I tell them: "Why don't you ask for people to begin going to the peaceful places. Ask for the peaceful people to go to the hills. Speak your mind only to the peaceful people. Your thoughts will reach them and you will find that people will travel to the peaceful areas to escape war. Then you will have a family to go to."

"I'll give it a go," he says. "I'll give it a go."

One after the other the children pipe up and say: "I want to go to the peaceful places too. I don't want to go to the towns and cities and where there is fighting. I only want to go to the peaceful places too."

I tell them: "You can't all go there."

The one who said he wasn't going, digs his heels in and says: "Well, I'm going to wait. I'm not going. I'm going to wait, so there."

I look around me. I know these are all young children and are representing young souls. There must be some mature souls, some evolved souls here. They too may re-incarnate. I look around to see where they are. I see over to one side, a large group, quite a large gathering of mature souls, bright souls, evolved souls. They are all talking together, discussing and debating, talking of mighty matters. They are in a debate.

I leave the children and go over to them. I say to them: "How about you? Are you going to re-incarnate and are you only going to choose the peaceful areas?"

One of them looks at me and says sadly: "No we have allotted to go into the war torn areas. We have allotted to go into the dark places on your planet and see what we can do to change the situation. We have chosen to be the pioneers, to go down and see how we can change matters so that these young souls have more space in which to reincarnate, have more peaceful areas than there are at present. We have a difficult job to do but we have decided that there is no alternative to this. Somebody must go and so we are going. We know it is not going to be easy and we know that not many of us will survive a full earthly span. We may have to come back before we are ready to. It does not really matter for we know that when we return, we will have done as much as we could possibly do."

The question in my mind has just arisen. I must ask them. "Are you going to be born as new babies or are you going to go in as Avatars, Wise men or simply become Walk-ins and take over another body?"

"Avatars are few on the ground. We have but few who can make this claim to be such a one. Of the others there is to be a mixture, so that there is a spread in time. Some of us will be born as babes. Others of us will become Walk-ins. We must arrange things so that there is a spread over time."

As I talk to them I can see a flickering of flame, lights. As I turn my head to look I see it is coming from the edge where the children are looking. I go back to them and look with them. They are looking at fires. The fires are alight on the planet. It is on fire in the troubled places. This too has a beneficial effect for it is a cleansing fire. Where there has been fire there can be rebuilding. Maybe there is hope after all, even in these places.

I say goodbye to the children and turn from them and turn back to the evolved souls. I put my arms on their shoulders. I give them a hug and wish them well. I turn from them also and walk back through the doors and back to the staircase so that I may return down to the earth below. Down to the troubled sphere.

JANUARY 21ˢᵗ 1998

I have orange. I am an orange flame, like a burning flame. I am walking on flame, all being blown in one direction ahead of me. I come to a steep slope. The flame sweeps down the slope, I follow. I keep going down. I am not hurt at all. For some strange reason my ears hurt and begin to sting. One ear in particular. My throat is tightening and aching. I am filling up with something, I don't know what. I watch myself as a column of flame. I pass through a door. I don't bother to open it as there is no handle. I pass through as would a ghost walking through walls.

I see a goblet, a silver cup on a table over to the left. I go to it. There are handles on either side of it, tall handles. I look inside and see it is golden, like a bronze gold. I try to pick it up but I can't as it is too heavy. It is as if it is fixed to the table. I can't budge it. I was going to lift it and take it with me. I try to drink from it but I can't, it won't move and I don't know why. It is fixed. I ask why.

"The cup hasn't been won, not yet. You can't take the cup until it has been won."

That is a little depressing. I walk on. There are corners here, passage ways which go in different directions. I feel as if I am underground. I go down one of the passageways. It is very narrow and rocky. It is like being in an underground cave, but I can walk upright and I can see, which is strange. I can see all the rock face. It is so narrow that if it gets any narrower I won't be able to go any further. It is like going deeper into a crack. Just before the crack comes to an end and I can't go any further, I see an opening on the right, like a large hole. It is too narrow to turn round and go back the way I have come. I go to the hole and almost fall into it. As I get through I have to be careful not to fall right down to the bottom, for it is a deep hole. I stand looking at it and thinking there isn't anywhere else I can go, except back.

Knowing that nothing can hurt me I jump into the hole. As I go I am caught up by currents of air. I float down like a feather in the wind. So there is no danger at all. I float downwards and wonder where all this is leading me.

A voice says: "When you go into the unknown you will always be caught. You will always be held safe no matter where you jump, especially into the unknown. You will feel as light as a feather and the feather will be blown by your friends to the place it was intended to go. It is rather like a child would blow a balloon in the direction it wants it to travel. We too do this to you whenever you jump into the unknown. Don't be afraid of new experiences. Don't be afraid to try new things. Don't be afraid to go where you have not been before. All these explorations will lead you to exciting things. It will also lead you to people who have a need for you so that you may continue to fulfil your pledge to humanity. You will be directed by us. First you must jump into the unknown and take that courage in your hands."

I ask about the book.

"The book has diverted you from further learning. The book has been a distraction. It will find its place in due course of time. There is more learning for you and more experience. This must take priority for the moment."

I am shown a picture of hands joining mine and others across the chasm.

"You will join hands with those across the seas. There will be a joining of souls."

I feel I must come back now. That is all I need for the moment.

FIGHT THROUGH TO LIGHT

I am standing on pine needles. I can smell the sweet, pungent smell of them. I feel the softness of them, spongy under the soles of my feet. Lovely, pure heaven. There is a pathway through dark undergrowth. I have to bend low at some points and move along. I can't see very far ahead because of the denseness. As I step forward there is always another step I can take. It twists and winds a little bit. Pine needles are still there, which is strange because I can't see any pine trees, only dense undergrowth. It is as if the pine needles have been collected and laid down specifically to make a path, for nothing will grow on the needles. So it leaves a path clear for me. It is very clever really.

I keep pushing my way forward through brambles now, all sorts. It is not the easiest way to go through. There is warmth here as well. It is comfortable warmth, exciting. I keep pushing and come out into a wider, clearer higher space. I can stand up easily and see the sky above. It is spacious here. It is like a circular, open circle as if it has been trodden down many times. The undergrowth is all flattened. It is a perfect circle, perfect.

I move to go and stand in the very centre of the circle. I raise my arms and slowly turn clockwise with my face to the sun. Oh, it's lovely. There is nobody here but myself. I can do daft things like this and nobody is going to take any notice, no public around. I turn full circle. I have had my eyes shut, but now I open them.

Ahead of me is a clear path and at the end of the path is a light. Daylight, but a light just the same. It appears to be the only path apart from the one I have just come down. I follow it. It is clear, easy walking this time. No bending down, no brambles catching on my clothes. I move very quickly, swiftly, regally towards the other end of the path because something is brighter there. The light is shining brightness not ordinary daylight.

Suddenly from somewhere comes a wind, a strong wind, fighting against me. I have to push very hard against the force, as if something or someone doesn't want me to get to the end. It is a very strong wind. It is as if I am in a wind tunnel and I have to fight against the force to get my way through. I am determined to get through. I push, push and keep going. The wind gets stronger. I *will not* be blown backwards.

At the end of the path, where the light begins, suddenly I am through. It is like pushing against a door which suddenly opens and you fall in. I have fallen into the light. I pick myself up from the ground. I can't see clearly, it is so bright. My eyes are blinded, I can't see clearly. The brightness is really great. I try squinting, trying to make out something through the squint. It is not as if the light hurts, it is simply blinding. I keep my eyes squinted.

The light comes from one source. I know that inside that source is a figure. The light is radiating from the figure. I can feel the presence of a person, a Being. It moves and is talking but I can't hear what it is saying. I can hear sounds but they are not sharp. My ears are not accustomed. He is talking to me and I can't hear, can't make it out. It is incoherent to me, like hearing an overheard conversation. Hearing voices but not actually what is being said. I ask to understand and to see. I stand and wait. A shiver goes all over me, a deliciousness. The voice settles into something I can understand.

"To be comfortable in this brightness, to see and hear clearly, it is necessary to keep your mind on your objectives, your spiritual attainment. Focus your mind on what it is you strive for in your own spiritual growth. What are the values you have set yourself? When you have decided the values and the quality of your being that you are striving to attain, may all your actions be to gain this attainment, to become the one you wish to be. May all your endeavours be geared to this end. It is not sufficient to be available for others, to assist them.

"What is required is the quality of your being when you are making yourself available. Being there is not sufficient. Being of spiritual endeavour while making yourself present adds to the results and to the benefits that others will reap from you. Keep your goals for your own self in mind and the rest will fall into place. You will not have to seek to help, because those who will require assistance will seek you. So you can see, my dear, the importance of looking to self. Do not neglect this aspect of your endeavours. Seek to grow. Seek to understand and by your very nature you will pass whatever you have gained on to others. Have something to give."

FEBRUARY 5th 1998

PAST LIFE AS JOHN BARTHOLOMEW

I can see the sea. There is a heavy swell, oily, not choppy. It is as if there is no wind whatsoever. The sea isn't flat, it is rising and falling, a swell. My name is John Bartholomew, looking for land. We are all looking for land, which is my job for the day. We have been looking for days. There is practically no food on board now. We have little water. We must find land. We must find land. There is no wind to take us. We are sitting still. Just the wind we need, no more. We are all sitting still; we are too tired. If a wind came would we have the strength to manage it? We are very tired.

I see a leaf on the oily surface. This must mean land. What is a leaf doing out here? I call everybody and show them. The leaf hardly moves for the waters are heavy. There is no current at all. Those who have the energy come to look. There must be land but we can't see any. My chest hurts. It hurts a lot. Like a heavy dull ache inside it. It is difficult to breathe. Very difficult to breathe.

*

What is interesting is that years later when I was in Seattle attending a class in photography I met a man who was interested in English naval history. He knew of a John Bartholomew, who was a Captain in the navy in the days of sail. The same one? I wonder.

TEXAS?

I am walking down a wide path with rough stippled walls on either side. It is stippled rendering. I go quite determined. There are wide gates which I go through. They are very wide and large. A big driveway. Keep walking, keep on. There is a way to go yet. It is gravel underfoot, not uncomfortable it is very well kept, this place, like the grounds of a big house. I come to the house with big imposing steps. I go up the steps and into the front door which is open, big of course. It is no ordinary house door. There is a hall inside. Polished floor. An enormous hall. In the middle of it is a table, a round table.

There are men sitting at the table, talking, discussing. It is a round table so some of them have their backs to me. I walk up to them and look over the shoulders of the ones who have their backs to me, to see what it is on the table. There is a big layout plan on the table, which they are debating and discussing. I feel this is my layout, my movements. There are big criss-cross lines all over it. It doesn't make any sense to me whatsoever.

I recognise it as America, where I shall be going. Lines crisscrossing. They are showing me the lines more clearly and pointing, there, there. I shall have to look it up on the map. From my scanty knowledge it does appear to be Texas which would seem I am going to after all. I can see where the line ends.

FEBRUARY 20th 1998

CREATE BY THOUGHT

I have green; there are leaves, big leathery jungle type leaves. Leathery and shiny, not the sort we get in England. I seem to be in the middle of all the leaves. It is thick around me so that I can only see leaves. I push my way forward with my hands. I have big strong hands. I am not looking at the rest of me for I might receive a surprise. I am not ready for that yet. I keep pushing my way forward as if I have done this many times before. I feel this is routine, as a pathway around one's house is routine. It is familiar. I am in the jungle. I come out to a clearing and as one would expect there is a hut. It is not a native hut. It seems to be built on stilts but doesn't have the look of a mud hut, but one that is constructed by a civilisation even though it is wood. I am not a native. I am white and not of this land even though it is familiar. I am still a visitor to this land. This abode, this dwelling has a veranda. I go up the steps and in through the doorway. It is not even dark inside. There are things on the table. It is well lived in. There are things hanging around. It is full of things.

As I look around a voice says: "Man has taken his mind and his creations into the very heart of nature. Nature has intelligence but does not think. It behaves intelligently without conscious thought. Mind of man has created and thought about its creation, it has a purpose for its creations. There is a purpose behind all his actions, his intentional actions. That is the difference, which is the conscious difference between nature in its pure form and man with the thinking mind. The message here is clear. If you would have creations which are to your liking then think before you act, so that you create what you desire and for the best possible reasons. Man is not intended to be haphazard in his development. The soul of man is intended to develop on a deliberate conscious level, aiming for the highest."

ENJOY LIFE

My passage down is rough hewn rock, boulder rock. I go down rough stone steps, narrow stone steps cut into the rock. It is going down into the solid core of the Earth. It echoes. It is steep. I am getting deeper and deeper in, isolated from the world. I am leaving the world far behind and entering a totally different world, totally different in every way. My feet touch the bottom, loose rubble, loose stone. I doubt if anyone has been this way before. Very narrow, only one way to go. I keep following, I don't know if it is turning or not. I keep moving step by step. I squeeze my way through in parts. It is as if the Earth has been split, not by man but by nature. It could just as easily close up again. It is a fissure I am walking into between split rock. It must go somewhere.

To my enormous surprise I see a little green shoot so there must be air and moisture. I can see, so there must be light, though where the light is coming from I have no idea. It is a little weed of some sort. I don't recognise the plant. There **is** a current of air. There is a current of air coming from the other end. I can see now the light from the far end. There is a soft breeze blowing into it. I arrive at the opening and squeeze out into sunshine, warm, bright on the eyes. I am standing on the edge of a cliff face. There is no way down that I can see. I am half way up the cliff face. I look around to see if I can find some way, some way without having to go back and retrace my steps.

To the right of me there is a little ledge, wide enough. I climb on to that and begin to work my way along holding on to the wall face. I mustn't fall for I'd have a long way to fall. I mustn't fall. Gradually I come to an easy slope which goes upwards. I climb. The rock is a little loose so I must be careful. I climb and hold on. After a while I arrive at the top. It is a grassy bank, like on top of a cliff. I crawl over on to this on my hands and knees, away from the edge. I look up and see a sheep looking down at me. I feel a bit stupid. I crawl past the sheep and then stand up. I feel safe now. No more trials.

A man who has been looking after the sheep walks up to me. He seems to come from another time. Old. His clothes are not of my time. He is not at all surprised to see me. He comes to my side and takes me by the arm. I let him. He walks me over to where there is a wooden bench and we sit down together. We look out over the grassy plain. It is a plateau for I can see we are high up. There is nothing to see but sky, grass and sheep. It is very peaceful with skylarks.

He looks at me – blue eyes. "Isn't this wonderful?" he says. "This life, isn't it wonderful? All you have to do is enjoy it. Don't worry about anything. As long as you have life and the sun and are healthy, what real cause is there for you to worry?"

"I have many things on my mind," I tell him, "many things, challenges, finances."

"Keep your mind fixed on the sun, the fresh air, nature. They are the good things of life."

My throat dries up and I cough. This takes me away from him. It is difficult to continue. I am waiting.

"You shall live a long time," he says. "As long as you are of the same mind then you will enjoy your life."

"What about my mission?" I ask him. "I am not supposed to just enjoy my life. I am supposed to work and achieve what I have come to do. I can't just sit back and enjoy life. If I could have done that I would have done it years ago. I wouldn't be pushing myself now."

"Your life would be very empty too, for you do have a purpose in life and you are striving to achieve success in that. We will help you. We will be with you. Just keep a sense of proportion about things. Don't let worry interfere."

MARCH 15th 1998

TACKLE THE FEARS

I am walking down a very steep slope, as if the ground is falling away from me. There is nothing to hold on to. It is a bit precarious. Very unsteady. It would be easier if I turned round and faced the surface. But I am facing outwards, digging my heels in and just going. I am out in the open, there is nothing to hold on to. There is nothing around me, nothing at all, just emptiness, a vacuum. At the foot there is a shingle path. Loose stones. Again not a very easy surface to walk on. I go on slipping and sliding a bit. The stones are quite big, not small. One could easily twist one's ankles here. I keep going, turn round the corner. There is still nothing on either side of me and I can't see anything at all. The gravel path goes into a hole. It is as if I am stepping through a hole, a blackness, an entry point. I walk through into the black thing that is in front of me. I can't see where I am going.

As soon as I step in there is a different scenario. I hear scurrying, a lot of movement. There are a lot of people, not people as we see them, but beings of some kind. Life, life, that is what I need to say. There are things here. I can't see them but I can hear them. A lot of movement, touching, touching. I can feel them touching me. I can't see them but I can feel them touching me. I feel quite safe because I know that nothing can hurt me. I don't think they intend me any harm anyway. They are just curious. They have never seen anybody like me. They've never seen anything like me. They are curious. They are not malevolent. They are prodding and pulling and feeling. Pulling at my hair, touching my feet. How do they touch? I don't know. I can feel pressure on my feet. I can't see anything.

I move forward hoping I am not going to tread on anything. I don't want to hurt anything. I don't understand.

"These are your fears, your anxieties, your worries. They touch you and pull you. All you need do is say 'boo' and they will scatter and run away from you. You know there is nothing to fear. You know your anxieties are not real, not valid. Send them from you and go forward as the person you are."

I do and say, "Boo, be gone," to them. Instantly I am alone. I am standing in a meadow, sweet meadow flowers, birds singing in the sunshine. I am on familiar ground. This is the Earth. This is my existence, this time. I feel good to be alive. The good 'can do anything' feeling. That is all I have to do when I feel anxious and nervous.

"Say 'be gone' also to the cough and the little physical irritants that beset you. You can also dismiss them as easily as you have done with your fears."

"I have tried that one and it didn't work. I will try again."

"Don't expect to succeed at the first go. Try again."

I ask for 'Two Suns Rising' [a guide] to be with me more. I ask because I miss his company and his advice. It is time for him to be with me. Once again as he did before, he is smearing me with oil and smearing himself with oil. He is rubbing oil all over me as well. I know this is a sign that he will be with me alongside my other helpers. He will be with me.

MAY 22nd 1998

HUGE PYRAMID GENERATING ENERGY

I have yellow with a tinge of green. I stand straight and tall looking down at my feet and at the hem of my gown. I am standing at the top of rough concrete steps. They are thick, narrow, not wide. Cellar steps with rough walls on either side. A very enclosed space. There is a cold damp chill to it. I descend into darkness. I don't need to see my way for I have my hands on the walls. My feet can feel each step. My legs are tired because I am not used to going down so many steps.

Thankfully I reach the bottom where the ground is fairly smooth, but rubble. It is not comfortable to my feet for they are bare. I am not accustomed to the rough edges.

I have to walk carefully. I feel my way along and turn off. It is easier now. The ground is smooth as if it has been swept. It is quite comfortable, warm. I can see and drop my hands from the walls. I can walk easily now, still with my gown flapping round my feet. I daren't look upwards to see what else I am wearing. I don't need to. I can see my feet and I know it's me. Big feet. I stride forward, flicking the hem of my gown with the movements of my legs as I go.

I come to a door, as I knew I would. It is shiny like Perspex shine, not glass. It is a brilliant colour, iridescent. I put my elbow to the door. There is no latch, no knob. It opens easily as if it is a board put in just to close the gap. It is not fixed. I walk inside and find myself in a huge... I can't call it a room. It is huge like a warehouse but it isn't a warehouse. It's a big building, it echoes. It feels empty but it can't be. I must find something here.

Over on the far wall I notice there are books lining the wall. It is quite some distance off. I walk purposefully. The wall is the only thing I can see to focus on. I move strongly forward to get to the books; they are packed in very tightly to the point where it could be very difficult to get one out. There is a stick on the table nearby. I pick the stick up so that I can reach. The books aren't meant to be taken down. I run the stick over them as one would run a stick along railings, making a noise. They are not meant to be taken down. Why are they there, then? I can't see the point of that.

I look around the huge empty building, like an aircraft hangar. I don't know what to call it. It is empty. It doesn't echo now. You could hold a hundred dances in here and there would still be room. I look around trying to find something that I can focus on. I see in a corner, a little crystal. It is glinting. I follow my eye to another corner which is a long way off. I see another little glint. I look all around and see a crystal in each corner. I realise for the first time that this is the base of a pyramid. It is so big I didn't notice the roof, the shape, because it is so big. It is inside a pyramid but completely empty. It is the shape of a pyramid.

Knowing pyramids I go to what I feel is the centre. As far as I can judge I am in the middle of the base. I am not quite sure if it is in the middle because it is so big here. I move around in a tight little circle and hit the spot. I know it is the spot. As I stand on it immediately a shaft of light comes down directly over me, as if I have set off some mechanism by being there. It is a gold light just big enough for me to stand in, no more, no less. It is a little blinding, wonderful. The light as it shines over me is like liquid gold. Around the floor I see the light keeps pouring and spreading across the floor and is pouring over me and spreading across the floor. The whole of the floor, the base is covered with light. Rather magical.

It does more than that. As it fills the base it begins to rise up as if somebody is pouring in the gold and it is going to fill the entire pyramid. I am in the centre. I have triggered it. I don't know what this means at all.

"It is necessary to trigger the beginnings. It is necessary for you to be the catalyst so that the input can take place. The input will fill this generator of energy so that when it is full it will generate sufficient energy and light to encompass the entire world. It will continue to generate for it is self generating. An enormous power house that is inexhaustible for as long as you remain at the centre to trigger this input."

I ask: "What do I do exactly?"

"You will continue to pass the knowledge that you receive by making your entry into our world. As the receptor you will then have what is required to extend this input beyond this generator."

"What does it mean, this staying in place?"

"Keep firm to your ideals. Keep firm to your purpose. Keep firm to your pledge to the spirit world and to humanity. Do not wander away from the centre of your ambitions and your goal. Stay focused upon your purpose and the input will continue to flow. Waver from it and the process will cease."

"That's clear enough."

"Do not doubt that the input is taking place. Do not doubt your abilities. Do not doubt that we are near, ever near. Do not doubt the synchronicity, the placements. The doubts of others should not affect your own purpose. The doubts of others are just that. They should not be taken upon yourself, for this would be the equivalent of one apple damaging a whole box load, if you allowed this to happen. So continue in your work with confidence and trust in us. Make your contact more in trust than you have been of late. Renew your purpose and your intent."

"Who is speaking to me now?"

"We speak to you as a group of those who have united with each other to focus our minds upon your thought process. We focus our minds so that what we wish to give to the world will pass through you."

*

Now I can go straight in without using the stairs method of going deeper into myself. Sometimes I still use the stairs but more often do not.

MAY 31st 1998

ENTRY INTO THE WORLD OF DEEPER LIGHT

I am in a swirl of green. There are two figures ahead of me, both of them stretching out their hands for me to take. They are all merging together in the one colour. I reach my hands to them and they take hold. Their hands are rustling, like taking hold of leaves. Strange, not what I expected at all.

I take hold and it is OK just a bit odd, weird, like taking hold of nature itself, two of them. I am not asking questions at the moment. They draw me in between them. With the hands closest to me they put their arms around my back, supporting my back and guiding me forward, as one would a blind person. They make sure I am encompassed. I am being taken, protected and safeguarded at the same time.

We all move forward. They know where they are going, I don't. I am like a blind person for I can see nothing ahead. They keep on. I am blind for all I can see is light and shadows. We go into some difference in light, a deeper light. How can one have a deeper light? That is the only way I can describe it. It is more intense and yet deeper. Odd! We enter the depth of light, richer, more vibrant, more profound. I don't know the words. I don't know the words to express the feeling. They have still got me fast, gently and tenderly now. We move forward and I am reminded of care assistants at a bathing place where handicapped people are guided into the water. A feeling of care and attention comes from them. I still don't know what this is all about. It doesn't matter. They are not there to talk to me. Wonderful, wonderful love coming from them. We move on into the depths of this light. We come to a sudden halt as if waiting for something. We are waiting for something. The wall of this depth of light is in front of me; I feel it more than see it. I feel it for I am in it and am merging with it. If I were to be observed I wouldn't be seen. It is … I don't know the words. I am standing in the light, of it, for you can't distinguish me in it.

Two doors swing open and there is a blinding flash. The depth suddenly changes. The brilliance makes me stagger. Now I know why they have got me held hard, why they have got me held quite tight. If they hadn't I'd have fallen. They have got me hard and fast so I remain standing. I can't describe the feeling of the other light. I can't feel anything. It is not hurting. I stand there adjusting, being held upright and moved forward. I step very gingerly to the brilliance. I feel faint. I feel faint.

I am dimly aware of hands holding me. I am in a blur, confusion and yet I must keep talking for the words are my link with my conscious mind. (Slowly). The…words… keep… me…safe, not that I am in danger. I must keep my thread, my connecting line. I feel so faint. Lost in it. I must keep talking, must keep talking. A hand is put on my head now, holding me, fingers outstretched covering my head. It is light and yet firm. I am charged, charged. The faintness begins to disappear. I feel stronger and can stand on my own now. I can stand without support. They still hold me, firmly. I can feel the grip. I feel their strength but now I am stronger than they. If I wasn't courteous I could release from them. I know they have helped me this far so I wouldn't do that.

I must listen. I don't need to talk to keep the thread. He is doing something with my feet. I feel a liquid over them, warm and soft and silky. It runs between my toes. I can't see anything.

"Welcome. Welcome to the world of light."

I am overcome with emotion.

JUNE 15th 1998

CHRYSTAL WOMAN

The colour is green. I am standing on loose pine needles. Soft and spongy. Very comfortable. I can feel them beneath my toes and the soles of my feet. Like walking on a spongy mattress, rather nice. I come to what appears to be a very steep slope, almost vertical. It still has an outdoors feeling. I must go down here. I slide down and the pine needles make it easy to slide. I slide quite comfortably down. I land on both feet at the bottom, down into myself, my innermost being.

I have landed in another world, another time. There is a lot of activity with people going about their various tasks. It is as if I am an observer. Nobody takes any notice of me. It is very strange, very different to our time. The clothes are different. I can't quite describe whether it is future or past. If it is past it is beyond our knowledge. Everybody seems to have efficient, practical clothing. Sleek and uncluttered, not like our clothing in the past. It is modernistic. Everything is practical. That is the feeling: practical.

I step into a world with clean floors. It is like stepping into another country, no, another world. I walk into it. I must find somewhere I can go in and meet who has the knowledge I have come to seek. That is the purpose of my visit, to meet with the wisdom I have come to find. I want to resurrect knowledge, to bring it back with me, to bring it back in my daily life in my own time.

Two people come up and hold me by the arms for they have seen me. They are not ungentle but are firm. They walk or guide me, one on each side, through the crowds. The crowds can see me now. I am an object of curiosity, unconcerned curiosity. I am walked firmly through a doorway into a front courtyard, up some steps into a rather large door. Yes. I am indoors now, inside. The two men holding me release my arms and allow me to walk where I want. I look around seeing what I can see. There is a woman dressed very tightly, she has a hat. Hat is not quite the right word for it. It is head gear.

She is a very strong woman, very upright and unbending. Before her is an enormous crystal, huge. It is nearly as big as she is. It seems to change shape as I look. One minute it is fat and the next thin. I don't

247

know how she does that. She is controlling this crystal with her mind. Her mind is intensely focussed and I can see rays coming from her, from her face and from her mouth. She opens her mouth and a blue light like a laser shoots out towards the crystal. She does nothing but open her mouth. I know it is done with intense focus of her mind and thought power. She is doing something that only she knows in her mind, only she can see. With sending the light to the crystal, it in turn sends it back, for it is linking. It is connection, like touching a probe. Once touched the current flows both ways. It is a conduit, no more. She receives as well but has instigated the action.

She appears to feel nothing. She appears to feel nothing, so intense is the focus. I am just watching. She will not take her concentration off the crystal to see me or greet me. I don't know what it is she is doing. I don't know more than that. Then she stops. The light stops. The laser beam of blue ceases. She shakes her head as if to free herself. She goes limp, not so upright, not so intense. She leans back in her chair, closes her eyes and then opens them again, normal.

She looks at me for the first time, says nothing. I look at her and don't know what to do.

"Come and visit me whenever you wish. Come and see my work whenever you wish," she says.

"I don't know what you have been doing, so it means nothing to me. It looks good but what is it doing? What is the purpose? What is the purpose of what you have done? I wish to know your motives, your abilities. I wish to know what it is you do and why you do it. What is your objective? *That* is what I wish to know. How and why? Maybe you can tell me these things. How and why? I will meet you face to face, for you would tell me how and why for the benefit of those in my present world, for the benefit, not of yourself but for myself and those in my world. You will tell me what, how and the purpose so that I will know all that you know. You will awaken in me the memory, the knowledge and the ability."

I don't know what she is doing now. Listening?

JULY 23rd 1998

IN AUSTRALIA – BE OF THE LIGHT

I have red and yellow. It is the colour of fire; active, not static. I am walking over fire, over hot coals. I can see a glowing, just a glow of red and yellow. It pours down like lava. I don't know why I have this colour or where the stream is flowing. I am flowing with it, down and out of the mouth of the Earth, out into the fresh air. I have risen with the embers of the earth. I need to know. I am flowing into all areas of cracks and crannies. I am flowing beneath doors into the houses. As I enter each place I become solid, real and tangible. I am immovable and cannot be erased. I want to know why I am here in Australia. Why? What do I have to do?

I am now me as I am usually, standing free, looking around in a great hall, vast, huge. An enormous expanse of space, but enclosed. If I were to raise my voice it would echo, it is so big. I look up at the vast dome above me, like a vaulted ceiling. I feel very tiny and insignificant. I know I am not alone here. As an observer I am alone, but as me the observed I know I am not, for I feel things around me, pressing me and touching me. Spirit forms surrounding me, spirit beings of all kinds, all kinds, spirits of green, spirits of the rock. There is a word I am trying to get, it won't come.

"Speak to me, Spirits of the Earth, spirits of the Origins of man." I look up and see my dear Andreas, standing there calmly and glowing as always. Smiling gently as he always does, he holds his hand out to me to go to him. I shake myself free from the spirits who are clinging to me, nicely but clinging. I walk towards him calmly, knowing it is right. I put my hand in his in a greeting. He smiles and we walk onwards together through a door he is to show me. He is taking me elsewhere.

I see light, another world, another existence. It is white light, deep light. We walk into it and as we do are lost in it. We become the light that we walk into and can no longer be seen, for we vanish into it. My mind is still active, as is his.

"I want to know what I am doing here, what practical use can I be on this journey? Tell me, what am I to do?"

"The only thing you have to do is be as the Light example. Be of

249

the Light and let others see. To achieve this you must think no wrong, do no wrong. Regard others with no judgement. Regard others as yourself and see them also as of the Light. Trust that all is well. The vibration of this Light in itself has a power to heal, to make well, to rejuvenate. The vibration of this Light consumes all ill, transmutes all dark into light. Being in and off this vibration light transforms all within range, at whatever state of readiness or awareness, all are transmuted. There need be no conscious effort except to think and act according to the highest principles of love and light. It is so simple. You do not need to strive to be, for you are. You cannot help but be."

"On the practical side, why here? Why Jenolan Caves and is that right?"

"The caves are of the Light and they will enhance yours, for their vibration transmutes, transforms and have a beneficial effect. Just to be is sufficient. Simply be."

"What about the psychic surgery, the meeting with spirit doctors and the others?"

"Follow the threads that are given you. The threads will unravel. Follow the threads and you will arrive at the point that was intended for you. Observe, notice. Do not disregard any lead or any information. Follow all leads. Negative leads will not be given to you. There is a purpose."

"I must finish soon for I am going to be interrupted. I thank you. I thank you."

I knew instinctively that I was to be interrupted in my mediation and so I was.

AUGUST 23rd 1998

A PORTION OF ME BACK TO THE PAST
AND PSYCHIC SURGERY

It is odd that I have a three way staircase with big broad steps, wide. It splits into three. I have never seen that before. I don't know which one to go down. I decide to use the middle one, it seems more direct. It is a narrower stairway with a rail on either side. It is not so narrow that I can touch both sides. I decide to go with my right hand on the rail. I can't see anything on either side, just the rail. There is a carpet in blue, like the carpet I have at home. I go down slowly, uncertain. I am uncertain of myself. I am not certain of myself anymore.

At the bottom there is the same blue carpet. I walk ahead expecting to find a turn off that must be there. Again there are several ways I can go, all of them looking identical, all of them looking exactly the same. They are spread out like a fan before me. There are seven. I decide to take the very first one on the left hand side. I walk down trying to get a feel for the place. It is interesting that the walls appear to be made of hands all reaching out. It is made of hands reaching out, not for help but to touch. They just want to touch, no more, no less. It's a greeting by hands all wanting to say hello and wanting to touch. I am confused by this. I don't know what that means. It doesn't matter.

I must keep walking. Soon I come to an opening. No door, just an opening with a curved top to it. I don't have to push a door as it is just an opening. You couldn't put a door into this anyway as it wouldn't fit. I walk through and as soon as I do I am on a glassy surface. It is shiny and quite dark. It is not transparent. It is polished like black marble. I can feel it with my toes for I have taken my shoes off. I look around.

"What is there here? Show me Father what there is for me to learn from. Show me the way forward. Please show me."

I see before me a tunnel, still and inert. It is big enough for it to take me. I go to it and although I can't see what I am stepping into I step in. Inside it is just the right size for me. It is eerie and echoes. I can't see a thing. I go forward into the tunnel, feeling with my feet, for I don't know how it goes, up, down, straight? Suddenly there is a whoosh from behind, a push. Suddenly I am shot forward by something from behind, like a great wind. Shot into the tunnel. I am now an observer of me as I hurtle down. I watch myself being hurtled down and yet not down, just along, lost, lost in time.

I am still standing here watching and yet I know I am gone. I can't understand that. "Show me what this is about."

"A portion of you has gone back to the past. A portion of you has gone back to relive, to re-experience." I know he is talking of my time in Atlantis.

"Why only a portion of me? I need to have this knowledge here in this consciousness?"

"The portion that has to re-enact will return to you and rejoin with you so that you will know. It may take a little while. Be grateful that you, here and now, are not that portion, for you would be changed by the experience."

"Surely to be changed by the experience is the objective?"

"We wish to add to what you are, not convert you, one life to another. This is the only way that we can add to your current lifetime by sending a part of you.

"How will I know when this has been achieved? How will I know?"

"Re-stabilise yourself, my dear. Settle your mind. Be at peace once more. Get your things in order and when you have done this, then may you be rejoined. If you are in a state of unease of distress you would not be able to withstand the knowledge. So we say, put your things in order. Re-stabilise yourself. Settle down and be happy. Know that all is in order. You do not need to fret about it."

"I thank you for that." I wonder how long it will take me to re-stabilise. The part of me that was the observer is now walking away from the tunnel. I am still in the place with the black marble floor, or black granite. I don't know the difference but it is beautiful. It acts like a mirror. Wonderful!

I walk around, not seeing. There is a table, a bench at one end, slightly off to the right. Ahead and to the right. I often see things in that direction. I go towards the bench with my arms outstretched with a feeling of 'at last I've found you'. On the bench lies a body. Head to the right and feet to the left. A body. I can't see who. I can't see an individual face I know. It is simply a body.

Somebody from behind takes my two arms, takes my wrists and pushes them forward so that they rest on the body. I am slightly bent over with my hands on the body. What am I to do? The body is inert. It might be dead for all I know. The hands came from behind, though how it manages to reach I don't know. The hands are holding mine in place and all kinds of energies are streaming through, really streaming through hard, not soft, but hard, purposeful. They shoot through the palms of my hands.

My hands are alive. My hands are alive. They sink into the body. The whole hands, both of them are sinking into the body until they are sunk inside up to the wrists. I can't feel anything except the energy. I wriggle my fingers. It is like putting one's hands inside jelly, moving easily and freely. It is not a problem to move. I don't know what I should be doing. I don't need to know what I am doing for the fingers are being guided by the hands that hold my wrists. The energies come through and move my fingers independently. I enjoy the experience of it. There is sharpness and tingling in my palms, like little knives, not unpleasant, just sensation.

I know now that the body is not a body of a human, a living human. It is just a dummy of some kind. It is there to demonstrate for me what is possible. It is an object at this point. I know this is training, reassurance. I am reminded of the mouth to mouth teaching where they use a dummy for this. This body is just a dummy for me. I breathe a sigh of relieve for I don't know what I am doing here.

The hands that are holding my wrists pull me out of the body. They appear to be the same, though I can't feel them at all. I can feel energy from the hands that hold me. I stand more upright. The hands that held me, release me. I don't know what to do. I have a pain in my chest and my head aches. There is tightness in my chest now. I don't feel good. I must release from this. I feel faint. It is over.

In Minneapolis. I am told to say these things. "The damages of the Earth will be removed and the Earth will run sweet again." I stand very stiffly at the top of the stairs. I move forward very jerkily, stiffly. Like a dummy, a mannequin. I jerk my way down like a doll. I don't understand why. I've been wound up so I can keep going. I go with difficulty. I reach the bottom. I turn my head this way and that as if I am not me. I am not in control. I am simply a physical manifestation, directed by remote control, a toy that is being manipulated. I turn down the passage for the controller knows. I go along and find a door. I don't hesitate. A hand comes out and turns the knob. I enter. As soon as I enter the artificial restriction on me drops from me in a heap. I am left standing free, the real me.

My eyes are searching everywhere, seeking something I can fix on. The walls are high and domed. I am in a kind of a dome shaped room, big. There is something over the far end. It is shadowy so I don't know. I must go to it as it is the only thing I can see. It is a long couch, soft and comfortable covered with a beautiful purple cloth. It is the only thing there so I sit on it. It is so long there is plenty of room for others. I am bidden to put my feet up and rest my head on one end. It is a chaise longue.

I lie there and drift. A voice is speaking to me, taking me back, back in time. The voice is taking me. I can hardly hear it for I am drifting back...back...in time. Back to Atlantis. I am drifting, drifting back. I wish to be as I was, with that knowledge now, for me to remember for all time, the assets and the learning. Take me to it. *Time passes and I have no memory of what happened because there is no recording.*

I can't stay for my physical body is bringing me back. I can't carry on.

PSYCHIC HEALING – ALL WORK TOGETHER

I have been given leafy green. I am an observer of me. I am dressed in fresh green. My hands are long and delicate. The pathway, the descent before me, has a rail on either side. It is a walkway through the forest. It has been put there specially to take me safely through dense forest. It is made of natural elements. It is all nature. I am reminded of the rain forest in Australia. It is like a swing bridge but it is not over a chasm but over rain forest. I hold onto both rails, ropes, and walk across. I enjoy it, although it swings.

It is crossing over one area of existence to another. I reach the other side and there is a figure waiting for me. It is impersonal. A guide, just that. He is to lead me down a path. I keep following behind, single file. At least I know I am being taken somewhere. I am being taken. Suddenly we come out from the trees. There is an enormous expanse of sky and beach. It is gentle. The seagulls are crying. The waves are breaking gently on the beach. It is warm, not too hot. We begin to go down on to the beach. The sand is a little slippery, soft and dry. It is not so easy to walk on. I follow, trying hard to keep up. I wonder where we are going.

We come to some steps which go away from the beach. Wooden steps, five or six of them. We go down these at the back of the beach into a little dip. There is a house, a wooden house on stilts. I think of the huts in Malaya where the houses are raised on posts to keep them off the ground, for ants I suppose and other creatures. We mount a ladder and I am shown into a doorway. Inside it is dark, not too dark.

There are a lot of people sitting cross legged on the floor. They are waiting for me. I have been brought to them. They are not primitive people. They are bright, intelligent and full of wisdom. I know that their knowledge is far superior to anything I might have, in spite of technology. I ask them why I am here. They make me sit down. They ask me to sit down, for they are also courteous. I notice for the first time there are people lying all around the edges of the room, if you can call it a room. They are sick. The men sitting on the ground point to them and they point to me.

They say "Do something."

"I don't know what to do."

"Do something and we will provide the energy. We will provide but you do."

I know this is referring to psychic healing, psychic surgery, maybe.

I ask, "Will you, can you and can I?"

"If we all work together, we all can. Know that we can and we wish to. Providing you are willing, we will all work together."

I thank them, for that was what I wished to hear. I get up and go and look at the people lying around the walls. Some of them are terribly injured. Some of them are wasting away. I shake my head and think, *it will take a miracle to save these people.* I ask for help from the Divine to be able to do something. I don't mind where I am sent.

I come back into the circle and sit in the middle. Each of the men here, shuffle forward so that they are close enough to touch. Each of them puts a hand on my head and on my shoulders. I sit quietly, I sit quietly feeling a change. A change.

SEPTEMBER 3rd 1998

PROTECTION FROM WIND FORCE

I am standing on the top platform of a fire engine ladder. It is moving about and I am in the little cage, so I don't fall off. There must be a way down for it is a ladder. But there is not. The fireman's lift thing moves itself around to a tall building. I get off onto a balcony. This is most odd. What do I do now? I must go along the balcony till I find a door, a green door. It opens easily for it is not locked. I go in to the building. No sound, nothing. No sound. In a room I find a baby, all wrapped up and asleep. It is the baby I have come for. Why did I have to do it this way? There is nobody else here, just the baby. I pick it up and carry it out to the balcony. I go back to the lift and get into the fireman's cage. I am taken down to the ground and the baby is handed over to some people. I don't know what this means or why I have been given this. It makes no sense to me at all. Maybe it has been left high and dry and brought back to earth? I don't know. I shall have to think about this.

It is quite clear that I haven't finished. It seems I am a busy little bee for I walk about. There are lots of people here. I find a shaft going down into the ground. I have to go down in there. It is not too deep. I get to the bottom by a ladder which goes down. At the bottom there are lots and lots of people milling around. Lots of people being herded down here.

I get sudden realisation. There is a wind coming, a strong force and they have all gone underground to escape being damaged. The baby was left behind and there wasn't time to go upstairs to get it. The baby had to be brought down so it too could go safely underground. Everything has gone below ground to avoid the wind that is coming. There is no time for long preparation, though people are still working on the surface, getting people below ground as far as they can. The only safe places there lie below the streets. There is not much space. The underground stations are all full. There are so many people and they can't all get underground. There isn't space enough to get everyone below ground so they must take their chances. There is no time. I am just making sure that people are safe, that they don't start fighting. I am telling them it's alright, it's alright.

I ask. "What is this to do with my request to go back to Atlantis? What has this to do with it? It is not what I was asking for in this meditation. It is not taking me back."

I am told: "It is doing precisely that. It is taking you back to similar occurrences. It is doing precisely what you asked for. It is typical of scenes enacted in those times."

"Why underground? I understood that the ground split. It is the last place that you would want to go."

"All they knew is that there was a nuclear fallout. All they knew is that they should shelter from the blast and from the winds, from the searing winds that they had heard of in other parts. They didn't have much choice, either stay above ground and be seared or blown, or take the chance that their area would not be affected. They had only heard rumours. What else could they do?"

"Why give me a modern setting to tell me this? Why not give the view of that time? I want to know. Why?"

"We use whatever means we can. We also do not wish you to jump immediately to conclusions so that you feel you are inventing the story."

MIND ONLY – TO SELECTIVE BREEDING IN ATLANTIS

I am going down steps very quickly, in a hurry. I am going down, down into my deep unconscious. As I go I can feel energies building up in me, as if I am losing myself and gaining another. These steps go down into the bottom of a hole, into another world. I am in a void. I am not on anything or surrounded by anything. I am simply there. A mind only. I am a mind only, a consciousness. My thoughts take me where I wish.

I wish to have knowledge awakened in my consciousness of the Atlantian time. That is my objective now. I see Andreas, I feel it is him. My mind has been with him. Although I am simply mind he can still reach me and I can still see. He takes me with him for I am protected by him. My mind travels back.

I am seated at a big, heavy glass table. It looks like glass for I can see right through it. Spread out before me are documents and photos or drawings. Faces, people. I am sifting and spreading them all out. I am looking at them all. I am choosing, making a selection. I don't know what for. Some are being rejected and some of them are being selected. They appear to be men.

I am a heavy woman. Large, physically strong and heavy. I am bigger than most in height. I stand and tower over all. I am very tall, enormously tall. I move away from the glass table and walk around to the end. I come round to the other side. There is a flight of steps. Just a little flight, four or five steps perhaps. I go down. These are my private quarters. There I have sexual relations with somebody, who it is doesn't matter.

I ask Andreas to take me away from this. I want to go where I can do some good. He takes my hand and we go into another place. There are quite a few children here. They are my children, my children that I have born. There are many children, many. I produce them easily but I am as a mother to them. I love them no matter how many there are for I do not have to look after them. There are people who do that, to attend to their needs. I have children almost like a machine. I have many children.

The photographs on the table were about selecting fathers for future children. Selecting them for their genes, for their abilities. This is selective breeding. I tell Andreas this is not what I need now. I need to know how to materialise and de materialise. I need these secrets and that knowledge.

SEPTEMBER 10ᵗʰ 1998

ON THE BOOK

There is rush matting on the floor, on the stairs. I am reminded of Singapore, of the jungle. It is hot and steamy outside. The rush matting goes all the way down. I don't have to go very far. Just a few steps and yet it feels a long way down. There are a lot of people at the bottom of the steps. They are milling around and making it difficult to go forward. I tell them I have to go forward and can't be waylaid. I push my way through them trying to ignore their hands. They appeal to me to stop and talk.

I move on into the jungle. I leave the path and go into the undergrowth. It is not easy. Why I am doing this I have no idea. As I go I get a weight and an ache, a pain across my shoulders for no apparent reason. I am not carrying anything. It is as if something is pressing into my shoulders, hard pressure. It is quite painful. I keep going through the undergrowth, getting a bit scratched here and there, getting hot and sweating. It is steamy. I push my way through a very thick part here. I come out to a clearing, as I knew I would.

There is a stream. The undergrowth has been hacked away. It is not a natural clearing, it has been cleared specially. There is somebody by the stream, bending over looking into the waters. Not that you could see anything in the waters for they are moving, not still. They are still clear. It is the movement that keeps them free.

I go to the man. He is dark skinned. I feel as if I am looking at the face of the aboriginal painting I have. If it is not him it is very much like him. This is an aboriginal which is a surprise to me. We are talking of jungle, tropics and yet I have an aboriginal face here. He is an old man, thin, bony and doesn't say much. He stands up and beckons me to go with him, which I do. He is going to show me something. He puts his fingers to his lips, telling me to keep quiet. We go along the path which leads to another clearing. There are children playing, play acting a role, which children do all over the world. Doctors and nurses, mammas and daddies.

They are engrossed in their play. He tells me to be quiet. He puts his fingers to his lips again. I can't ask him any questions, but I want to. I mustn't because he wants me to be quiet. They are enjoying themselves and don't know we are there. If they knew we were there they would feel inhibited. We must keep out of their game so that we don't spoil it for them. The children amazingly turn into the pages of my book. All separate pages of my book. They are all playing, dancing about and enjoying themselves, it seems. I am told to keep quiet again and leave them to their play.

I ask, "How can the book ever get published if I leave it?" The aboriginal mentally tells me that when they are tired of their play they will settle down. They will settle into their correct order. Then I can go and pick it up and it will be OK. I wonder how long it will take them to be tired of play. The aboriginal shakes his head *as if to say, all these questions. Why don't you just let them be?*

I ask now, in my mind, is this the first book or the second book? I am not getting an answer.

NATURE ALWAYS WINS – THE POWER OF LIGHT

The ground is rocky, volcanic, hard on the feet. I pick my way over, trying to get a firm foothold. I didn't expect this. I asked to go to Atlantis. I didn't expect this. I am having to go down, bend over and hold on with my hands to stay secure on my feet. It is very hard going. There has to have been a volcanic eruption here. It is cool so it is not too recent. It hasn't had time to weather down. It is still extremely rough. I make my way across, asking to go to smoother ground. I quickly come to the edge of the flow, for that is what it was.

I am on grass now, on the slopes of a hill or mountain. I am on slopes for my feet are at an angle. Keep walking. This is not what I wanted to see or where I wanted to be. I am told I **must** see this. I **must** know this. So? – I could find this scene anywhere in this time.

"What does it tell me? What are you telling me?"

"Man has long had the power to create his world according to his actions. Man has long had the power to activate nature, to interact with nature, to affect nature. Man has long since, long past learnt how to manipulate nature but we tell you that nature will win in the final outcome. You, Man, may think that you have all things at your fingertips. You may think that you have the ability to order things according to your wishes, but it is nature that has the last word. It is nature that is the master, even over man and his ways. Nature will not be subdued, will not be dominated. Nature's will is stronger than anything you can perceive."

"I want to know why this [meditation] is not answering my question and taking me where I wanted to be? I want to have the knowledge that I had in times of Atlantis so that I may use this knowledge. I want to know how."

In answer to that, my mind is taken to my hands again. I look at my hands. There are lights coming from them, spears of light coming from every fingertip. The whole of my hand is glowing so that the glow is obscuring the hand itself. I put my hand out to touch the land. My hand disappears into the ground.

"The Power of the Light is strong. The Power of Light is the force. Remember that. The Power of the Light is the energy. The Power of the Light."

"Does the Light know what it is to do?" I ask.

"The Power of the Light has intelligence within it. It contains knowing. It does not operate in words. It operates in simply knowing the order of things. It knows the correct order of things. It knows the perfection of all cells and wherever it touches, perfection reigns. Where it reaches, perfection reasserts itself. It can do nothing else for it is touched by the Power of the Light. All you need to do is carry that light within you and direct it where it is needed. It is that simple."

I think about that one.

"To carry the Power of the Light you must be of the Light. To enable that Light to flow through, you must be of the Light. By that we mean you must behave as of the Light. Be the perfect being that you see so often. Do not view but be. Do not be just the observer, but become. Of course this requires dedication and action according to Light's principles. You must earn the Power of the Light by being worthy of it. You will know, you **do** know how to be worthy of being a vehicle for the Power of the Light. All men, if they so desired and so acted, could be vehicles for this Power of the Light. Some have it already. You will know these when you meet them for there will be a glow that shines through the physical form and out so that eyes can see. If you carry the Power of the Light within, you will be perfection in mind, heart and in all ways."

"That is a very high thing to aspire to, not easy for us to have all of that. Is it possible to have some of that light while we strive for the wholeness of it?"

The Light that is glowing from around my feet, speaks. "Think of it as a darkened room and when one lights a candle, the light is there but may not fill the entire room. It allows one to see where one is going. If you place more candles within that room the light becomes brighter and the going is easier. You may see more detail. When full light has been turned on you may see clearly. When full brightness is placed within that room then walls may disappear. You would not see them, for the brightness would obscure the physical, you would not see the physical. You would see only light and the light would penetrate the structure that forms the room. That is an answer to your question. Whatever light you can arrive at, that you can achieve is of value. Whatever light you have within you is helpful.

"Do not sit in darkness. Do not live your life in darkness for you

264

would see nothing, you would know nothing, and you would interact with nothing. You may achieve the fullness of obliterating light, obliteration of the physical. Light is what should be aimed for. This is what should be aimed for at all times, not merely that of Atlantis, but for all of your existence in time."

"It is a lovely answer. How do I achieve that now? How do I achieve that vision?"

"We have already answered that question."

OCTOBER 10th 1998

HEAL CHILDREN OF THE PAST

This is very odd for I am wrapped in a palm leaf, an enormous leaf, huge. I am cocooned in it. I have hopped my way down the stairs for I can't do anything else. I look a bit like a penguin. I can't put out my hands to touch anything because I can feel my fingers fast against my legs. I hop down and before I get to the bottom I turn into a bird, a kingfisher. I fly off. I feel nature is having a say here. The kingfisher flies up and settles on a branch of a tree. It dives down into the water below it, underneath the water. It brings up a fish it has seen from a distance. I haven't got a clue what this is telling me. We have had nature and the water. I don't know. Am I wrapped up in things?

I don't know what this is telling me. I feel it must be a very symbolic message, one I must give attention to later. I am now transferred to a normal me, walking along, looking, looking to see where I can enter. I find an opening, which is a concealed opening. It has big leaves hanging down, jungle type leaves covering it. I can push these aside and enter. It is concealed but I knew it was here. I step in through them.

There are lots of native men, brown men sitting on the ground. Old men, young men. I can't see any women at all. As I go in they scramble to their feet. Why do they do that? They are all standing now. They come forward and pull me by whatever they can hold, my hands, my clothes. Some of them are behind me pushing me. They clearly want me to go with them.

They take me far back away from the entrance. It is not exactly a cave, an opening made, an enclosure. We move back, back away from the entrance to the far corners. Lying on the ground are children, sick children. They are too weak to get up. Some of them are dying. They are the children of these men. There is much wailing from the mothers. The children are there, helpless and hopeless too. The men and the women have tried and failed to help. They look to me and point, making sure that they can see. They wave their hands over the children. They don't speak but are trying to tell me this is what I must do. I must heal the children. I must heal the children. The children are of the past, as are these people. They are of the ancient times. I must heal the children.

If I heal these children now, then the future that we are in will be improved. Very strange and I don't understand it. I must heal the past, their past, not my past. I don't understand but I must do it. I walk around and through them, passing my hands over each child, even the ones that are dying. I do simply that, no more. I pray for them to be better. I pass my hands over the mothers too. All of them. That is all I do. I pass my hands over them and I pray and ask for help and assistance.

As I pass my hands I am weaving a blanket of covering, to cover them. I am making it with the passing of my hands. I can see streams of vapour coming from my hands as I pass along. Vapour, something coming from my hands. I don't know what it is exactly but you can see it. As it leaves my hands it drifts down and settles over everything, forming a film, a blanket, a filmy blanket over everybody. They are covered with this now, all of them. As I look the covering seems to dissolve into the forms, soaks in. Like water droplets on the Earth it is absorbed by it until you cannot see it.

They begin to stir and show more signs of life. They begin to get up, to stretch and smile and to cry too, for they now feel whole and well. The mothers gather the children to them. There is a reunion. The fathers stand proudly around. There is rejoicing. The babies are picked up and hugged, fed, for they are rejuvenated, renewed, re-energised. There is rejoicing. I walk away from them and turn back towards the entrance. That is why I came. I still don't understand it, but that is why I came.

OCTOBER 26th 1998

SOUL RESCUE

I am at the top of stone steps. They are quite deep, not very wide with sharp edges like concrete. It is outside. I can't see the bottom. I go down. There is a rail at the bottom. It is not meant for comfort, this. Each step is deep. It is quite difficult but not impossible. I can't see the bottom. There is no particular colour. It is just grey. There is greyness about everything here. As I do down it gets darker. Although I started outside I am in some sort of hole. There is darkness about everything. I get to the bottom. There are concrete floors again. It is smooth as if it has been laid especially and fairly recently too, I'd say. It hasn't had time to get dirty or marked by a lot of feet or the weather. It is quite clean. The walls are very bare, again concrete. Very austere. No warm human touch.

I turn off to the left. The same thing! A corridor, freshly done, very barren and stark. I come to the only door. I am reminded of a barricade, very forbidding. It is not meant for just anybody to enter here, only those who know must enter here. It is like a safe door with bars across, reinforced. There is a padlock on it. The key is still in the padlock, which strikes me as a little odd. I unlock it and take the key out. I go in.

I vaguely see people or shapes. There is something here. It is very dark. It is as if whatever or whoever is here is holding its breath. They are all a little scared. They are scared of me. They don't know who I am, or who has come through this door. I can almost feel them cowering back against the walls. I just feel them there. I can't exactly see them. They are just shapes, shapes. I can't tell if they are adults or children, people huddling against the walls. They can't get away any further from me than that. They are very frightened of me.

I walk very slowly. It is so dark in here. As I have done once before, I know I must get their trust. I sit down in the middle, on the floor cross-legged. I lean forward slightly so that I don't tip back. I sit and I wait. I simply sit and ask for help. Meditate and ask for help. Meditate and ask, and draw in the forces of light. The light is needed here. The light is needed here. I am drawing in the light and asking the Divine Beings to shed their light in this dreadful place. I ask that the fear be taken from those around me.

I sit and a wide beam, gradually intensifying in light and strength shines down on me. It is wider than me and casts a pool of light around me. So I am seen and they can see me clearly, though I can't see them. I sit quietly with my eyes closed, waiting, waiting and asking for help from the angels. I feel little touches on my cheek and my hair, like little butterflies. I know that the Beings of Light are here, for it is a gentle and comforting, reassuring touch. I continue to sit and wait, and wait.

I hear movements from those who have hidden themselves against the wall. They shuffle forward slightly. I can feel them coming on hands and knees, not standing but shuffling forward. I am surprised how many old people are here. Old and haggard. There are the young macho boys, rough characters. They are here too. We have the pious ones with their noses in the air, supercilious ones, and frightened ones, unsure now, where they were sure before. Because a few have moved forward the others do. They creep closer and closer, still not standing, still afraid.

I continue to sit and wait. I wait for them all to come and settle. They too wait. Movement continues as they move in closer. They are on the edge of the beam of light. They haven't entered it yet. Their faces are lit up with the glow as if sitting round a fire. They daren't enter the light; they are touched by it but are afraid to come too close. They draw a little closer and can come no more without entering the pool of light, and without getting close to me. They don't want to get too close for they don't know who I am. They wait and I can see their faces. All kinds.

I turn my head to look. This frightens them, the movement frightens them. They are frightened, terrified of what will come next. I just look and smile at them, hoping the smile will reassure them. I wait and smile and ask again for help from the angels. Suddenly the beam of light that surrounds me widens. It expands into a larger beam and all those sitting around are caught in it now. They are blinded. This frightens them even more. They cover their faces.

They gradually realise that the light hasn't hurt them. It hasn't hurt them at all. Their eyes, little by little, become adjusted. They look at each other for the first time. They regard each other, some with interest, some with loathing, and some with tears running down their faces. But they are taking notice. They are taking an interest in something other than themselves at last. It has been a long time since they took an interest in anything other than themselves.

I stand. This takes them by surprise. It doesn't seem too bad for now they are interested. They stand for the first time for a long time. They stand up. The light expands even more. It is light from the angels. It fills the room and shows the bare walls. One by one the people there begin to fade. They dissolve, they disappear, fading and not to be seen. The room is now empty and I am standing alone. The job has been done and I now can return. I thank all those Divine Beings and cry.

269

NOVEMBER 5th 1998

GUARDIAN ANGELS

I have been given silver. I am going down steps which are ribbed, like reeds placed along the ground. There is nothing to hold on to. It is a little unsteady. The reeds, the ribs of which are dark green and very flimsy, are almost not solid at all. It is precarious going down here but these are the steps I have. These are the steps I go down in trust. I go down in trust, as I must. Nothing to hold on to. My hands are outstretched for balance more than for anything else. Eventually I am at the bottom. Now what?

There is a very steamy feel, tropical, very hot and humid. I can hear the insects in the jungle, the high pitched screeching. I feel quite giddy. I feel very giddy as if I am going to go right off. My head is spinning, spinning… *faintly now.* I feel weird.

I stand still for quite a long time. I can feel insects biting. My nose is running. I can't stand here forever. I begin to move off in any direction. It is just jungle. I move forward and find my way through. I don't know where I am going. I push my way through. It is tough, tough going. I come to what appears to be an easier way. It is not even a pathway. I push through the thickness which is everywhere and break through into a space. It is a natural clearing, not man made in any way. An open space at last. There is even grass.

I stand sweating and ask to be shown what I need. I ask for proof of what I am. Immediately two enormous figures appear before me, huge giant figures stand before me. They are fighting angels all kitted up with their swords. They are fierce. Lovely faces, but there to do battle for me. They are there to protect and fight for me. Why, I don't know. Their role is to look after me. I don't understand. They have come to look after me and to protect me. I don't understand why and I still don't know who I am.

"You are our little brother."

"Brother? I am a woman."

"You are a woman in the flesh. But you are our little brother."

"Oh. And what is my name?"

"Matthias. You are Matthias."

"Can you prove this to me? Give me proof."

NOVEMBER 9th 1998

ANOTHER ASPECT OF SELF – *conquer the world with love.*

I have wooden stairs and am dressed in ordinary clothes. Wooden rail to hold on to, not even polished. There are bare boards on these stairs, like an empty house. I must go down. The walls are bare plaster, not even painted. I don't know if this is a new house that hasn't been done up yet or an old one that hasn't been lived in. I don't know. There are no furnishings at all. I walk forward and turn off.

It is surprisingly a long corridor, lots and lots of doors stretching as far as the eye can see. How am I to know which is mine, for heaven's sake? I walk along and feel, for I put my hand out on either side. I feel them as I arrive at them. I come to one which has a different feel to the fingertips. It is silky, warm and silky. It is quite different to any others. This intrigues me. I look for the handle. It is a beautifully small, ornate knob. Not a big thing, more for a cupboard door. I turn it and go in.

Over on the far side, hanging on the wall are gold chains, pendants, chains of all sizes and weights. They are beautiful, lots of them, as if this is a place where they are hung when they are not being used. I ask what I am to do. I see one which strikes me more than the others. It is a beautiful, heavy red stone. It stands out from the others. It is magnificent, a very deep, bright red. It draws me. I take it off the hook and put it round my neck. It feels good. What does this mean?

I take a step back from the other chains and separate myself from them. I feel I am going to keep this pendant. It is alright to take it. I turn around, away from the others. I see a man beckoning. Beckoning! I can't see him clearly. As there is nothing else to see I walk towards him. As I approach he holds out both his hands and grasps me by the elbows in a greeting. I know this is alright. I thought for a moment he was going to kiss me on both cheeks. He looked as if he wanted to, as if he might. I wouldn't mind. He doesn't do that. Why doesn't he do it? He is warm and friendly.

We stand with arms held for a little while then he releases me and turns away. I must follow him. There is a chair. Oh dear! This is a chair up on a little platform. I feel an investiture here. This is an investiture, whatever that means. Oh, to be invested with something. I am to sit on the chair.

271

I sit on it feeling rather embarrassed, rather silly in my ordinary clothes, out of place. My feet don't even reach the ground. They are swinging a bit off the ground. I must look rather silly here. He doesn't think so. He hands me a rolled up parchment. He hands me a glowing globe. It is the world. It is lit up from inside. He puts that into my lap, not into my hands but on my lap. It is quite safe. It doesn't roll anywhere. Then he puts a blue cape over my shoulders. The blue shimmers, shimmers beautifully, as if it is alive. I feel better having it on while sitting in the big chair. It is more appropriate. He makes the sign of the cross on my forehead. As he moves his finger I can feel the energy from it. The energy impresses itself in my brow in the sign of the cross, an equal cross, equal arms. I feel giddy, I feel a little sick. I don't know if I can stay with this. I am going away… away.

(*In a new powerful voice*) I am transformed. I pick up the globe and hold it aloft for everyone to see. My clothes begin to glitter. Suddenly not ordinary, mundane. I am another being. I am transformed. I have a new energy. I must use this energy to greater purpose.

"You have become another. You have now a greater knowledge. You have ability to change things, many things, many forms, many ideas. Work for the Light and do not forget who you are. You are many things, many aspects of self. You choose which aspect you wish to present, to use. You have a choice of many aspects of self. Use them wisely."

I climb down off the chair with legs a little shaky, a little wobbly. I still feel me, ordinary, everyday me. The man, the Being takes my shoulders and kisses me now on both cheeks. He couldn't do it before. In some strange way I feel as if I am a man. I don't look like a man but I can feel, I can see a man being kissed here. The man is me. I am a strong heavy man, very powerful and yet this has to be me. For he or I have just come off that seat, that chair. He is like a knight in armour, invincible, invincible. Now what? Now what do I do?

"Go out and conquer the world."

"That's a bit strong."

"Conquer the world with love."

I feel a little sick and had better come back.

NOVEMBER 12th 1998

BE WITH NATURE

I am bathed in a sea of sunny bright yellow. I am almost lost in it for I am of the same yellow. It is beautiful and fresh, sunny, clear. I have a great lightness of spirit. I trip lightly down the stairs, skipping, feeling joyous. It is not important what the stairs are made of this time. Everything is bathed in golden light. I arrive very lightly, like alighting at the bottom. Even here everything is bathed in a golden light. It is a glorious feeling. I move along and into the passage. It is like moving into gold. There is nothing of a texture anywhere. I could be anywhere. I keep moving forward, seemingly because I must move. I enter my space.

Here the colour is more of autumn; a deeper, rusty colour. Golden but with a deeper shade. I quieten down a little, I feel a little more reserved. There is some feeling of awe. I look around. I am in a wood. There is a little fawn, creatures are around me. Nature, natural things. There is a quieter, quieter feeling.

A man steps out from the trees. I almost laugh for he is covered with leaves, autumn leaves. It is as if he is dressed up for camouflage. But he is always dressed up this way. He is a man of nature. The leaves are him though he is a big strong man. I am reminded of the Green Giant but this is not the Green Giant. The man is big and is a part of nature, mainly a symbolic figure. But he is very much alive. If I touched him I would touch the leaves. I know he is solid underneath. We stand and look at each other. He is amused. You can see the amusement at my impression of him. He won't laugh but he is amused, there is no doubt of that.

He turns and I follow. We scrunch our way through the leaves. We come to a little brook, just about enough water to go over the stones. He tells me to drink, to drink from it. I get down to the ground and cup my hands to the water and just about manage to fill them. I drink. As I do I change. I change somehow. I want to go away from me, out of me, leaving the physical me asleep somewhere. I am free. I am free now.

I seem to drift and lift out of me. It is rather nice. I am free. I can go where I want… Something is happening. My physical body is feeling things. I have a headache and I feel sick and yet I am free too. I don't understand this. If I am free why am I feeling physical discomfort? I don't understand that. I don't understand what all this is telling me. It is very nice but what am I learning from it?

This man puts his hand out, touches me. I know in that instant that I must have more connection with nature. I have kept away from it. I need to be with nature more if I am to experience all things. I know what he is telling me now.

CHAPTER ELEVEN

NOVEMBER 5th.1999

IN A VILLAGE IN GOIAS, BRAZIL *an agreement*

High guides are with me. I ask to be with the spirit doctors, to see what they do. I ask to leave my body to be with them and remember. They take my right hand and walk me round the crowd meditating in the room. They wave my hand at several of them.

I get closer and closer to Joao's spirit, closer and closer to him and join into his body, entering his body along with the doctors. The line passes by. I watch several souls, all kinds. I feel great compassion, almost crying. I do not heal anyone but watch. One is deaf − a lady. I am told to blow through one ear to the other. A cloud, a mist comes out. To recognise her afterwards, for proof I am told she has a fringe straight across − shoulder length hair − dark brown. I straighten the fingers of one arthritic lady − old.

I even agree to use the knife if required. Several entities pass through me. Try to remember, try to hold onto it. Say I *will* do this work, am happy to do so. I see acres of people suffering. Need to help. I can't hold it any longer.

I must remember this is just one part of my mission. There is more, equally important, if not more. I am reminded on this journey, that the people on this planet are our responsibility, as we have created them and now must look after them. *All* peoples. We cannot create children and then abandon them while they are still young. We entered into this agreement in the beginning.

2000

FEBRUARY 20th 2000

I am standing in red, strong brilliant red. It is not a weak affair. It is the colour of blood. There is a ladder in front of me. I can't see where the ladder is leading but I must get on it and start to climb. I feel the rungs beneath my feet and under my hands as I grasp the next rung. It is an ordinary ladder but I can't see anything except the ladder so it is a bit scary. I can't even see the wall that it is propped against. I get what must be near the top and find I am getting out onto a ledge or platform of some kind. I am up high but where I don't know. It feels spacey as if only the platform is there. I can't see anything around it. Total trust is needed for this. I am higher, symbolic I know, but much higher.

I hear the sound of music, like trumpets blowing but not Celestial trumpets – music, a tune, songs and things, playing something specific. As it is the only thing, I go towards the sound, making sure I don't step off into nothing, making sure the ground is in front of me, something to stand on. Now there are voices calling me, calling my name. I head in that direction. I am blind to my surroundings. Head on, head on, keep following. The voices now. Activity beyond my sight. They want me to join in the activity. What is this telling me?

I come to an area that is brightly lit. I walk into it and see lots of things and people – active – lots of bustling and yet it is calm and peaceful at the same time. Everybody knows what they are doing. They are all busy but knowing what they are busy at. There is no confusion here. A man whose head was bent over something looks up and beckons a finger at me to come near. He is an old man but heavy set and broad, solid and dependable. I walk towards him knowing he is fine. He reminds me of Neptune. He looks at me with beautiful blue eyes, steady. So calm he is, so calm. You look at him and know that he knows everything. He knows what I am thinking. He knows me inside and out and it is not unsettling at all. There is love in his face and it makes me want to cry. Such love makes me want to cry. Love like this does not exist on the Earth plane. Love such as this is rare in a physical world.

"You will soon be in this world of love, though you will not die. You will experience the world of love while still in physical form. Wouldn't that be wonderful if all were to demonstrate this? How absolutely wonderful that would be."

"What can I do to help bring this about? I don't seem to be doing very much on a big scale but just organising my own activities."

"You are going to be given the larger work. Rest awhile for you will soon be plunged into the wider field. Rest awhile. You will soon be taken up into a larger plan. All that has gone before has been preparation for this. Don't be anxious. Open yourself daily to us. Open yourself to us daily. Do not miss for we have some information to give you on a regular basis now."

I must, I must, I must. I want to. I will communicate daily and carry on with trust. This lovely man takes my hands and raises them to his lips and kisses them. It is a gesture of affection for a child. I feel like a child before him. It is a wonderful feeling to be the child instead of the adult. It is nice to have someone who cares.

MAY 16th 2000

BOTH SIDES OF VEIL

I am in a warm climate, feet in sandals and a very skimpy, short brown dress, more like rags. I walk forward for I do not have to go up or down. It is a dusty and dirty road under hot sun. I keep walking forward. I feel I am in Africa. A tall, long, lanky man comes to meet me. He is a tall African leader, a spokesman or whatever. He has come out to meet me. He shakes my hand. He has been expecting me: Mgulu. I don't know if this is his name or a greeting. That is what he is saying. We walk together with people all around us. It is a place I have to go to but it doesn't tell me where. The thought, *Mbuto*, comes in but I don't know if this is right or not.

I go down a very narrow path. Sometimes I have to squeeze through. I am very slim. Anything larger could not follow. I find another opening on the right which I expect to find for I know it is there…it has always been there. I have been here before. I go through, squeezing between the rocks into what seems to be a big crack. Once I get through it is a big place. Nothing large can get through here and although I know this place like home I don't know why I am here now.

I look around looking for something, some clue. Two big men come from the back and greet me. They know me. They are huge, rough men. I feel I have gone back in time, back to time. They call me Hedwyn.

"You survived then in basic conditions and you will survive again. So will many others."

"I don't understand. What about the new dimension? I don't understand. I need clarification."

"You will exist simultaneously in the next dimension and in this dimension. You will travel to and fro, helping those that remain here. You will be aware of both sides of the veil. You will be invulnerable. Nothing can touch you for you exist in the next dimension also."

"Is this true for me now in this present moment?"

"It has been true for a long time. You are of another realm. You know this already. Your problem is that you have not made contact more closely with the other dimension. You are able to do this and travel freely from one to the other. Why do you not take the opportunities that are offered to you? What holds you here?"

"Maybe I can't return to here where I am needed."

"This has been set many, many years ago. You are here specifically to assist. You cannot be barred entry. You can travel to and fro. Do you not know this? If you do this you will bring gifts from the other dimension that you may use in your present one here. When you get the next opportunity to enter then do so. Do not fear that you will not return. Travel freely from one to the other."

This message may have come because I had an entry point shown to me and was invited into while in Australia, walking in national forest land. I was not expecting it and not in an altered state and ran from seeing the portal in the land. I have regretted it ever since.

MAY 23rd 2000

I walk along, underground between dark rock walls. There are rainbow glints here and there. I begin walking on an upward path and come out high up on a craggy mountain, well above the tree line.

A voice says: "Why are you looking for a way down? Why don't you stay awhile and enjoy the wonders here?"

I do and look at astounding scenes of beauty. Then a huge bird flies down to me. It is larger than I. It is a bird man with an eagle's head but a man too. My thoughts immediately fly to InterPlanetary Being Horus and Osishoo. He speaks a language where I can't understand the sounds. He wraps his arms/wings around me and flies up with me. He sets me down high up in a hollowed out space – like an egg. We stay in this, comfortably enclosed. He wraps me right inside his wings, like a mother bird does to her chick.

He says, and I understand: "My little one. You are always protected by me and many others and will come to no harm. Horus and Thunderbird and I are of the same place. We are the same."

I know this is Osishoo and that I am his child. I feel enormous love.

Osishoo

JUNE 29th 2000

I have been taken up to see Matreiya who looks rather different to my expectations. I ask about Solomon. I wish to see what he looks like, for I know he is there. I am surprised to see he is a very large man, a very imposing one. A good feeling but much larger than I expected. For some reason I always thought of him before as being small. He is imposing, strong and virile; a fine figure. Something is happening to my vibration and I hear the voices:

"Hold her. Hold her down. This is powerful stuff."

It is odd because I can view this. I can see my form undergoing this and yet I am still here watching. Transformation is taking place of my form, etheric body, I don't know what to call it. I go quiet. I stop resisting.

Those holding me, Solomon and Matreiya, step back as there is no need to hold me anymore. I change before their eyes and before mine. I grow and am a space Being. I am humanoid but not as I am as Shirley. I am not of the planet Earth. I have a large head which appears to be too large for the rest of me. I am changed. The eyes have clear vision. I can see differently now. My eyes are not as they were. There has been a reversal back to what I was. This is for the better. It is not deterioration. The deterioration came when I entered human form. Now I have taken back my form. I can now enter this soul wise when required. I don't understand the process here. I don't understand how I can be two things.

JULY 2ⁿᵈ 2000

READY TO FLY

I am being fed like a chick. I am being fed just like a bird. I am already quite well grown. My legs are thick. They are bird legs. Interesting! I am high and about to fly. I am ready to take my last feed from others. I am ready to launch off this safe nest that I have been in up to now. I am to try my wings. I thought that was what I had been doing already but it seems that all I have been doing is flapping and strengthening the wings. Lifting off a few times but not really in flight. Now is the time. Now is the time to take flight.

I launch myself off and find that I can cover vast distances in a brief space of time. I can see a long way and cover a lot of land. I am on my own. The parents must get on with their work now. I feel this is symbolic otherwise it would not make too much sense. What must I do now?

RA SPEAKS

I feel a great presence within me. He speaks: "All things are possible. All things within the mind are made manifest. You can manifest whatever it is that you desire sufficiently. There are no limits. There have been no restrictions put upon your mind. It is time that you realised that whatever you desire and put before you can be made in reality, is made in reality. If you desire peace for your world then construct it. Do not take the view that it is impossible. All things are possible. All things can be done. Know this to be so. You are with me on my beam of light.

"**I am Ra** and I speak to you as one who travels the light. You are one who carries the light, the one who assists me in my work for mankind. Know that you travel afar to many corners of your universe. Know that you travel far in your consciousness. Know that your soul has no limit in time or space. You will learn to take your physical form with you when you engage in these journeys. Believe this to be so and it will be. You are in no danger of losing yourself. You are in no danger from adverse realities. Do not give attention to those who would cast doubt and fear in your mind. While you have me within, you are at all times safe. You will experience me again in Egypt. I will present to you Thoth."

It was while I was staying on Aruba on January 24th 2000, that I had a message connecting this incident. Again I was not meditating or in a deep state. I was trying to get ants out of my clothes. I was told to write and this is the very powerful message I got.

Shifting sands, shifting sands. Smooth movement of land, vast land. Nothing is recognisable, nothing is left of former times. Move on, move on. The new is fresh, the new is welcoming you. Forget the past, forget the now. Look ahead. It is almost here. Can't you see it coming? Do not be caught unawares. Do not waste time. Get your mind settled in peace and readiness. The change is for you. You will do this with no company alongside except me. I am Ra, the greatest of all. Come with me. Be with me on my beam of life and you will know all.

AUGUST 17th 2000

AFRICA

I am standing in elephant grass. I am assuming that where there is elephant grass there are elephants. It is very tall but this is the path I must tread. I wend my way through since I can't see over it. I keep walking because it can't go on for ever, not even elephant grass. I clearly am in Africa for this is not India because I come to a round hut, typically African. The grass is all around it and is set in a clearing. You would never see it from a distance. You would have to be up close or in the air to see this hut, no, a collection of huts now.

I walk up to the first hut that I can see. No people are present, nobody I can see at least. I go inside. It is very dark. I can't see for the moment. Then I see two children on the far side, a boy and a girl. They are nervous of this white stranger. I don't think they have seen a white person before. Their eyes are adjusted to the dark and mine are becoming that way. They crouch against the wall of the hut. There are no adults, just the children.

It is no good me trying to reassure them, for they don't understand. I sit down on the floor and wait. I wait for their curiosity to get the better of them. Time passes. Eventually they get up from where they are sitting and begin to come nearer. I see they are both crippled, maimed. They were not born like that. They have been maimed. One is minus a foot, the other one minus an arm. They are not in good shape. They make their way towards me, eyes big and round. Because I do not move they feel comfortable but are still nervous. I try not to look directly at them because it is too confronting. I look at the ground and see them out of the corner of my eyes if I can.

I put my hand out and look at them and smile. They are not sure. I keep my hand extended. The little girl puts out her hand and touches my fingers to see if I am real. She explores my fingers with her little hand, the one she has left, and begins to feel my hand more, then my arm and shoulder. Because I don't move she comes closer and starts to touch my face. The little boy watches and doesn't want to be outdone by his sister. So he too comes forward, touches me and then becomes bolder for clearly I am not going to harm them. They allow me to give them a hug. I draw them into my arms and rock them back and forth. They start to cry, then they begin to sob. The sobbing gets louder and more intense, deep, deep sobs from the very core of their being.

I look up and find that adults are there after all. They have heard the crying of the children and have come to see what has caused it. They must be used to it by now. I am told they are not used to it for when there is deep suffering there is no crying. There is silence and patient resignation. They go beyond crying. I smile at the adults as they stand in the doorway and they come into the hut, as many as can crowd in.

Crying with emotion now I don't know what I can do here, except to be here and give them something from the outside world that isn't going to hurt them. This is a place that is not reached by aid association, for this place is hidden and is not reached by the outside. I ask spirit if I can bring some hope, some light by being their contact. I ask for the rainbow bridge that has been suggested to reach down to this place and for it to be a bridge for the angels and the light so that they can travel this bridge when they wish. I ask for something better for them.

I am to take them. I am to lead them to this bridge and to encourage them to go over it to the arms of the angels. I am to go there.

AUGUST 26th 2000

AFRICA BABY ELEPHANT

I had not yet been to Africa, and yet you would have to be a fool not to know it is suffering; it has always suffered for hundreds of years, if not longer. People have been suffering for all kinds of reasons. The climate is not always conducive to good health and yet it is so vitally important to the whole of the world. The dawn of civilisation is not true. The dawn of mankind – maybe. There are many theories on this. Is this where Eden was, or is it just a fantasy? Maybe it was somewhere else. Who really knows? All that is known is that there is suffering over all over Africa. There is hardly an inch where there is not maiming, fighting and killing, corruption, greed and great poverty and starvation.

I am drawn to Africa and have been since I was a child. I read book after book on African adventures, all the Rider Haggard books. Africa was put into my thoughts and feelings at a very tender age. These feelings have surfaced very strongly in me. It began with dreams. Not each night but frequently enough to be noticed.

I have this dream and in the dream is a baby elephant that I have enormous love for. I know it is a dream for the elephant gets onto my lap. This would not be possible in this reality life. The elephant climbs on my lap like a baby. I stroke it, I stroke its cheeks and caress it and send it enormous love, for that is what I feel for this baby. I speak to it and it answers me back. We all know elephants can't speak in our language but I hear it in my language. We hold conversations. I am jealous of the elephant. If feel possessive of it. There are others who have tried to entice it away. There are film crews who wish to use it for their purposes to make a film. It is such a sweet little thing. There is another person who wishes to have it for herself. I do not want to part with this elephant for it is my baby. I stroke it and I love it. The love that I feel for this little baby elephant is greater than the love I had for my own children as babies. How can this be? A mother's love is so enormously strong and yet I feel the same for this baby. I would die for this baby elephant. I would die for what this represents.

286

I ask the baby: "What can I call you? I can't keep calling you baby elephant."

He says: "I am the spirit of Africa. I am the emblem of Africa, for where else can you find African elephants. You can find Indian elephants but they belong to India. Here I am the African elephant and the symbol of Africa. I need nurturing and caring. I need love."

I say I still haven't got a name. I must name it for it is my baby. All the while this conversation goes on, I am stroking it, loving it and sending it enormous love; deep heartfelt tenderness for this elephant that is suffering so much. It has only come twice so far in my dreams, for this must be a dream. And yet at the same time I am aware of this reality. What does this all mean?

They want to take the elephant from me. The film crew want it. They want to make sensation out of the events. But there is no feeling, there is no caring from them. It is sensation and attention from the world but not in a helpful way. Who really cares? Nobody really cares, but it makes good news. It spurs some reaction to provide aid but it does not address the deeper issues. The hurting, the maiming, the killing that goes on. The help is superficial, surface only and while these good people do their utmost they can only scratch the surface. They have to go deeper to the heart of the baby elephant, to the children, to the core of Africa.

I come to realisation that I am finishing my dream as the film crew try to entice the baby out of my arms and under the focus of their cameras. I awake out of this second visit by my baby elephant. I must wait for the next dream for it can only come and talk to me in this manner.

AUGUST 2000

ANGELS/BIRDMEN

I am standing at the top of a hill looking out over vast plains. It spreads as far as the eye can see on a clear day. There are no mountains, but flat all the way round going off into the haze of distance.

"What am I doing up here?" A great bird comes flying out of the distance right up to me and alights next to me. It is a man bird, a bird man. He is taller than I am and speaks to me.

"You are to come with me. You are to go where I go."

Knowing I cannot fly, I climb upon its back and hold on tight to its feathers. I lie down across its neck and put my arms around it holding on tight. I know it is a man and yet it is a bird that flies. Interesting! Maybe that is where the stuff of angels comes in.

Maybe. Now that is a thought that has not come to me before. It takes off and soars up higher before it flies off sideways into space. It flies over the vast plain, so high that the details below are not clear. It is too high, it is too swift. We appear to be flying sideways which is strange. It is covering great areas, going a very long way. I don't know where we are going to arrive. I seem to be on the bird for a long time, so long I am getting sleepy. It is similar to when you are on a bus on a long journey, you eventually doze and forget to look at the scenery. I have become comfortable and relaxed and still we fly. Still we keep going. I am taking it all as a matter of course now that we will arrive somewhere and at some time. I am very dozy now.

I wake up after a long time and realise that we have landed. We appear to be in a city of some kind but no city that I have ever seen before. There are tall, shining, crystalline structures, nothing but light and colour. It is beautiful, clean and smooth. There is nothing dirty or gritty here. It is clean, like being in crystal that has no grit in it. It is pure shining, smooth, silky. I am standing alongside the birdman. He begins to walk for he does have legs, human legs. He is, after all, similar to the angels, like a man and yet with wings. Now I see and I walk with him. Where am I going? What is this all about?

We walk into what appears to be a crystal and yet it is a building. As we walk in I see other beings like him, lots of them. Are they angels or

288

are they birdmen, bird people? I don't know the difference. It is difficult to tell the difference. I am the only one there that is not a birdman and yet I feel at home. I feel completely at home and that I have come home. *I cry with emotion* We walk through crowds of them with no problem. We are accepted as we walk through them, lots and lots and lots of them. I feel as if I am in the land of the angels, beautiful bright shining colours everywhere. There is a feeling of great peace and joy. Peace above all things.

We enter a room where some of these angel/birds are looking over a map spread out over an enormous table. They are pointing at various parts of the map. It is a map of our world, the Earth. They want to show me where I must go. They point to where I must go. One of the places is Africa, but not just one part of Africa as I have been told, but all over Africa. That is a huge task. How can I do this?

"You can cover this easily for you too can fly. You too can cover vast distances in a few moments. You do not need to be physically present. You do not need to take an aeroplane to be there. You can cover vast distances in your mind, in your thoughts and in your deeds. You can work your magic wherever your mind takes you on your travels. You will also travel there physically but do not think you have to set foot in each of these lands that is Africa. You will do this in many ways. You will write about Africa, you will influence the minds of peoples through your writing about this continent."

I argue that I have no knowledge of this great continent. I have never set foot there. I have no knowledge so how can I write knowingly about somewhere I have never been?

"We will give you the knowledge. We will give you the information. It will come to you. You will find it. It will be presented to you in a variety of ways. Do not concern yourself about this. You must awaken men's minds to the importance of setting this vast land on a course that is healing. We will assist you."

"Hmmm! It sounds good but I'd like to see the evidence of this now. I ask now for you to give me evidence that this is about to happen and is not just within my meditation. I want some sort of proof to show me that what I am getting now is correct. This is not a doubting of you but a cross checking to make sure that I am not self deluding."

"We will do what we can in this for it is an important mission, one that you need to focus upon for the present time. There will be more."

They ignore me now and continue to look at the map and pass hands over various parts. They are setting things in motion. They are organising with their own energies and directing their thoughts. They are able to do this. They are planning their own actions as well as mine. So I will have these birdmen with me, I know that. When I travel I will do it with them alongside, with them watching over me. I am quite content that this is so. I have no-one who will make this journey possible for me and I don't see how I can do it otherwise.

"It will have to be done over the next few years. It will not be immediate. Attention of the world is elsewhere but it must return to this land, vast though it is."

A great energy comes over me and I know I have someone mighty with me, giving me the energy.

Since that time I have visited Zimbabwe, Kenya, South Africa and I know I am not done yet.

DECEMBER 22ⁿᵈ 2000

MANY PARTS OF A SOUL

Two figures have joined me on my journey. They have fallen into step beside me one on each side. Two male figures and yet they feel like angels, Light Beings. We go up the steps. I am slightly ahead of them. All I can see is a light before me but I can't see where I am going. I ask to be told who I am as I approach the light. All I can see is the light so I ask again, *who am I really?* I step into the light and am shown a mirror. I go and stand before it. I see a figure, a male figure, extremely powerful. It is very much a male. I look to see what I am dressed in. It is difficult to see for the figure merges in the light. I know it is a male. It is hard to see the outline for it shines. I am human in form and yet there is something not quite of the human race. I don't know.

I look around to see mirrors all around. Each reflecting this main one. Each looking slightly different, the same figure but not quite the same. I am a composite of many parts, many of my essence. It explains why a part of me can be in the Galactic council giving commands and yet also here on this Earth. How I can be elsewhere, working with the sick.

"Parts of you are playing many different roles, all for the moment, all in the present time, no past, present or future. They have all come together and are working in different areas at the same time. Whenever there is a need here, the part of you that is required comes forward instantly and fulfils the role that is called for. The man steps back when that need is over, therefore there are many things and still you have not seen all for we have not shown all. The past of you has come forward into the present. The past abilities, the past knowledge and that which others see in you are these parts. That which puzzles you when others see you for many purposes are the parts which step forward and become one with you in this incarnation. That is what is seen. It is time for you to recognise that you are many things in one body, not many souls, not different entities but all parts of the same essence of you. All have come together in this moment, in this period of time. All have united with you so that you are now complete in your incarnation. You have united all aspects of you."

"What about the future?"

"These lie waiting to be discovered by the conscious you that is currently incarnated. You may, with application and with dedication, step forward into the future if it is felt to be of benefit. So often it is not of benefit and we would advise against this for the present time. Your actions today would be influenced to the extent that soul growth does not take place. It would be rather like having answers to the questions before taking an examination. We wish you to learn and to continue to learn as you progress through a series of events. However you have your past and the variations of you united. Now you can call on any one of you in any given circumstance. There is nothing that cannot be done now. When you are called upon for action you know that it is within your capabilities to call upon that part of you that has already learnt."

"Can you please tell me about my visits to the Galactic Council? I wish to remember my time on board the Galactic meetings. I wish to know so that I may act with knowledge upon this planet. I wish to know the connection with Solomon and the connection with the ancient gods of Egypt. I wish now to know my role in those areas. I am aware that I ask a lot but I ask so that I may conduct myself for the benefit of this planet, so I may give to those who come to me the maximum that I can. I wish to open the minds and to do my task with the DNA."

CHAPTER TWELVE

APRIL 2002

DARWIN

I have asked the question again about the books. I am taken by the hand to a man writing. A man from the past writing with an ordinary pen, not a computer. He is right handed I notice. It's not me. As I approach I am walking with an angel. He looks up and sees me. He sees the angel too, for he is not of this world. The angel whispers in his ear. She has repeated my request to him. He looks up with interest as if to say 'Ah yes, we have another writer, an aspiring writer.'

I look at him and nod in agreement. I'm a little in awe of this man. For he is a writer, he has been a good writer. Old time, I am not good at history and I can't pin a period for him. He is going to work through me and help me from spirit. But I wish to write books of a spiritual nature to help others. I don't want to write things that are not in tune with my work. I am telling the angel this because although the others are nice and good I need to get my message over, to understand what I do, to understand the connection with the stars. Can this man do this?

She leans over and whispers to him. He looks thoughtful.

"Connection to the stars eh?"

I say: "Yes this is important. This part is important."

"We will see what we can do. I will call in reinforcements."

"I need to write about man's journey in evolution." Now I have hit the right chord. I am speaking, I believe, to Darwin. I tell the angel his theory of evolution is different to mine.

She looks at me and says: "Yes but he has been here a long time and he has learnt otherwise and he will assist you with mankind's evolution. You don't need to worry on that score. He has broadened his outlook."

He looks pleased because he hears what she says.

A DIVINE STATE

This is a serious request to spirit. First I have been told to make a link with them, before I ask a question. Otherwise it is like leaving a message on an answer phone before and not after the long beep. I had never thought of it that way before. I will repeat my questions once I have made a link.

Something else I have just discovered – gosh, after all this time. The reason I get more when I speak is similar to that when mediums in the church need the sound of the voice to help them give the messages. It is when I begin to speak that it is something in the voice, the vibration perhaps brings an opening, brings the connection. It is only when I begin to speak that I get the link.

I am getting answers to my questions about the book and although it is contrary to my idea, it makes sense. It is to write the 'How To' books: how to meditate, how to channel etc. how to do this that and the other. For these will be the most help for others and will pave the way for the writing that I really want to do on a deeper level.

"You have been given this opening and this recognition in order for you to go forward in confidence, knowing that you have the ability to do all those things which we have put before you. You have the ability to do all those things to which you aspire. That is the difference. You know that all things are possible, for have we not told you this? All things are possible also for other beings. They simply do not awaken themselves to this fact, to this awareness. So do not deny what we have told you. Allow this to be.

"Your next question is, 'How do I achieve all these things? How do I put into practical manifestation all these things which you have told me?'

"We say to you, just know that it is possible. The barriers which you have erected will crumble before you like dust. You alone can do this. You alone must know that all things are possible. You must feel, you must accept and all things will be possible for you."

"I want you to show me please, show me with pictures. Not simply words, but pictures for my mind's eye, my origin, my original place."

I walk to a brilliance of light. There are moving lights so bright I cannot see the source of the lights. There is brilliance of beings. There are no words for this. Divine light each. There are many beings here, each so bright that a form is not possible. It is energy form but you know there is intelligence in it. There is a being in the centre. I wish I could find words, it is just beautiful. The lights! I walk into it, one can walk in. The lights are all around so that I too am obliterated. It is like walking into a mass of light. Any denseness I have is no longer dense, else I could not be here. I feel touching. I am touched but nothing solid, just a knowing I am touched and caressed. Warm and love, such gentleness. This is my source. This is no place. This is a state of being. This is no place in space. It is a state which has no fixed position. A divine state everywhere, everywhere and at all time. Not even a moment in time but all time.

EVERYTHING AND NOTHING

I feel the left side of me is being pulled up through the top of my head. My eyes are being pulled up out of their sockets. It is uncomfortable. The words of the Atlantian Sital came to me: 'There is nothing you cannot do.' I see my guides. Although the pressure is still there I am with them, I can see them. Osishoo is a lot taller than the others, head and shoulders above the rest. I can see them standing there and I am there too, looking very ordinary amongst them. Osishoo, my father, sweeps me up in his arms as if I am nothing. I don't have a physical form – I am spirit. He holds my energy form to him. My energy goes into him. I am inside and yet I am aware of him as if looking at him from the outside. It is a hard thing to describe. I am now part of him and able to observe and be absorbed at the same time.

We are rising up. Everything is receding below us. It is like going up in a rocket, only slowly. All the others are still down there. We seem to be in nothing now. All we have is our mind, our consciousness, nothing else. We are nothing, nothing to see, nothing to touch, just our minds, just our awareness, nothing else. It is perfectly alright, for we are everything.

He speaks to me. "Why do you want to know?"

I answer: "Because what I know can help all those down there."

"Why do you want to know when being in nothing is all that counts?"

"It's all that counts for us. What about those all the way down there who don't know this and don't feel this? They need to be helped into the nothing too."

He agrees that that is my role. That is my job. He wanted me to experience the nothing and the everything. It is the same.

I ask if I can take some of the everything with me back down there. I want to give everything to those down there.

We begin to drop down and other things appear. I begin to feel colour, sensations, awareness of something more solid, awareness of breeze on the skin, awareness of sight, sound, awareness of the senses coming back. We settle gently back with the guides again – in form. We haven't really gone anywhere; we have simply experienced not being in a form and just being a mind. Intelligence, energy. We haven't gone anywhere except in this way. We have simply vanished.

What is bizarre is that I don't think that those present knew. To them we were always there. Our vanishing, our going had no place in time, no time in space, it simply was. It was continuous to everybody else. We hadn't gone anywhere from their perspective or from the perspective that was separate me.

ET's SURVIVE IN THE EARTH

I am in a glowing orange, standing at the top of my stairs looking down. Parts of the stairs are rough and parts of it are smooth, like the peel of an orange. It is a weird surface, dimpled. The handrail is knobbly. A peculiar rail – this is nature. The means of getting in are not stairs at all really. It is a means of getting down. There are boulders and it is more of a climb down, not a walk down. Down I must go to find myself.

It becomes easier as I go further. At the bottom it is shingle. I walk forward shifting on the shingle as I go. I follow my nose and turn off looking for some means to get in. There is a crack, an opening between two boulders. This is it. I climb through. There is no difficulty but I must climb over. This is physical.

I feel the presence of others here. I can't see anybody but I know I am not alone. *Show me what I need to see.* I feel the others are from another planet. They are not of this earth. I can just see them now – shadowy. There one minute and not the next. I have to be quick to see them. It is like trying to see a shadow that is moving. If I am to communicate with them they must show themselves more clearly or stay still. They are inquisitive. They are all over me, little ones pulling, investigating, curious and not harming me at all. I do not feel frightened of them. They are just tasting me in a sense, feeling the vibrations of me and deciding if I am alright through a sense of touch. They use touch and vibration to decide. I realise now that they cannot see. They are blind. They sense me in the same way that I sensed them. They can't see me but can sense me, which is why they are feeling me much as a blind person would do. They operate through the mind.

"We will teach you how to survive in the Earth. We will teach you not with words but with knowledge and ideas. A knowing so that when the occasion arises you will simply know what to do."

"Wouldn't it help me to know in advance?"

"No it would not help you for you would tell your mind and your subconscious that it is impossible. But when the occasion arises, you will know and it will be possible. It does not help to have advance knowledge of this. Information will be there when you need it. We did not always exist inside the Earth. There was a time when we lived on the surface also."

I am confused now. I can't think clearly. Something is going on. Maybe input is taking place now. I can't think of anything else.

Is the message for future times to come?

DECEMBER 24th 2002

COMMAND TO WRITE

The stairs down are of fur, soft fur, deep fur. The walls are also clad in fur, a soft and comforting animal feel. I am being protected from the elements, from outside danger. I am in protection all the way. It is very soft and comforting but I am alone. There is nobody else, just me. Keep going down in bare feet. I can't see myself, but I know where I am. Down at the bottom it is as I expected. It is a cave, a comforting even temperature cave. Even the floor is soft to the feet. There are no sharp rocks. It is smooth and comfortable. Although it is deep underground it is softly illuminated. I can't see where the light is coming from but I can see my way for it is a soft dim light. Again warm and comfortable. I must find a way out or a way forward.

I turn to the left. The walls are smooth and soft like clay, not rock but clay. No sharp edges. It is very solid just the same. It is not very wide. I can't imagine there being a door in this passage. It gets narrower and there are times when I must squeeze through gaps. If it gets any narrower I won't be able to go forward, even with the mind. Right at the end when there is no way forward there is something to the right where I can go in. Not a doorway, an opening. It is the only way I can go without going backwards. I feel it with my fingers. Others have been this way before, many others, which is why the sides are smooth. It has been trodden this way before. Many hands have touched the walls. I step through. The entrance is thick, like going through a mini passage.

I ask to be shown what I need to see and to be told what I need to hear. Sitting in front of me is a whole row of people. Men, wise men sitting there waiting for me. I can't see their faces clearly, but they are human. I know rather than see they are looking at me, waiting, waiting. They have been waiting for a very long time. I ask to hear what I am to hear.

"Why has it taken you so long to make contact with us? You have considered it and have rejected. You do not trust yourself to make contact and yet we are here waiting. We have always been here waiting. When you come to us come with some intent. We feel your intent. If you wish to know you need to come to us and ask."

"Well I am asking now. What do I need to know?"

"You need to know that you are loved, that you are not alone and that you have still to do your work."

"I wait for inspiration for that work. What am I to do?"

"You are to write. You are to write what you wish to write. If we wish to bring anything else into your writing we will do so, but you are to begin."

"There are so many things I could write about. What shall I start on?"

"Write your heart's desire. Write what fills you with joy to write. Write what releases you from pain. Write of the anguish you feel at times. Write of the revelations and the trials and the despairs. Write of the wonders. Write from your heart. If there is anything we wish to add we will do so. From the writing will come teaching, for the writing will teach, will unite all peoples."

In answer to my pleas for help came this. "My dearest one. Of course I will write for you if you wish it. I will write of the beauteous things, of wonders that man has yet to comprehend. I will write such things that all will be inspired and will feel great joy in the inspiration. Allow me to penetrate your mind so I may do this. This is the beginning of a great union between us. Allow yourself the time to make contact. The title is to be *The Book of Wonders.* " Spoken by Sechem

Please note I have not written this book yet but he has given me the start of it. From Sechem The Book of Wonders

"You are aware that space journeys take time. You speak of this planet or that as being so many light years away. We witnessed the birth of your planet Earth. We watched and wondered how this new being would progress. You were recorded in our charts of the Heavens, much as you do today when you discover 'a new star'.

"With the progress of our time we would learn how to cross the barriers through our non-physical consciousness. Understand that from our viewing through physical eyes and instruments, taking into account the distance in light years, what we were seeing was already very old history from our perspective. You had already advanced, though we were not able to see that advancement. Not, that is, until we had learnt how to cross the time barrier.

"So here we are communicating through mind. Is it not wonderful? To make things clearer to you we will explain. Many, but not all of those

300

you communicate with through the mind, are in the same position as I am now. They have traversed the time barrier and, although on some distant star or planet, are at the same time with you. They are watching over the results of their earlier interactions with you, to assist their own species to flourish and expand further into the Great Cosmic Arena. You might liken it to your own exploration and settlements in lands previously unknown to you. Like you and your continued movements from your homelands to other parts of your planet, we continue to traverse the space between us.

"Note however that our form such as we have on our home planet cannot comfortably physical exist as we are on your planet. Therefore we bring our essence, our minds, our cultures, our abilities and our ethics and enter the newly conceived human. Entry into one cell is all that is required to make the transition.

"I will tell you first of my homeland. It is filled with music, laughter and joy. So you ask why does anyone wish to leave such a place? In fact my love, we do not leave it behind. Many stay where they are. Some in their attempts to travel and further our species take these joys and delights with them. We try to give to other parts of the Universe some of the pleasures of our world. We have large populations on our home planet that do not do this. As we said earlier, we, like you, have our explorers and adventurers who are willing to share and teach."

Me: "I need to know where you come from."

"Why? What difference would it make to you? No matter. We come from the group known as the Pleiades. There are more members of this group than have yet been discovered. One smaller planet is hidden behind a larger one. Because of the orbit it remains hidden, unless viewed from a different angle. This new angle has not been achieved so far by your astronomers.

"What is of interest to you is the knowledge that you have walking among you many thousands of us, conceived in the manner of which we have spoken. This should bring delight to your hearts for with our entry introduction of new genes is possible. The genetic makeup of humans is forever altered and is to continue. It cannot now be eradicated. Who would wish to do so? We are humanoid and have form similar to yourselves.

"We will give you a little story enacted on our planet. Shall we call our home XX? Two kisses of love and yet referring subtly to chromosomes. For the purposes of familiarity we shall use your terms 'man and woman' or 'male and female' as you do on Earth. In this way you will not be overly confused in trying to remember our terminology."

And so that is all I have so far. Maybe later I will get more from Sechem.

DECEMBER 2002

PIXIES AND ELVES

There are round, smooth pebble stones. The walk is through trees, dried crackly leaves and brittle twigs. It is autumn or winter. Everything cracks and the air is dry and thin. I am walking through a winter forest. Because it is winter I can see through the trees. I come to a slope down. It is off the path. I slither down the slope into a great pile of leaves at the bottom. I can't stop the slide. It is like a funnel, for I slide into the spout of the funnel and fall out the other end. It is warm and cosy – underground. There are people here. Not normal people for they remind me of elves and pixies. I don't understand this at all. Show me what I need to see.

"Although we are human looking we are another species, a completely different species never to be mingled or matched genetically. We will always remain separate in form. We belong to this Earth and are citizens of the Earth every bit as much as you. Therefore we too have a right to feel and to say what we feel about the doings on the surface that damages so much."

CHAPTER THIRTEEN

JANUARY 2003

ON WRITING

As I stand at the top of the stairs I feel I am in a flame, right inside a flame. I am not looking at it but am inside it, completely surrounded. It doesn't feel bad, it simply is. I don't need to walk down the stairs because the flame just flows down. No steps, just flowing down. I don't quite see what this is telling me at all. I stop at the bottom and am upright now. The flame is still with me – turning gold. Like a pillar of light. I move forward deliberately following my pattern. I look around – tall walls, glittering walls. It reminds me of a cathedral or church. It has a high vaulted ceiling. It echoes a little here. I walk along – this *is* a church or cathedral. I turn to the left down one of the many passages. This one is wider than most. It is gold and like being inside a huge cathedral. I turn to the right to a little door. It is not meant for the public. The public come into the cathedral but not through this door. It is dark, heavy, stained wood. It is studded and heavy to open. It has a ring to open it and I turn it and it operates a lift catch. How do I describe it?

I go in and it creaks a bit. I have to stoop to get through. As I ask to be shown what I need to see there are lots of men, all writing away at different tables. Busy, busy, busy. Some are from our historical times, dressed in olden days. Some are very modern, some are very science fiction, Star Trek type stuff. Others are clearly from the angelic realm, glowing as they too write. There are so many of them here. Ooh! I've even got some Gods from ancient times writing. This is telling me something. What is this telling me?

"All these words, all this writing is already done. They will come through you. You will write what we say, what we ourselves have written."

"I don't see this. The words are still on your side. They are not with me."

"Be patient. The words will come. When we begin, no longer will you have your visits to other countries. When it begins no longer will you accept offers for readings in other countries. You may still accept them according to your own desire, for this will give you some release from the writing. Once we have completed our job and pass through you what we wish to say, then you will travel once more. You will continue to travel to promote our work."

"These are lovely words. I wish I could feel it. May I have some proof please that is not within my meditation? I need some evidence that what I hear is true."

"We give you evidence from the mouths of others. We understand this is not enough. The evidence will come when you begin."

"With so many writers won't the style be a bit muddled?"

As I watch, all these writers stand up and put their pens down. They link arms. They don't hold each other's hands but link arms. Impenetrable, unbreakable in the way they have done it.

"Strength in unity. The energy and the message will be the same from all of us. It will be the same and will run smoothly through the current we send you. The tenure, the tone will be yours as it comes through you in your words. The message comes from us. We intend this and it is so."

As I feel despair that I have nothing coming through in the way of writing, they all begin to pound on the tables they were writing at. They are chanting, "Write, write, write." They are quite determined. They will need to impress me very strongly. I have no idea where to start or what to write.

I see myself again as the pillar of gold flame and they begin to circle me. The flame goes right up into the sky. They keep circling, circling clockwise. A great circle. As they do their own light forms a band of light around me. It is all very nice but what is it telling me? A band of light surrounds me.

305

APRIL 1st 2003

AGAIN ON WRITING

I am dressed in pink. I don't feel at all solid. I am like flubber, not quite firm in shape. But I have a shape of some kind. It is a weird feeling. The stairs are not straight. These go round and round like a spiral staircase, only more than that. Spiral staircases are usually short. This one is long. I go down with an odd feeling. It is as if I am not level, I am on the slant, leaning over. By the time I get to the bottom I am giddy and have lost my sense of direction. I stand up and go forward. I imagine it is a bit like being in a bouncy castle. The walls are rubbery and malleable. I walk on quite easily considering. I find an entrance, which I go down. As soon as I go in the entrance I leave this rubbery toy thing behind.

I am on solid hard ground with hard, rough walls on either side. It is not smooth, not manmade. Rock walls. I walk along and come to my opening. Although there is no door I know it is my opening. It couldn't be plainer if it had an arrow painted on it. I squeeze through into my space. I ask to be shown what I need to see.

I see a pile of books. I look and there are more books appearing all the time. As I turn my head to look around there are yet more books appearing.

"All these books have been valuable to each person who has read them. If you want to have your book amongst these then you have to write. It won't appear by itself."

That's telling me!

I am in rose pink. The rail at the top of the stairs is soft and silky. Nice to touch. The stairs are wide and shallow. It is easy to go down but they slope away and I can't see the bottom. I am wearing soft luxurious slippers, close-fitting, not loose or floppy. I am dressed in flowing finery. I have the figure that I would like to have; slim, in good condition and not at all old. I go down the stairs with perfect poise. At the bottom there is a huge hall, high ceiling, very wide and polished on the floor. It is a huge, empty place. I look for a door or passage on the left. Yes and there it is, very well lit. Compared to the hall it is narrow. There is plenty of room though with lots of pictures on the walls... I go down there. There is lots of interesting stuff. It is a huge mansion or museum or something... I come to an archway on the right, very posh – it has doors, big wide doors that open from the middle. I push them open and I step into my space.

There are several people round a table, all of them finely dressed. The table is big. They are at the far end of it. I go to see what they are looking at. It is out of time. There are pieces of a jigsaw puzzle. They are putting the puzzle together. There are at least seven of them each holding a piece. They are looking for the right places to put their own particular piece. I will know the puzzle when my work is complete.

They look at me and hand me a piece. I also have to put my portion in. They will put things in place. I can't see the entire picture yet for it is not finished. This tells me I am in pieces and haven't got it consolidated. I need them. So I ask them to put the pieces in place for time is going by and I am getting older.

"Don't be concerned. You will see the whole picture when we have done our part. We have to put our pieces in at the appropriate time and not before."

NOVEMBER 2nd 2003

LEAGUE OF NATIONS

My stairs are more like a ship's gangway; the sort one uses to get on and off a ship. I am in long white clothes. It is not exactly flowing but is strong cotton. I go down the gangway. There is a car waiting for me, a black shiny one. I get in pulling my long clothes in so that they don't get trapped in the door. I don't know what this is or where we are going except that I am expected.

"You are going to the League of Nations."

"I didn't know that it still existed. I thought it was old and finished."

"You are going to a meeting of the League of Nations. It has been re-formed to meet a common occurrence. It is not a threat but a happening, a global all over. This is why the League of Nations has been re-formed, for this does not affect only one country but all countries, large and small. You and others like you have been called upon for it is finally recognised that you are the ones who can communicate with non-human beings on the planet. You can communicate even though you do not know the words. You are able to understand the thoughts and intention and are not fazed by an [odd] appearance."

We arrive and there is an armed guard all around. I am escorted inside the building. I don't know the building but it is not important. Armed guards are everywhere. It is not necessary but people might come in and they don't want that. On the platform are many different interplanetary species, humanoids all. Many different kinds and they are all twittering and communicating with each other in their own way. They appear to be in harmony, though some would be frightening to others. I have an impression of arms and legs and different heights. It is weird looking at them for they are different, very different to us, except for one or two who are similar and who have voices and can speak as we do. They have the mouth and throat structure the same. They will be the spokes people for the others. What am I doing here?

"You will act as a kind of interpreter, an intermediary reassuring those in power in the world, assuring them that there are more benefits to be gained by co-operation and inter-action than by denying access to the general populace. This will go in the media while these visitors remain in safe custody until the general populace become adjusted to the idea of their presence."

"This sounds all very well but, and we know that this is ahead of this time, I don't see how I as an ordinary individual can come to the knowledge of those in power."

"They will have heard of you through your talks and your books."

"I don't have any books published."

"You will write of this."

I am currently speaking many different interplanetary languages and understand the gist of it. I am not alone in being able to do this.

NOVEMBER 23rd 2003

THE OVERSOUL

I am sitting with a picture of Alvadeon [a powerful guide] before me. I need his energy. I am holding a crystal, a long one. I feel the presence of my guides and energy of them. I am simply talking so that I get the energy going. I decide to do the stairs. They are flimsy, almost made of wire. There is nothing very solid. It is a thin rail like wrought iron but is just wire instead of iron swirling round. I look down – it doesn't look as if it would bear my weight. I go down carefully and holding on to the bits of wire, even though they would not support me if I fell. Everything is in silver, silver light. That reassures me for, to me, the silver is always truth. I keep going down. It is dark on either side of the staircase. I can't see anything. Whatever might be there is not important else I would see it.

I can smell cooking, probably from outside the house. I keep walking down trying to keep my mind on the job but the smell of cooking outside keeps invading my nose. Someone is having bacon. My thought runs to the double-glazing. Can't be much good if I can smell bacon from outside the house. I bring myself back to the stairs. What am I dressed in? A silver gown, flowing, draping. I am very tall, not the me that lives this life. I am extremely tall and fine, almost regal looking. Very straight and upright. I have a purpose here.

I get to the bottom. It is all in silver. It is fairy-like in the sense that there are tall walls, gleaming. All this has an unreal feel. I keep walking forward and turn off to the left. The passage is very narrow and I can touch both sides if I put my arms out. This is not meant for a lot of movement but for one individual to pass at a time. The ground is solid, at least that will not give way. The walls are solid too; cool to touch with the occasional rough edge here and there. It is like walking through crystal – rather nice. Let's hope the crystal walls don't move or I will be squashed. Silly thought!

I almost glide forward and come to my opening on the right. It is not exactly a door but a panel that is glowing with light played over it in different colours. I can't see any means to open it. It is a patch on the wall with the different colours marking it so I can see it. I suppose I could try walking through. I step into the glow that comes from the colours and walk through. It is a portal. That is what it is. I am out of time here.

I pause to go deeper. The energy is building. My eyes are hurting. Both my eyes are under pressure here. I wait knowing I must go deeper into this...time passes and questions surface in me. So many things I want to do but without one particular drive to get started – scattered.

A voice says, "You know that you have the ability to be inter-dimensional and to be all those things that are seen by others. This is proof to you and to those others that one particular life is simply just that. Each is many personalities. *(My head hurts)* You are multi, you are many things and when you are seen as such. It is all aspects of you making it clear [to others], bringing forward all you have been and all that you will be in one. You are demonstrating to others your Oversoul. Or to put it another way, you are demonstrating the unity of all consciousness in one. You do this by connecting with the records of all time, for this is when it happens, does it not?"

"I want to know the purpose of all this. What about the books? What about the Little Owl Cards, what about the workshops? I am living in this world. I need to make an effect on this world. These small meditation sittings are not sufficient to do that."

"If you wish to make an impact then you MUST write the books. You must get into it. Do not procrastinate further. You have done this long enough. You have rested overlong."

MARCH 15ᵗʰ 2004

AFRICA AND BEINGS FROM OTHER WORLDS – PROOF

My stairs are steps down the side of a mountain or hill. I hold on tightly to a bamboo rail. It has been placed there, not grown there. The steps have been made too with all natural things. It is hard on the feet as I go down because the bamboo pole that holds the earth in place has sunk down behind it. The bamboo ridge is still there. It is not easy, quite steep. Steamy jungle, insects, the sound of insects, shrill. Oh my head hurts as I go down. The energy gets stronger and stronger. At the bottom it is a very narrow space. It looks like a pool. I wouldn't want to go in that. It is not clean water. I look for a way round it and step around the outside, holding on to various bits of trees and twigs. I don't want to fall in, as it is deeper than it looks. It is not just a puddle but is a very deep hole. I don't want to fall in the hole. I work my way round, holding on. On the other side there is a well-trodden path. A lot of beings have been this way. Whether it is people or animals, animals probably who don't mind drinking from this water. It doesn't feel safe but it is the only way I can go and I know I am alright.

There are two men, natives with spears. Not much in the way of clothes. They are not short, but tall. They have been waiting for me to arrive. As I draw close to them they stand on either side of me. Clearly I am to go with them. I am being escorted. The path widens out now. It is getting brighter. We go to a village where they have been expecting me.

"This isn't answering my question whether to focus on the cards or go abroad. This isn't telling me."

"Well this certainly isn't England, is it? And if it isn't England then it is abroad."

"I don't know where this is."

"You have already been told that you will go and you do know where this is. This is why your plans to go to Australia, to America are not being fulfilled yet. We are leaving the way clear. We are leaving the way clear. This will be arranged."

"Am I to do nothing then? Am I just to wait? Africa is a big place.

Do I do nothing and just wait?"

"Just wait."

The men take me to a hut. Bending low I go inside. It is a round hut. It is not Masaii . It is a very round hut with a pole in the middle. There is a very old man dressed in his finery. He has been dressed up with regalia of some kind. He is sitting, as he is too old to stand. I don't understand this at all.

"When you do go to this place you will be under his protection. You will not be in jeopardy from any adverse contingencies. You will be under his protection and that will be strong enough."

It doesn't feel very comfortable, and what am I here for? What am I to do? I have lots of pictures now, dancing people. A white man. A lot of very rapid movements blurring with the speed of it. I don't quite trust this message for I can't see how it can come about or what I can do.

"It is here that you will meet beings from other worlds. It is here that you will record, take notes and provide evidence for the world to see at large. Not only are you under the protection of the old man but also those who are present from other worlds."

*Shortly after I was invited to Capetown and from there went to Zimbabwe. I was the only guest in the hotel and very soon I had a queue of local people lining up for healing. It was a humbling experience indeed. My flights to Florida were cancelled due to hurricanes in that area.

SEPTEMBER. 17th 2004

BOOK SIGNING

I am in purple – not dressed in it but surrounded by it. I am tall and not short as Shirley is. I am wrapped in a purple colour and it is difficult to see through it. I look for the stairs but there is nothing. However I am standing on a platform with a grab rail on either side. I imagine it as being similar to the top of a ski jump where you leap off into space. I take the leap. It is a bit like flying with the wind whistling past, visions of land rushing past, but my focus is ahead and down. I land safely as if I have not done anything. I look around and all I can see is purple. I am

313

in purple all together and it is difficult to see through it. It is a clear colour, not muddy. Beautiful!

A hand comes through into my vision, reaching for me. I hold it and it pulls me into an embrace. I can't see who is doing the embracing but I can feel it. I don't know how to deal with this. There is a table piled high with books, my books. I sit down and the books are all in front of me. It is quite clear that this is a sign and this is a signing. There is a lot of happiness around from the spirit world. A lot of back slapping and congratulating. I feel this is a good sign for the energies are very strong

SEPTEMBER 20th 2004

LAND SLIP/EARTHQUAKE

I ask to be shown what I need to see. They show me people going up what appears to be scrambling nets going up a cliff face. It is land that is fresh, not an old cliff. It is a break in the earth and they are scrambling up so as to be on higher ground. There has been what you would call a landslip I suppose, but it is an earthquake thing. They are trying to get to higher ground for where they were will be covered with water. They must go higher. I don't know how this leaves people who are low lying.

"Where is this?"

"This is along all known fault lines and also in lands where there have been minor quakes in the past. These will become more than minor but not as great as on major fault lines. Excessive rainfall will also cause these slips and will not all be caused by earthquakes."

"When is this to be?"

"We are speaking of the next two or three years and not all happening at once. There will be enough happening to cause comment and concern."

"What can I do?"

"Go back to your original purpose, that of explaining that this life is but one. Explain that the continuation of the soul will always be, and that the quality of one's being is of the paramount importance. How one conducts oneself through life in the physical, internally and externally, is of importance for a better continuation of the soul's journey, irrespective of conditions on the physical plane. Adhere to the Commandments, in particular to that one of 'Love thy neighbour as oneself.'

"Write about the continuation of the soul of one individual amongst a group of souls. Write about the soul's journey through one lifetime after the other in a continuous thread. Write from your experience and you may entitle it *The Thread of Life*.

CHAPTER FOURTEEN

JANUARY 29th 2008

INTERGALACTIC DELEGATION

I am standing on artificial carpet, the sort you might have outdoors. It's a bit rough to the feet. It is red. I see steps going down, no walls, nothing to hold onto, just steps pure and simple. I am perfectly safe. They are not wide steps. The carpet, where I said artificial is plastic – most odd. Ah now I see what it is. These are steps going down from a craft, I don't know if it is an aeroplane or what, but it definitely is a craft that flies. These are steps that open down onto the ground. This craft is quite high and there is nothing to support the steps except the actual craft itself.

I go down and although there is nothing to hold onto it is safe. Weird! I am at the bottom now. It is concrete and open space like you would get at an airport – very much a landing area. It is just open space so I am looking for a way to go. To follow my normal routine I turn left because it is my patterning. I can't see anybody or anything, just open concrete space. I go to the left hoping to see something or somebody. Oh! I see on the ground little arrows, just like you get at some airports. I follow the arrows and they indeed do turn right.

They lead me into a collection of buildings. I am reminded of Bournemouth airport. Nothing big, nothing grand. The doors open as I reach them. There is a welcoming committee. Groups of men, only men. It is a committee of some kind for they all look as if they belong to each other. They are all happy to see me. I am led by them into a vehicle, one of those long sleek jobs that you'd get in a city. We all fit in. I haven't got a clue who I am or what I am or where I am going, except that it is very organised.

Again this is really odd. We are driven to an official building of some kind. There is a delegation of people there all waiting for me. I still don't know what I am supposed to do or why I am here. It is a long drawn out thing this but they all look happy to see me. I am expected. I am not arrested or anything which is nice, for that thought did go into my head.

At last I ask "Who am I and what is this all about? What am I doing here?"

"Don't you realise you are not of the Earth? In this scene you are recognised as a being from elsewhere. You are seen in your true form and respected for your true form, for there is now acceptance of such as yourself from other planetary systems. You are representing the Galactic Commands. You carry the insignia of the Galactic Command and as such have authority. In this you are recognised and accepted and are able to speak with authority to delegations from a variety of countries across your globe. The craft you arrived in is indeed a craft from space, all of which is brought into third dimension so that it may interact with those of you on Earth. It comes from your command of the Galactic Fleet."

"I want to know who am I, apart from being an Intergalactic Being? Who am I really?"

"In which state do you wish us to reply? If we reply for third dimensional understanding, you are a being from space. If we reply from the idea of consciousness and essence only then that is truly what you are, merely an essence, an intelligence, a consciousness that may interact at all levels, with all peoples when appropriately called upon."

"So in this scenario you've given me, what help is it? What help is it to Shirley who is currently embodied as an ordinary human being?"

"It will give her a deeper understanding of her role. It will encourage her to believe that anything is possible."

"That is a lot to take in and I don't now know what it is I am supposed to do at this delegation. I feel very much like the Shirley that is an incarnated human being."

"Open your box. Open your Shirley mind and extend it into other realities. Extend it into far reaching possibilities. You know very well everything is possible to the mind. All that is required is application to that portion which knows all."

FEBRUARY 12th 2008

UNA, BAHIA, BRAZIL

I was on a Fazenda near Una Brazil and about to give a workshop to a group of twentyseven people from Slovenia who did not speak English or Portuguese. There was to be one interpreter, thank goodness. The event was to take place in an amazing pyramid. Being anxious I went into a meditation to see how it would all work out.

I am wearing a light cotton shift that reaches down to my feet. I am on soft white sand. Ahead of me are very broad white steps which are covered with the sand that has been blown onto them. There is a rail on either side but I can't reach them. It feels like a beach with steps going up to get off the beach itself. Everything is bleached by the sun. There are more steps than you would expect. I am going up but cannot feel what I am treading on. I can't see what is around me. I am constantly rising. I want to meet my helpers for tomorrow's workshop. I want to have assistance with translation of the language.

As I am thinking and wishing this, I am still going up. Eventually I reach what appears to be the end of the ascent. There is a broad platform, very white as if bleached. I walk along looking for something I can relate to. It is the entrance to a big hall, what I can only describe as a Celestial Hall. Many doors. I am to choose one. I choose a golden, glowing one. It is a door, not a passageway. I go up to it and find I can pass through without actually opening anything. I walk into golden light. There is so much gold all around. Soon I come to the expected turning on the right – it is my pattern. This too is golden but with a more intense feel, almost solid. This too I pass through, into what appears to be space. Figures now walk out of the light, coming towards me. They are here to help me.

I ask, "Will you help me tomorrow?"

"We are always here to help. We will influence your thinking but will watch to see how you handle the situation for this is but the first time of many to follow where you will be speaking to many different nationalities. We have told you this before. It is a learning process so you can choose words that can be easily understood without ambiguity. We will be there to assist each one attending, to give them the experience of their lives."

Each walks up to me and gives me a hug. They are all human. There is no distinguishing feature.

"Yes you will learn to communicate with us even with your eyes fully open as you are doing now. In fact it makes it easier to communicate with you when your attention is elsewhere as it is at the moment with the birds and the nature around you. The words are coming to you without being pre-thought. Is this not so? You see how much easier it is, if you put your mind elsewhere. That is the lesson for you. That is the next step in learning to speak for us. Perfecting an art always requires practice, does it not?"

I ask to go to my subconscious, my soul being. I leap off from where I am. Waiting for me at the bottom is a man. He looks wise. He takes me by the hand. We walk together. I am reminded that I need to see where I am. We are walking along between walls of blue, like a vapour, not solid. It is a very clear turquoise blue. It is the clarity of the colour I feel.

"I am taking you further away from your consciousness so that you can communicate more easily with us on a much higher level."

As we go deeper together ... "Ask of me what you will."

"There are so many things. I would like those skills and gifts that I have had in my past lives to be brought forward into my current life so I can use them, so I can be more effective."

"You know full well this is not always allowed and that you are the sum total of all the lives you have ever lived. You are the sum total of all things you have ever been."

"Yes but there is a certain amount of forgetting so we start fresh each time. This lifetime I need these skills because the Earth and humanity is in crisis. I need to bring forward skills so I can be more beneficial in this life. It may be the last time on this Earth plane."

My head is getting very tight and achy.

I hear him asking: "Are you prepared for the onslaught of what this means and for the work that you will be required to do? Are you prepared?"

I say: "Yes I am. I will deal with it in the best way I can."

I do not feel they have met my request.

MAY 18th 2008

I am standing at the top of stairs. My clothing is a tunic which is tightly belted. I have sandals on my feet. The banister is like brass, highly polished. It is not brass but it looks like it. The stairs are rough wooden ones – straight down but I can't see the bottom yet. I could be going into a cellar underneath a house, or a building. I go back in time here. I feel a weight on my neck, on my shoulders. The thought comes that it is a wooden yolk.

Thoughts are racing through my head. This is a period of tyranny, tyranny of power. Rome. This is the yolk of Rome. I have no idea why – this maybe just a symbolic presentation of what is happening today: oppression. When I get to the bottom there is a sweet stream. I call it sweet because it feels so light, fresh and cleansing. I have to walk through the water – there is nowhere else. I follow the stream at ankle deep. It is easy walking. It is beautiful. I feel different. I am released – I am free. I am free to go where I want, to do what I want, to be who I want.

"The choice is yours. The choice is always yours. You can be of service or you can simply enjoy being who you are and living a pleasant life. To be of service requires dedication, application and sincerity of feelings, not because you should or because it is required, but because you wish to. This must come through emotion, the need to be of service."

TO A PAST TIME, ORIGINAL BEINGS , SPACE CRAFT

The stairs are covered in red plush carpeting and the banisters are set into the wall on one side. It is smooth like marble – nice and gently rounded curves. I am told I must continue talking and not stop to think, just let the words come. As I go down the stairs I am not thinking about anything. I go down, down and am not even looking to see where it is leading.

"Keep talking, keep talking, keep talking, it doesn't matter what you say. Keep talking all the way down."

At the bottom it is all soft and squidgy, a bit like stepping onto marshy ground. A bit unusual! It is squelchy, there is grass but it is squelchy and waterlogged. Too much water when so many have not enough.

"Look for your opening. When you do find it, keep talking. You must keep talking."

There is an arrow pointing the way. I follow the arrow. It is very broad, this arrow. It has been placed there with natural means. Leaves, twigs. It is a native thing. This is native!

"Just keep talking."

Yes, I must follow. It is undergrowth, a jungle walkway. Ahead of me is a little man. He is beckoning me. He is a little, I was going to say aboriginal but he is not Australian. He is a pygmy perhaps.

"He is an original of the Earth not from another planet. He is an original of the Earth."

That is strange. I don't come across them very often.

"They are originals. They don't come from another planet. They are descendants of ape. They are the original beings!

He is beckoning me now. I follow and don't know where I am going.

"Don't think, don't think!"

I am still in undergrowth and must follow the little man. He sees me as from the future or from somewhere he doesn't understand. I am from his future. I see a space craft. I no longer call them UFO's for they are identified by me. This is where I belong. I go up to it. There are others like him around it. I know how to get in. I think myself in and at once I am inside. It is big inside, bigger than you would expect. It is a bit like the tardis idea. It is all constructed by mind. This is a mind, time and travel machine. I have been brought back to it because I got lost. I was lost in his world. I am now found.

"What am I like? I am not very tall. I can shape shift."

"When we travel we can confine ourselves into small spaces, when we arrive we assume our natural physical forms."

"That's a clever trick!"

"Anything is possible."

"So what is my original form?"

"We would have to take you somewhere else to show you that."

"Do it then."

Immediately I am taken onto another planet. It is a long journey.

"How is this helping me to deal with the planet Earth?"

"You asked the question, what are you usually like? We are simply reacting to your question."

I look at myself. I am a bird being. Tall, if I put my arms out I am very wide. Wingspan! I AM a birdman and yet a humanoid as well. My face is not that of a bird but is similar.

"Take me back to where I was. I want to know how I can be of help on the planet Earth."

"You must broaden the minds of others. Tell these things are possible."

"They won't believe me."

"Tell them anyway. Tell them as a story, a make believe. Actually sow the idea in their heads. Even as make believe you are a shape shifter. In your current life you retain human form every time your consciousness is with the planet Earth. When you work for us you retain that other consciousness so that the two do not mix and confuse things. You are more things than one. You can be many things."

"So how can I be of help on Earth for that is what I am there for?"

"You must speak. You must continue to draw others to you. Do not sit down and waste your time."

I am back here, very quickly, very quickly.

I go down. At the bottom there are a lot of corridors going off in different directions. I am in a circular space with entrances fanning out. I don't know which one I am supposed to take. The floor is tiled. I choose the second entrance from the left. It has a greenish tinge to it. It is a small corridor, not wide but just enough room for me and perhaps one other. The floor now is smooth, not tiled and cool to the feet. The walls feel close to and are smooth as well. It doesn't look as if it has any openings. I come to my expected doorway. Again it is very narrow with no bumps or lumps. I don't see any means to open it but I can see it is a doorway. I look hard and notice a little indentation. I put my finger in it and as I do it clicks and the door swings open of its own accord.

As I step inside I know I am not alone. It is a bit dark and I can't actually see anybody yet until my eyes adjust. I know I am not alone and am straining hard to see. I can feel the odd movement and the odd rustle. I feel the place is full of spirit beings. Then somebody takes my hand and the hand that does this is soft and pulpy. It is squidgy. It is taking mine so I don't have to worry about taking his and hurting him. Somebody takes my other hand and pulls me forward. I am obviously not intended to see. We move forward and I am trusting because these two know where they are going and can see in the dark. My eyes are not used to this. I ask for more light which they obviously don't need.

It becomes a little clearer as I ask. They have forgotten that I need more light than they do.

(recorded over by mistake so is not finished.)

CHAPTER FIFTEEN

APRIL 3rd 2009

CONTINUE MY JOURNEY

At first I thought the stairs were artificial grass but with a bit of exploration I realise it is carpeting that looks like grass, close woven matting. The sort you would get to go down to a swimming pool to make sure you don't slip. It is very artificial and green. There is a rail on either side. They are making sure I don't slip. There is a pool at the bottom. It is flashing different colours, very strong colours – nothing weak about them. They flash blue, red, orange – all flashing as if they are lit from below. I have to walk through and don't have to submerge myself.

As I walk across it I feel the colours shooting through me. It is not unpleasant but is like electric currents shooting through me. I am being charged by whatever the colour is. It is easy walking and there is a slope out on the other side. Someone waiting for me. It is the nun I was told about earlier on this week. She helps me to get out and puts a cloak around me. She is not the one I am to meet but is taking me there.

I feel this is to be an important meeting. We hurry along corridors and paths. We are outside now. There is a building but it is almost not real. It is there but you feel as if you could walk right through it, like a mirage building. But she knocks and something opens so we can walk right in. It is a totally different world inside. All colour. Nothing is very solid but wafting and waving about. It is like walking into a wavy dream. But I am real and so is she.

I see the presence of many high beings. They have an aura and blend with each other and move about. I feel they are masculine with a sense of authority here. I can't get them to slow down enough for me to see clearly. I know they are trying to present themselves in a form that is meaningful to me, for they are pure light. To show themselves they must condense a little so I can see them. I feel honoured to be here.

One reaches out and touches me. I shiver. The shiver goes right through me and I feel deliciously charged. It is wonderful and another one does the same. Again it goes all through me. It is wonderful. They are coming into me now, similar to when I channel. I can feel them in my head.

Me: "I wish to know what I am to do in the future. I wish to know many things." The energy in my head is almost more than I can take. Very intense, almost painful.

Forcibly: "We cannot allow you to step down from your work. We cannot allow for you to sit back and retire. We would request that you stay in contact with us each day and not just occasionally as you have been doing. We wish you to communicate with us more often and we will then take you further. How can we do this if you decide not to contact us? We are working with you. You know that. Do not doubt it."

Me: "I want to know something more definite, more concrete."

"If we were to have your book published you would then be extremely busy and would not always find the time for the tasks we have for you. So we will programme the timing of this book. There are some elements in it which should be altered. But you know this already and that will come later."

We ask you to continue to be of service until the end of your days. If you wish for good health then we tell you that to remain in service is your best option. You do not need to fear that you are not strong enough or awake enough or physically enabled enough. We will ensure that you maintain a high standard of physical and mental well being. We can only do this if you continue in our work, if you do not you will resume normal aging process. You will resume normal human activity, which in itself is satisfactory. But this is not your role in this incarnation."

Me: "I wish to do deep trance."

"We have covered this before. Deep trance is not always an efficient way, for so many safeguards need to be in place. We wish you to continue to travel, to continue to visit even those areas that you are not actively enthusiastic about."

Me: "Then you will have to put them in my way for I am not seeking them."

"They *will* come your way. What we have in mind will come your way. You will grow stronger. You will develop stamina that is required for these journeys. You will have resistance to all and any inconvenient illnesses, bugs and influences. You will be resistant to all these things and many will wonder why you *never* get ill. You will remain in good health at all times. This is dependent on you continuing your work."

I feel his arms around me and I am ushered into a crypt. There is a large book on a stone bench. It is like a book of ages.

"Your name will be inscribed in this book for the work you will have done, not only in this incarnation but in previous incarnations, many times. Your name will be inscribed."

Me: "What is my name?"

"You ask for tangible proof. If we were to give you this there would be no peace for you. We could not then preserve your anonymity. This is to be preferred, is it not."

I do feel the presence of someone in me very strongly but this kind of proof I already have. So perhaps something that is tangible to me alone? I go down the stairs. There is nothing at the bottom. I look around until I see the entrance to the left. The passage is lit with little glowing lights. A soft glow, very soft, very gentle. The passage itself is small, wide enough for me to get through but not wide otherwise. The lights are a bit like the lights we get as emergency lighting – soft and just enough to see.

The opening on the right is another soft, gently lit way. It is not bright but just enough. All I have to do is just push and the door opens. When I get inside the air is brighter. Rocky ground. Although I am inside what appears to be a cave it is very open. It is just an entrance or exit. Exit into something much bigger. I come out into glorious sunshine. I am on a mountain looking out over the scenery. Beautifully lit, not sharp but soft in glorious sunshine. Everything is there.

It is a glorious scene coming out of confinement into the open. Although my way has been lit enough for me to follow, where I have come out is absolutely glorious, another world. I feel my hand being taken. We walk together down a nice little slope, easy. This is a different world. I am in a different world, not the same as before.

"If we were to put you into this world too soon you would very quickly become bored. Although it is a delight there is nothing that you need to do and being a soul of action you would certainly be looking for something you could have an effect on. You would be looking for this or that and would not be at ease. So accept where you are in your world. Accept that it is giving you what is comfortable and right for you as a human being. That action is keeping you alive, keeping you vital and giving you a purpose for your existence. Here in this world where everything is easy, everything is smooth and a delight you would lose purpose for being. You would simply be and that is not enough for you. You know this. To be is not yet enough for you. Your life is one of service. Who or what can you be of service to in this world? That time will come even here, but it is not for you yet."

I am assuming that service in a spirit world could be as a guide to those still incarnated or stuck in their own progress, and I certainly am not ready or able for that now.

I am dressed in a cotton shift, white full length with a sash cord around the middle. Bare feet. The steps are in stone, very worn. The handrail is a heavy chain threaded through eyelets. Iron I think – not a firm rail but it is something to hold onto. At the bottom is a flagstone floor. This feels like a crypt or cellar or below a church. The walls are plain and unadorned. The opening on the left is a little door, it is very old. I think I am in a church. Through the door is a passageway. No windows, just a passage with stone walls. It is not cold and quite dry. It echoes a little. I must find the other door on the right.

When I arrive at the other door it is a bit bigger. It is like a church door and has an iron ring. I twist and turn it to open the door. It is dim inside – not very well lit. There is an old man sitting at a table bench hunched over something. It is an old book he is writing in. He has robes on with a hood so I can't see his face. My bare feet don't make a noise but he looks up as I approach.

He is brilliant, beautiful and not old. He is blond with blue eyes and youthful. He is like an angelic form hiding beneath the dark robe. He looks at me and I notice even his lips appear to be red. He smiles as he looks at me. He has been waiting and knew I was coming. I ask him to tell me what I need to know.

"Sit down, sit down."

I sit opposite him. He takes his time.

"What do you think you need? What is it you wish to know?"

I take a little time to think about that. "Am I doing things the right way? Am I right in pushing the workshops and the books? Is this what I am supposed to be doing? If I am not then I want it made clear to me in one way or another where I should be heading and what I should be doing with the few remaining years I have. I don't want to waste the years."

"Although you are fed up with travelling and we can appreciate and understand the reasons why, you will continue to travel in spite of the inconveniences and the trials that come with this. We wish you to move about the planet as before. Your energies, even when you are not aware, will have an effect on the land and environment and the people that you meet. We wish you also to continue to teach even when you feel it is not having a lasting effect. Even if you have one out of ten going forward as a result of your teaching, it will have been worthwhile and will expand outwards for others to take up the baton."

I ask: "What is my connection with ET's and the space beings."

"You are one of them. The role you are playing on Earth is just a part of your activities in your soul. You are also active elsewhere at all times, not just when you sleep. We wish you to expand your mind and allow your mind and thoughts to embrace the pictures that come to it. Embrace them as being your reality and things will then become clearer. We will try to give you scenes where the other parts of you are working so you can understand what it is you are and what it is you do."

It seems I am to continue to put up with airports and uncomfortable accommodation.

JUNE 5th 2009 2.30 am

DO NOT GIVE UP

The stairs appear to be a kind of rattan, handmade, native made. It swings down like a kind of chute. It is very well made so that there are steps but it is all enclosed in one. It is unsteady and not fixed to anything. I have a feeling of Malaysia or Borneo or somewhere like that. It is very hot and steamy with noises that you get in a jungle.

"There are so many worlds even on your planet. So many different environments from one place to another. Stop complaining about your life. Stop complaining. You have it easy compared to others."

It is very true and I have been complaining. Eventually I get to my door. As I go in there is a blaze of light, so bright I can't see at first. So bright! There are figures in there waving at me, calling me over. As I become accustomed to the light I see those from other worlds, not this world. Osishoo comes forward. He is clearly so different from the others, so much bigger and more stately. He is beautiful and reminds me of an angel. He has a presence about him, a calming one, a gentle and loving one. He is very much in charge.

"Do not give up as you go forward. Do not give up on what you are here to do simply because of little difficulties along the way. If you give up now then you will regret it as you go into your other lives. Now wouldn't that be a pity? Keep going forward, keep striving, and keep alight the spark in you. Do not be downcast by the Earthly difficulties or your age. Your age is nothing compared to what you have done before. Your age is miniscule in comparison to other lives. Miniscule!"

I feel as if I have been thoroughly told off for having my little concerns. They are insignificant things really.

JUNE 18th 2009

I MUST WRITE – RECORDS IMPORTANT

My steps are like circles cut in half, semi-circles – stone steps with the bulge outwards. They are a bit crumbly and I am reminded of ancient Egypt or Greece. They are crumbling and I see have not been well maintained. The ground at the bottom is rough, crumbly rock. Not debris exactly but broken up rock that used to be a building. That is what this is − rubble. It is uneven and has been here a long time.

I look for the opening and it is more of a pathway that leads away from the area of brick and stone rubble. The path leads down a hill so the building, whatever it is, must be up high. We are now going into countryside, vineyards, tended places but very dry. I keep getting reminded of Greece, not that I know Greece very well. It is a hot, dry, Mediterranean climate.

As I walk I see a tall metal gate, leading to a dwelling I assume. It is old again, rusting. I can get through quite easily and feel I am in a hurry now. On either side of the walkway are statues of marble and granite in various poses. I am in a hurry to get to where this is leading. It has to be somewhere grand, or that was grand.

I suddenly realise that there are two people, one on either side of me. They are men in old costumes of scribes. This is to do with writing. I am reminded of people like Homer, Plato and those wonderful Greek philosophers who put pen to paper.

"They didn't just think, they put it down. That is what you need to do. It is not enough to just think and know. You must put it down on paper else how on earth can you pass this on after you have gone. You must put pen to paper."

My reaction is, "What a journey just to tell me that. I know I must write."

"Yes, but you are not doing it. You must put pen to paper. After all the events that have destroyed civilisations, what is left but the words of the Record Keepers? The words that have been passed down keep going when they strike a chord. Those of your world are trying to decipher words still laid down thousands of years before. Still your Bible is in production. Words laid down thousands of years before. Words laid down in the records for all to see, they are the things that endure. Even the teaching that you do, even that does not survive beyond the moment or in the minds of those you teach. Words laid down continue onwards. Can you not see that the writing is important so that it may continue?"

JULY 6th 2009

WAY STATION IN SPACE

I am in a silver close fitting suit. I don't look like me and am slimmer. This feels like a space suit but very tight fitting. My stairs are modern looking – shiny and they don't look as if they belong on this Earth. There are hand holds on either side of the stairs which are extremely steep, almost to the point where I might be better going down backwards if I was in my own body here. I go down facing out quite happily because of the hand holds. I can see it so clearly but to describe it isn't so easy. It is like when you are on a small ship and you go down from one deck to the other.

"We ARE on a ship. This is a Space Station, not the same as NASA has. This is a Space Station for interplanetary beings. That is to say, not from just one planet but many of their inhabitants are here. It is a Way Station. Some might call this a Mother Ship but it is not that. It is a Way Station, a stopping off point, embarkation for passages of interplanetary travel.

"You are one of those who organise and run this. You give the directions and organise. My goodness me, you have many roles here because your mind is clear and can function on many different things at once. You are able to see what is required and direct. You are of course, not alone. You are not the only one running things here. There are many others who have tasks allotted to them."

"Why the close fitting silver space suit?"

"This has properties that make it easy to enter the various chambers we have on board here. A variety of systems that you might call 'airlocks'. There are adjustment chambers for different species from other planets. Each one (chamber) is different to the other and is relevant to the species requiring an interchange or a preparation. The suit that you wear enables you to enter any one of these without harm, for you too are a species that cannot always interact physically with all or any of the others. Not all are giving off the same energy waves, emanations and radiation. So adjustment must be made before they can enter the rest of the ship, or travel as they are here to do. This is why it is called a Way Station and not a Mother Ship." (Note: I went on a Mother Ship later.)

"I don't quite understand how this works. No doubt you will tell me at some point."

"You might call them decontamination chambers for not all the wave lengths, the energies, the attachment in terms of physical emanations are compatible with the environment they wish to visit, that of the Earth. There has to be a decontamination process to avoid contaminating Earth itself or any they might meet. If we didn't do this there might be effects upon the flora and fauna and living beings. The energies are not always compatible. This is why we have a decontamination process in these chambers. We have chambers allocated to each species from certain regions of the cosmos.

The suit that you and we all wear when we engage in this work is impervious to the energies from a whole range of species from other planets. We are not adversely affected by the varieties that visit this Way Station."

"I would like to talk about my role on this planet Earth as a human being. How on Earth (excuse the pun) would it be arranged that I give talks around the world. At present I have no means or contacts for this."

"Hold it in your mind that this is possible and we will arrange it. You need to meet an individual who will take this on board for you."

"I can't help feeling that publication of the book is key to this."

"It certainly will help."

"I'm not getting any younger and if it takes too long I will be ready to leave the planet myself so I won't be able to do the talking. 2012 is rushing up on us and the opportunities won't be there. We are speaking of three years now. Three years to get the book published and to do the talks. You'd better get your skates on I'd say."

VISITING SPACE BROTHERS

My journey down is very similar to Badbury Rings [in Dorset]. I am going down – at the bottom it is like a very tall mound with a moat. There is a doorway, an entrance to a tunnel I believe. I go into the tunnel. It is quite a tight fit, earthen. It has been manmade and is not a natural thing. I walk along the tunnel, at times brushing both sides with my clothes. I am going into the heart of things. Soon I get into what I feel is the centre. There is nowhere else to go for it is the centre. I look around. What can I see? There is a shaft. It is a very small space but there is a shaft going up from where I am standing. It is going up high and at the top there is a crystal. There is a blue light cast from the crystal. It must be large because it fills the hole.

I stand wondering what to do next because I can't go anywhere. I rise up like going up in a lift, only I am not standing on anything. It is a form of transportation. I move up, I move up, I move up. I feel quite comfortable and I am now in blue. The light from the crystal has enveloped me in blue. I pop out of the top.

"Why couldn't I have started from the top?"

"No, you cannot do that. You must do it this way for this is our system. This is what you might term a 'lift me up Scottie'. It cannot be activated from outside but only from the centre, from the bottom. That is the only way you can do this."

The scene around me is changing. I am not in the sky I am in another land, another dimension, another time. It is very real. Nobody is surprised to see me though I have just arrived. They must be used to this. I am just another arrival and there are many like me.

I seem to know where to go. I don't need to be led. I walk along a definite path. I am quite determined and know exactly where I am going. I go to a building. Not as we have but it is circular with a spire on top of the dome. I walk into this. I am to meet with a group of people here. I have been invited but am there by choice. I don't need an invitation. It is my right. I don't know who I am here.

I am shown into a room; I suppose you could call it that. There are mostly men sitting at various work stations. I march up to one of them who is very tall. He is an Extraterrestrial, Space Brother.

"We are all Space Brothers, a space family unit. A space command. You have been asking to meet with us," he says.

I say forcefully: "I meant I wish to meet Space Brothers physically here on Earth, not up here in another time. What I need is to be adjusted to those here on Earth, even if they come in human form. I need to be linked to them so that we have something in common between us when the work begins. It is important for how else can I help the unaware ones if I myself have not had the experience first?"

"You are having the experience."

"You misunderstand me. I mean on Earth, physically on Earth as I am there, so that I may be comfortable with them myself before others can be made comfortable. You can understand that surely?"

It seems I am able to speak to him in this way for I have some authority here. They don't seem to understand the need of a human being.

"I am here as a human being. I wish to interact fully with the Space Brothers on Earth. It is all very well meeting like this but it does not prepare the human being that I am for the work I must do [said firmly]. This is a request."

"It is noted."

"I would hope it is more than noted because I need some action here. I need some answers. I need one of your kind to help us understand the languages that are being given to myself and others here. We need a teacher for this in the same way as you would have a teacher in the classroom when learning another language. We need an intermediary. If we are to become intermediaries ourselves we must have more assistance from you here."

"We have noted."

I am getting frustrated now. "Noting is one thing, doing is another. Maybe I am being presumptuous here but I need something more, much more."

One of them stands up and waves his finger at me. A wave, a current envelopes me all over so I am changed. I am changed now forever.

"I have another request. If I am to continue working well past my eightieth year, I need to be rejuvenated. I need my body and mind to be regenerated, for I hold a physical body that in the normal process would age. I need the body to regenerate. Also the brain needs to be regenerated and not die as is normal with human beings. I have taken this body and it needs to be regenerated mentally as well as physically."

"It is noted."

"That is so annoying. You must assist me in my work for you."

"You forget that the work is also for you."

"I haven't forgotten but it is hard to separate the two. Or should I say it is hard to unite the two when I am living a human life – with a human family I may add, that looks to me to be human in all aspects."

"You will not find it hard, for you have the memory of the human form that you took and all it went through including all the human mental and emotional aspects."

Since then I have been given a new guide that is to help me with speaking and interpreting different ET languages.

"Do you have anything more to tell me?" I ask.

"Your next journey, albeit for a holiday, will also be used by us for you are going into troubled areas. Almost every step of your journey takes you into a troubled area. We will use you to change the energies there, to have a ripple effect wherever you go. Think of it as walking through a field of energy and your entry into that field sends out ripples in the same way that a duck swims on the water continually from one part to another. As it does it disturbs the energy pattern. This is what we require, for the energy patterns to be disturbed so that they may be regenerated. You have chosen this trip for a holiday but it has a deeper purpose than that. You are to change thoughts and energies as you go. It should be easy for you."

"You are not human are you?" I asked this tall Space Brother.

"I was once."

"That's interesting. Who were you?"

"I am now Serapis Bey."

"Ah! So Serapis Bey, you were human – and now?"

"I am a Space Friend."

All of this was conducted on an equal basis with neither being more authoritive than the other. I feel I am one of them simply reporting and asking for certain conditions to be changed or met to make my job easier. In the meantime I must be human. I am going to leave it at that.

I had an amazing year of travel which included Egypt, Aden, Oman, Jordan, India, Sri Lanka, Thailand, Malaysia, Java, Indonesia, Cambodia, Vietnam and Hong Kong.

OCTOBER 1ˢᵗ 2009

SURVIVAL OF THE FITTEST

I am in a long shift gown in green. The stairs are narrow with a rail on either side. There is just space for two people side by side. It is rough hewn, nothing polished or marble. As I go down deeper and deeper, I hear rustling on the side. I know we are outside and I have the feeling it is like being on a forest treetop walkway with wooden steps coming down from here. I am at the bottom now and it feels like the bottom of a sink hole. Not much space. It is earth. Just discernable is an opening that I can get through. It is covered with branches, brambles and if I was any taller I would have difficulty and I would have to bend over. I walk along looking for another opening on the right. And there it is, just an opening in the undergrowth.

As soon as I step through I am in another world. It is a completely different world and nothing like the one I have left behind. I almost forget to ask: "Take me where I need to be, show me what I need to see." As I ask I see a row of little lights on the ground, marking the way. It is just enough to see and no more.

"Where am I going, where am I going?"

"You are entering another world, another time, another dimension."

As I ask again there is a barrier, a wall, an unseen invisible wall. It is enough to stop me. I have to ask permission.

"May I enter through this veil, this barrier?"

"Enter."

As he says the word I find I can walk myself through it. It closes behind me. I can't see it do that but I know it does. I am in another time. There is air and everything is shimmering blue. I expected it to be sharper but it is shimmering. I think it is because I am not used to it. My view of it has not settled.

There are large human beings here. I didn't expect humans; mostly male, though there are some females.

"This is a vision of what can be for your future. This is not fixed. It is an aspect of a possible world which is why it shimmers. For this time has not been set yet. The size of those you see relates to the strength required to exist in this world. Only the strong will survive and we mean

STRONG physically. Those who are not strong cannot endure this reality and so will pass on. What you are seeing is a possible future. As we have said it is not set."

"I had hoped to see a future that was more likely."

"There are many possible futures. You know this already. This is but one. Know that if things do not go well those who survive will need to be strong physically for it will be survival of the fittest and not according to the mentality or technology or the ability to see ahead. It will be survival on a daily basis."

"Can you not show me another possible future for us as a human race?"

"You will need to go in a different direction."

"But **you** led me on this path by following the lines."

"We showed you the way but you did not have to follow."

"I am asking now to show me another way." My mind will not accept anymore so I come back. I come back.

OCTOBER 19th 2009

TUNE IN HIGHER

I have a picture of lots of young people all going in a hurry in the same direction along a street. I am caught up in this and I am young too. I don't want to go with them.

A voice says: "If in doubt, don't."

I realise they are all heading in the wrong direction and I don't want to go in the wrong direction. I turn and face the other way, against the stream of people. Looking ahead I see peace, serenity and empty countryside. All the masses are going in one direction, into hordes of people. My direction is into peace and solitude. I want to know why now.

I am getting huge pressure in my head which tells me I am making a high connection here. The pressure I am under now is getting me readjusted. I am being re-tuned to higher forces. My way is not of the masses, not with the herd. I must tune in once more to the higher communication.

OCTOBER 20th 2009

The stairs I have are wooden boards. It is like pre-war houses. I can see the sides of the stairs where it has been painted but there is no carpet. Someone is either moving in or moving out. I feel it is moving out. There is a brass railing. It has been nicely cleaned and is not dirty at all. A lot of people have been up and down here. At the bottom I am still in the old house. It is not grand, just old. It echoes because everything has been taken out of it. It has been emptied and whoever was here is leaving. I am in the corridor now which leads to the front door.

I step out into the street. There are lots of people waving in jubilation, celebrating. They are very happy about something. They are dancing and laughing and joking. It feels like when the end of a war is declared and they are released from all the fears and troubles.

I step out into the crowd. They are slapping me on the back and hugging me as I am part of it.

341

"It is jubilation over release from fears and they are happy in the moment since they do not know what is ahead. Nobody really cares for the past has gone. The past has gone. All that can lie ahead is better than what has been."

"What has this got to do with me? I can't see a connection with my desires."

"The past has gone for you too. Rejoice in the moment for where you are. Rejoice in the jubilation that is in your heart now. Know that ahead is better, much better."

A very tall man takes my arm and pulls me out of the crowd. He leads me to a quieter part. We go up some steps in a higher building. He holds my arm as we go up together. I know he is alright. He has the sense of someone with authority, someone who knows what it is all about. He even knows what the future holds. We keep climbing the stairs. They are softer and do have carpeting. We go up floor by floor.

I ask: "What are we doing? Where are we going?"

"This to be your new hall of residence. From here you will see far. You will oversee the activities that are going on below. From here you will receive higher messages. From now on this is your hall of residence."

OCTOBER 27th 2009

ENERGY HOT SPOTS

I am going down a twisting chute like a candy bar that curls round. I
land at the bottom where it is all cushiony and soft. I get up and dust
myself off. Clouds of shimmery dusty stuff swirls all around me. I look
around me and see an opening just visible above the swirling clouds of
dust. I can't see what it is like but walk in that direction. The floaty
sugary stuff stays behind as I walk into the corridor. I am clear now and
hear bells. Some are light and some are heavy. Sounds like the sort you
would get in a monastery or church. I feel I am more outside than I am
in. It is a bit like a cloister. I come to a few steps up to the right into
another door. There is a huge vortex in the middle. It is absolutely
massive and is an energy that I would have previously called a hot spot.
This one I can see and is swirling round.

"Why can I see this when previously I just knew it was there?"

"When you find a hotspot of energy if you had eyes to see you
would see this very thing. It is a vortex.

Knowing that I can step into an energy hotspot absolutely safely, I
do that now. I am stepping in now. The only sensation I feel is in my
body. My head feels as if it is going to explode. My total focus is on the
body. There is someone or something pulling my hair up so that my
spirit body is pulled up out of the physical. I leave from the top of my
head and I am free to go up wherever I want.

KEEP WRITING

My stairs are like a corkscrew. A corkscrew penetrates more easily than anything else. There are walls on either side to stop me getting giddy. I can put both hands on either side to guide me down a very narrow stairway. I make no noise as I go down because there are rubber strips on each edge. I can't slip and it makes no sound.

At the bottom now. The ground, the floor is like glass. Very shiny, unblemished and totally black so it reflects like a mirror. The shiny floor flows into the gap I must take on the left. It is seamless, like molten rock that has solidified into a perfect surface. It reminds me of some black crystal but I can't think of the name at the moment. Obsidian?

The walls on either side of the passage almost feel as if they are alive. It is as if there are faces looking out from them but not distinct enough to say for sure. It feels as if they are behind the wall looking at me, like in a one way mirror. I come to the door on the right which is like glass and reflective. Everything is reflective. I give the door a little push and it swings open easily.

I look around me at a large space. There are wall hangings. I am not sure if they are paintings, tapestries or other objects. It feels ceremonial where one enters an old place and all things of the past are hung up there as a record of memories.

It is very grand and palatial. I stand there wondering what to do next and how this can relate to my current concerns. There is a figure at the far end beckoning me to go over there. The far end is quite a long way. It takes me a little while to go there. There are no obstacles and everywhere is smooth, shiny and clean. It is just a question of covering the distance between us.

I stand before him now. He is depicted as a figure from a pack of cards like the king or knave. It is just a depiction for I know the real him is behind or inside. It is a façade. He takes me by one finger – the forefinger on my left hand. He takes me forward into a little room at the back. A room at the back is very much more enclosed. I want to know the answers about the books and whether I should really bother my time with any more.

I ask the question. He points to what I can only call a forest of pens, stood on end like trees.

"A forest of pens, and like trees, each pen produces branches. Each word that they write produces more growth, more branches which spread and drop seeds. Then new growth appears, all coming from the pens. I think this is a clear answer to you. Write even if you feel the books are not going anywhere. Continue to write."

"What am I to write? If feel I have done all I need to do. Where is the inspiration coming from?"

"The first thing is to sit down and write and inspiration will come. Ideas will be put into your head."

"That is all well and good. I have been given encouragement for so long now and still nothing is happening."

"It is happening all the time that you are writing. Every time you sit down and write and go over to look for subject matter your own growth is proceeding. It is never ever a waste of time."

CHAPTER SIXTEEN

MARCH 29th 2010

PREPARE FOR FUTURE

I have been given a rope and bamboo stairs. It is flexible and not rigid like a ladder but are stairs. I have to go down backwards. The bottom is rush matting. I turn round to see where I am. I appear to be inside. It is a flimsy rush matting type of building. I walk along on soft ground and go carefully. I come to the door on the right. It is very quiet. I push open a matting door. It is very dark inside. There are people here, Africans or at least dark skinned people. A whole group of them. They have been waiting for me. They have met in secret as if they don't want anyone to know they are there. There is a huge gathering of them. I don't understand this. Tell me what this means.

I feel the weight of something on my hand – very heavy and solid. It is placed in the palm of my hand. It is a heavy book. What is it?

"It is a record of our nations, not just one nation but our history. We have knowledge that goes back much further than your history books. We know much more. We know of the events to come and yet you worry about insignificant matters when the world is at a turning point. The order of priorities will be reset. We understand the need to focus on the present so that you may carry on, enjoy and endeavour. But look further and prepare. Prepare well in your mind and in your heart. Prepare in delightful anticipation."

"I don't wish to ignore the present for that is not living in the now and we have to carry on. We have to carry on and experience the presence too."

"Yes, but hold in your mind delightful anticipation so that your thoughts are not in the negative. You can prepare in this way and send healing whenever you can and to those who need it. You will continue to speak."

I ask if it is important that I travel and do the books.

They unroll a map of the world on the floor. They are pointing to all points of the globe which I take to mean that I must still travel.

APRIL 11th 2010

ANIMATE OTHERS

I have ended up in a shop of some kind. It is a toy shop with lots of dolls and puppets and things sitting around on the shelves. I wander around the shelves looking.

"What am I doing here and what is this all about?"

"You are to pull the strings and to push their buttons, for until you do they are inanimate. You are to bring them to life."

The pressure in my head is getting stronger and stronger but I do what he asks. These toys and puppets begin to relate to each other. They move about, get on and interact and are motivated.

APRIL 19th 2010

INNER SPACE BEINGS

The stairs I have are covered in a sisal type of matting, very worn. The banisters are of wood. It keeps coming to my mind that it is a colonial house in America. The door to the right is heavy with a very heavy latch. It is in dark green. As I step in there is a big hole in the floor and is not at all what I expected. There are steps going down. I must descend into this hole. I go down several levels. It goes deep into the ground and I realise the house is just a cover and one would not expect this here. The hole goes right the way down, a long way.

I already sense in advance what I am going to meet. I know I am going to meet beings not of this planet. They have been told of my coming and there is a lot of twittering and noises. Somebody is going down to them. I just know this because I have been before. I recognise I have been before but it is the first time I have realised it. I am a friend and they know me as a friend. Their twittering is comforting. I don't know what this is all about or why I am here.

I am now at the bottom. It is very modern, very high tech, lots of instruments all very clean and furnished. It is high tech and clearly very advanced. It is massive. I am one of them. It is very busy down here with lots of beings doing things. Some are humanoid or human looking as I am. They are tall and in wonderful shape and in good condition considering where they are. I want to know who they are. The name is given but I really don't know if it because it has been hinted at by somebody else. Nefelim! I could have this totally wrong and there are other names I can't pronounce. *(There followed a lot of their language which is impossible to write or put names to.)* I will have to learn their languages. I accept that it is friendly and they all have a job to do. It is something to do with preparation for underground activities. They have been here a long time. *(More of their language.)*

Eventually after some procedures I realise I must leave straight away.

DREAMS

"I wish to know the meaning of re-occurring dreams I have of going somewhere, maybe an office, a hotel or some other building, another village or place and not being able to find my way back. I always seem to get lost going back to wherever it is I started from. I always wake up before I actually do get back."

"It is not our intention that you go back to where you were or where you started from. Our intention is that you explore, that you do not try to go back as you have been doing. We wish you to go forward to see new venues, to meet new people, to spread your energy beyond where you began. You are not intended to stay in one place."

"I thought I was doing pretty well in all the travels I am doing."

"We are not only referring to journeys on your planet. We are also referring to your work. We wish you to go forward to expand your work."

That doesn't feel like the right answer to me. That is because I often do not remember where I have come from or even the name of the place I started from. I can't remember where I have been.

My stairs are plain wooden boards, unvarnished, unpainted and untreated. They are very wide and when I ask why they say: "They are still in preparation. These are not ordinary stairs, they are very wide and are yet to be covered with carpeting and have finishing touches."

I walk down the middle as they are too wide for me to touch the sides. At the bottom is swampy grass, squelchy and not what I expected at all. The path to the left is a track and gets onto dry land. It is a well worn track, narrow and closed in. I can't see the sky because the undergrowth covers it over. It is more like an animal track.

My right entry is where I have to scramble over a big boulder and slide down the other side. They speak: "You have lost your way a bit and have stopped following the threads, the little trails that lead you somewhere."

I am trying. I follow him as he goes off into the undergrowth. I am trying hard to keep up with him. To my surprise I get to a clearing with a table set out. It is a long table. It is the council with a lot of men/Beings on the other side of the table. I have seen them before. I have been before them before. I hesitate because I am not sure what I am here for this time. I walk up to the centre man and I assume the wiser one.

He hands me a scroll, a parchment. "Here are your plans. Here are your onward projects."

It is rolled up so I can't see but he is handing it to me. It is lengthy and the others are all smiling. It is as if I have passed a certain period of my work and this is the next stage. It would be helpful if they could tell me what that is instead of leaving it scrolled up so I can't see.

"Look out for the threads. Look out for the signs and make sure you follow them."

"I suppose that means making sure I meditate more."

"It certainly does. You must widen your area of connections. You must spread your connections as far as you can. You have restricted yourself for too long."

I ask that they put some of these connections my way. Place them so I can see them and follow up.

MAY 14th 2010

MORE TRAVEL PLANS

I have made my journey down and am in a business centre. I arrive at a door and there is a name on the door. It says 'The Director'. I knock before I go in and someone from the other side calls out: "Come in." On the other side is a panel of people, all men. It feels like an interview board. I feel there are six people but I can't get a fix on their faces. They are in control. I ask them for direction and they push a file over to me. I open the file and inside there are flight tickets. What a surprise!

"You are still to go to America and also other countries."

I am looking to see what countries. It is not clear and I feel Japan.

So I ask: "Will you make the preparations? Will you put things in place for me?"

The men from the table come round and slap me on the back, shake my hand and congratulate me. It would seem they are pleased with me and I don't know yet why. It is their assistance I need if I am to go. I need the doors opened and the invitations to come. That is what I need.

A long trip to the Orient and Texas was in store for this year.

JUNE 5th 2010

TEXAS

My stairs are a bamboo ladder. I am going down a rock face, an earthy wall. I appear to be in a typical canyon area. My path to the left is a gap between two high rocks like a pass. Soon I come to a turning to the right. There is a little figure beckoning me just in case I missed it, because I could easily have walked by. It is an obscure pathway which I could easily have missed. He is beckoning me on and we come out to a drinking hole. It is not that big and is a watering hole. Water in dry lands. Very precious. He is pointing at it. I have to drink it.

"It is very precious."

As I get down to drink from it, I drink and it disappears. It just isn't there anymore. It was there just for me. I stand there between the rocks and wonder what to do next. High above me there are eagles. Hugh big birds flying around and circling. I know they are eagles and not vultures because I can hear them screaming.

"You are standing in a vortex of energy. They are circling above for they feel it. They know where the energy is strongest and where they can soar on the thermals. You are standing right where it begins. You ARE to go to America even if you do not make your compensation financially. It is Texas that is more important to you than Washington. You might even, if you wish, skip Washington altogether. Just do Texas. Remember the energy and where it starts and that is you. So being there, you are the fulcrum of the energy that we can use in a place where it is much needed."

JUNE 6th 2010

TO THE CENTRE OF THE EARTH

I seem to be wrapped against the cold. The stairs are ice stairs, cut into blocks of ice. I have gloves on and spikes on the soles of my shoes so I won't slip. I don't understand why I have ice. I go down very carefully. There are walls on either side so I can hold onto those, although they are ice as well. There is a reason for this. As I go down it gets warmer and I am now getting too hot in all these clothes. The ice has melted, showing bare rock. I get the feeling we are going to the centre of the Earth where it is warmer and closer to the core. I begin to take my outer clothes off and my boots. I sling them around my neck as I probably have to come back the same way.

Someone has been here before because there are lights strung up. Yellow, white, some are blue as I go down. Down to the centre of the earth. It is easy going. I have a lot of questions. I keep going down, down, down. Soon I am at the bottom. It is solid ground and a bit rocky. There are crystals and minerals but they have the dirt on them and are not all in their polished state but as one would find them in a mine. I am walking carefully so as not to damage any of them.

I find the tunnel that must be here. There it is! This has been designed for it is clear cut, smooth, used quite often, quite polished smooth. I look for the entrance on the right. In fact it is just a bend to the right so I have to turn right any way. I don't want to get lost. It is comfortably warm. Not too hot. Living quarters? That is what I see, living quarters and not just for one person but for many. It is big big!

The energy in my head is increasing a lot. The thought in my head is, *here I am wondering about how to promote the books, how to get the word out and yet there are things so much more important to focus on. So much more.*

"Your desires that you are worrying about now will fade into the background as the other more important matters take over."

The big Indian guide that I was told about appears. A big muscular man. He takes both my hands and puts them together and draws me to him so that both my hands are touching him. It feels nice and comfortable and warm. I am to take his energies. It is to be one with him.

"You are one with me. You have always been one with me. Whatever happens you will be under my protection and guidance."

I still don't know how my work is going to change. I really would love to know.

"Don't you see? When you begin any work with connecting people together, call for me and think of the unity so that we work together, so that healing, clarity and explanation of things come through me to you to them. Use me. You so often forget to use us who are here. Call on us. Call on us and it will flow through you. Use us more."

JUNE 26th 2010

ARABS AND TEXANS

I am in deep velvet. Everything is in velvet including my clothes. I feel strong, powerful energy. It is very deep blue velvet. I can't quite get the colour. Beautiful! At the bottom of the stairs it is soft, plush, like a very special place. Everywhere is hushed, quiet and reverent. The passage off to the left is small, just enough for one person. You could miss it if you weren't looking. It goes to a secret place. There are a few steps up with a handrail on either side, again just enough for one person. The door opens before me. I don't have to touch it.

There are several men sitting on the ground in a circle. I am reminded of the Arabs, my Tuaregs and all those tribes that came once before. They motion me to sit. I do but I am not very comfortable sitting cross-legged any more. Somebody brings a cushion for my back which supports me. I am the only female here. They have all thrown their hand in; the cards and what they had in their hand are now in the middle. Someone has shuffled them all.

I don't understand this but I am to take a card out of the pack and that is the card I must go with. It turns out to be confirmation for me because it is clearly an American with a big Texan hat. No mistaking that. I asked for confirmation and that is how they have given it to me. So clearly I have to go there even though I don't know the reason.

"Stay a week, not three or four days."

Thinking of this later I have put two and two together. Oil – Arabs and Texas. Oil is the connection but I feel a stronger meaning here.

THAILAND

I have a beautiful turquoise type green. The ladder they have given me is a rope ladder. Straight down. I feel the roughness of the rope as I go down. I see myself going down holding on to the rope. I see myself as a figure rather than me. It is a person without details. I can feel what that person feels. I can feel the rope under my hands and beneath my feet. As I go I feel the energy increasing. I feel transformation in my face and am entering another state.

I land quite heavily, solid and with shoes on. No bare feet. The ground is solid and it is an empty place. The ground is solid and smooth and I don't feel enclosed. I must look for a turn off to the left. There are little markers set in the ground to the left. I follow those. The pathway is laid out for me. I can't see anything around me, but the markers are there. I walk quite confidently and soon come to an archway on the right. It is an arch made out of wicker and bent into shape. Quite pretty! I have no door, just an entrance under the arch.

I stop because I know there is an invisible wall. There is an energy barrier here. I can feel it with my hands. It is to see if I can pass through; to see if I have the energy that is right. I walk through it very easily and am now in a different world. A world of light, gaiety and light. Quite a different world. It is like walking into another time.

"Show me what I need to see."

There is an elephant all dressed up like an Indian elephant in finery. It is painted, festooned. There is nobody on it. It is ready for some procession or something. The elephant is from Thailand not India. The elephant is picking things up from the ground and throwing them all over the place.

"He is demonstrating his own right. He is demonstrating his own will. This elephant represents the Indonesian countries who will demonstrate their own will, who will not be led and used. They have the right to lead themselves."

"That is not what I expected but it is what I have been told [in this meditation]."

JULY 23rd 2010

ON TEXAS AND CROP CIRCLES

I was in bed with spirits urging me to get up and meditate. As I was clearly in conversation with them I said: "Why can't we do it here?"

"Because you will forget what we say if it is not recorded."

I argued a bit because I did not want to get up then. However they persisted. My head was very full with energy. It clearly was important.

My journey:

The stairs are jagged rock. These steps have been put in a long time ago in order to go down a very steep mountain. They zigzag and are made of very strong rock. I don't know if the rock has been there already or has been carved and put into place. It doesn't matter. I am going down in sandals. To do this in bare feet would be foolish. The sandals are firm and just enough to cover the soles of the feet, kept in place with leather thongs.

I am not in too much of a hurry because it is quite steep and at almost every other step there is a turn. It is a real zigzag down. I wouldn't like to be going up. I keep on going.

I have to state that I have been urged to go into meditation for the past hour while I was in bed having a real conversation. They were insistent that I get up and meditate because I would forget it without a recording. My head is very full, so full I can hardly think.

Still going down as I am thinking all these things. There is a grassy plain at the bottom. I naturally turn left instead of going forward. Doing this I am going round near the base of a mountain. I know there has to be pathway or something to the right at some point. I can hear cows mooing and birds singing. It is warm and pleasant and not at all dangerous or threatening in any way.

My right turn is a path. A beaten path. It leads me into … oh I see what it is. I was struggling to find a word for it but I recognise it now as a crop circle. It is a proper circle not one of the odd shaped ones. Being low down I can't see a pattern.

"Go in to the centre." A very strong voice tells me. I go into the centre of the swirl and stand quite still. As I do a great shaft of light

357

comes down. I can hardly think or speak. I have difficulty in speaking but my training is such that I must. I am disappearing. …

I then have a long bout of coughing which keeps my focus on me and not what is happening. I have arrived. I have arrived. It appears to be a space craft. Now whether this is my imagination or real, I am not sure. I am not alone. There is a lot going on. It is a very busy place. I am not speaking of one of the tiny pods that I would normally see or have been on.

For those who don't know this would be called a Mother Ship. Osishoo appears.

He says without speaking: "You will be returning home soon."

I don't quite know what that means and he repeats it.

"You will be returning home soon."

I wanted to ask about Texas and what this has got to do with me going to Texas? My mind is in a turmoil now of thoughts.

"Do you mean I will die? Do you mean that my soul in this body will return and there will be an exchange? What do you mean?"

"It is tied up with Texas. You must prepare before you leave."

NB: I had a great time in Texas.

AUGUST 1st 2010

A WRITER SENT

"Why can't you let me sleep?"

"Well you said you wanted to write. That was your declared intention. We sent you a writer and you sent him away"

"Yes well it was 1.45 am and I preferred to sleep."

"In that case you had better give yourself time in the day when you are not taken up with other things so you can listen to him then."

"It seems to me that the things you are telling me have nothing to do with the kind of work I do. In fact it has no real subject at all. That is no good, is it? So here I am sitting downstairs at 2.00 am hoping to make sensible contact. I have to say feeling a little foolish talking to myself."

"You know very well that talking to yourself is not foolish and where you get the most information."

"So who is my mystery writer?"

"Now you know that if we gave you a name you would be looking up his works and then you would be just a copy editor, a copy writer. It would not be fresh; it would still carry the old style. You need to get into the habit of allotting yourself a set period of time where you can sit and let the thoughts come without interruption from elsewhere, without having to go off and do something else. If you are serious about writing then you must put your part into it. You must find the time."

AUGUST 30th 2010

SHARING

"We are going to talk about sharing, not just about valuables, business, things you have; but sharing yourself, your knowledge, information, chitchat and anything you have learnt. That is sharing. That is what is required, sharing of your innermost being with others, without fear. Keeping things to yourself for fear of others using what you have, or of gaining an edge over you is not appropriate in today's world and in the world that is to come. You will not be diminished by letting a part of you spread over to others. You will not be diminished by sharing what you know."

AUGUST 31st 2010

CLAIRVOYANCE

The stairs I have are broad. It is the size you'd get at a theatre or cinema. The carpeting is rich green. I am going on my own but there is plenty of room for others. I see myself tripping lightly down. I am a lot slimmer than I am usually, younger. At the bottom there is a door facing me, a big door, double doors. They are right in front so it is clear I have to go in. I push them in the middle and they open quite easily.

On the other side are lights, high up as you would get in a theatre but very high. They are so high they are not casting a lot of clarity and are not fully on but dimmed. I realise we are in a theatre. People are already in their seats. The place is packed. I walk down the centre – I have been here before – I know this. I am the one that has to go on the platform. I know I have done this before and am not nervous. I go up the steps at the side and out to the front. I am a lot younger than I am in today's life. I have done this before.

Someone hands me a mike. It is a handheld mike, not one of the modern behind the ear things. I look very calmly over the big audience. Spirit comes swirling into me from the back. It actually enters and I simply observe this. I am watching it happen. I am doing clairvoyance. Then I start to lift off. I am floating. They know this is going to happens as they have seen it before. I am spirit.

"Why are you showing this to me?"

"You have done this before and because of that you can do this again. You know that. It is time to put it into practice. It is time to open yourself to what you were."

NOVEMBER 2nd 2010

LISTEN

The stairs I am on are alive. They keep moving in differing directions and are moving while I am on them, very like the Harry Potter films. I am holding on to both sides, on a rail. It is like a fairground this. I don't know if I am going up or down or where I am on the stairs. It is a fun ride and nobody can see where it is ending while they are on it and can see only when they have left the stairs. I keep holding on. It is pointless trying to walk and is enough just to hold on.

Then I see I am at the bottom of somewhere and I step off onto firm ground. They continue the fun thing for there are little lights along the way on the ground. That is all I can see, little lights. I follow them and they lead along passages with firm ground. Coloured lights everywhere. They take me to what I now call my space. No door just an opening with little lights all around it. It is a definite invitation to go through.

Inside is vast emptiness, but is not really empty, only for sight. I can hear thoughts. I can hear everything that exists, a cacophony of sound in what appears to be empty space. There is so much going on here – so much – the entire world. No, entire worlds, all are making their sound. Making and leaving forever their impressions on everything. I listen to this for a while until it becomes too much. I ask for an explanation.

"Everything that occurs in existence remains for it to be found [discovered], sought after, ignored or whatever you will. It is all there for you to make use of, all of it. Speaking of sound, even your clearing of throat is a sound. Even that remains if you wish to anchor to it. You can let it go, as all beings have learnt to let go of sounds that do not serve them and yet can tune in to those sounds which please them and makes them feel whole again. Listen for the sounds of angels. Listen for the sounds that you have tuned out, the Celestial Beings, listen for them. Listen to the innermost workings of your mind. Each thought also has a sound. Every thought produces a vibration which is felt somewhere, sometime, in some manner. Be sure your thoughts are pure and of love."

I have standing before me what I can only call an angel. It is very

362

still and just looks at me. Beautiful, golden, shimmering, giving off a light all around like a glow. One hand up, as if blessing me.

There is a whole group of men, clearly guides or high spiritual beings. They are all shining, but are not all in white. There are different pastel colours. It is a large group and I can't separate one from the other. What am I to do with this?

As usual there is a spokesman who comes forward. He has strong hands and holds them out to me to take mine. He draws me into the group so that I am surrounded by them.

"What is it you want me to do? I am not clear about what I am to do. I just keep doing the same things over and over and over. It is the same pattern of work. I am waiting for your answer."

"It is during your travels that you will meet the individuals that you need to take you further. Keep your eyes skinned for them so that you may recognise this possibility. This is on all of your travels; for if you do not recognise during the first one we will attempt to place someone in the second until you do realise what is being presented to you. You are to continue writing and it will become clear in the months ahead. We do ask that you maintain contact with us in your meditation and your thoughts. We ask that you teach your mind, that is, to fill it with the subjects that you are interested in so that you have the foundation that we require to take it further. So even reading matter is of importance for the procedures to come. We know you are confused as to what you are to write and wonder if what you have in mind is the same as we have. It will become clear."

CHAPTER SEVENTEEN

JANUARY 25th 2011

BANDING TOGETHER

I am at the top of my stairs after a conversation with the guides. I am wrapped up in some kind of furry outfit, like an Eskimo. The stairs seem to be ice. I am in a very cold climate. There is no worry about slipping for whatever I have on my feet is a nonslip sole. I am going down a long way. I still need warm clothing even though I know it isn't so cold now. I don't feel cold.

I get a strong sense that I have gone back to past life in a colder climate. This is a journey back and I am told maybe a journey forward too. I don't like the sound of that. At the bottom are ice tunnels. Perfectly calm and smooth. There is no door to knock on, just another entrance. I see a guide, also wrapped up in furs.

He beckons me: "Come forward, come forward."

I feel I may have been related to him in a past time. I am a female and he is a male. I am not sure if I am his daughter or wife. He has the commanding position. I do as I am told and come forward.

"In past times we all banded together. We gathered together to support each other no matter how difficult things became. We survived by this means and people of today will do the same. You will also use the animals for your survival as we did."

I stroke the outfit and it is soft and silky. It is no horse skin but possibly bear.

"You need it to keep warm. If you don't do that you will die. **We** knew that"

March 19th 2011 4.30 am

JAPAN/NUCLEAR

I am wrapped in what looks like an orange jumpsuit. I am standing on plastic kind of flooring – smooth and shiny – very hard. It is like a walkway with a slope down. There are handrails because it is not that wide. A gangway? I don't know what the word is but it is like plastic. I am wrapped in a working suit, orange.

"You must use the mind as it is a protection and notification to others."

It is a winding pathway. It goes round curves. There are no angles, just soft bends as it goes down.

"I can't understand what this is about."

"It is so that you can't see what is around the corner. It implies a certain trust in carrying on, knowing this is leading somewhere."

This is really weird as I don't know where I am. I am going down but not steeply. There is protection. The curves are also a slowing down device for anything that might be coming up because it is harder when you can't go straight. I don't know what it is talking about but I must follow the thread they are giving me.

I am still in orange. I feel quite strong, much younger. I feel much younger than my current age. Then I come against a thick wall, blocking the way. Remembering that I am only mind I just walk myself straight through it, no problem at all. But the wall is there for others too, not just for me. Not everybody will know that it is not an impediment.

I am in a different place now. It is softly and gently lit. The few lights there are, if they were not there it would be black. Oh, these are emergency lights, the sort that are put on in a plane if there is an emergency. There is a soft gentle hum. I don't know where this is leading me but it is going into somewhere that requires work, specialised work. Oh I see! My mind keeps going to the nuclear disaster in Japan. This is something to do with that. That is why I have a protective suit but this is a mind job. I must remember I am not physical.

I am in the heart of things now, in the very heart of things. There are a few things I must do. I see a few disconnected pipes. I put them together. I do this with my mind, but using my hands. I am snapping them together and am tightening the rings, like a screw on. I am tightening it and making sure it doesn't come off. There are quite a few of these and I must do them all. I am now opening a flow which allows the coolant, whatever they use, to come through. I do this now and it starts to flow all around. It is a coolant and is designed to bring the levels of danger down. Where all this is coming from I don't know, but this is what I must do.

I stand here watching it take place. This is a place no one has been to before, not even in the mind. Nobody has been here, nobody would go there. I know I am alright. This is a massive place, there is nothing small about this – *(disturbance of tape)* – there are switches, I turn some of them on. Things are starting to happen around me. There is a glow and a vibration, a physical vibration such as a noise would make. It is a noise that is produced by the vibration.

I am just here. I don't know what else I must do. I must stand my ground. The gentle hum continues. Things begin to change, more organised, if I can use that word. Now it is time to leave. I turn round and see another way out. There is a thick casing of a wall. I am to walk straight through this. This is to tell me and remind me that I am not physical even though the experience feels physical. I pass through easily. It is thick and seems to go on and on and on. Then I plop out the other side into a much cooler environment. Air! I am out of there. Then some hands come and pull me away. These are spirit guides, the angelic realm. They pull me and are attending to me. I feel that is quite sufficient for now.

APRIL 19th 2011

SAFETY IN THE EARTH

I am going straight down on a bamboo ladder, all tied up with twine or creepers or whatever is natural. It has been constructed by those who know how. It goes down on what appears to be a rock face from the surface down into the earth. I get the feeling there will be many such ladders down leading to deeper places which will be safer from whatever is going on at the surface. It is not permanent but is a safety measure for a short period of time. For example, against strong winds, hurricanes, tornadoes.

"You are much safer down in the earth than on the surface."

I follow my usual route left then right. There are a lot of people, indistinct but very busy. They all know exactly what they are doing. It is a comfortable, warm, cosy feeling in here. I don't know what this it telling me. I am reminded of gnomes such as you see in a Santa Claus thing, when they are sorting out the presents. They are happily going about their tasks. They are short, round, happy.

JULY 17th 2011

SAFE PLACE WITHIN EARTH

I am standing on purple velvet, very thick and rich velvet. It is like carpeting in velvet. The banister is knobbly so you can't slide your hand down it, metal like gold or brass. As I go I realise there are a lot of people watching. I stop and take my cloak/coat off and put it over my head so I can't be seen. That is a bit odd. As I get to the bottom there are people, energies, intelligences, whatever. Some of them are interested, some are just going about their business. The place is absolutely packed, seething almost. I work my way through until I come to the passageway on the left. I can just about see it through all the others that are here. I slip into it. Nobody seems to notice that I have done this.

It is calm, quiet and dark. Not too dark so I can still see where I am going. It is a narrow passageway, very narrow, almost both shoulders are touching either side, it is so narrow. I push my way along. The passage almost feels like a crack, something that has broken apart and has allowed entry into it. Like a crack or fissure in a rock. It is still quite dark and I have to feel my way along on the right to feel the opening. I turn into it not knowing where it is going. The only place I can go is down a ladder, fixed to the wall so there is no fear of it falling.

I keep going down. It is well hidden for safety, for security.

"You are allowed for we know you are safe [to know this]."

I come to a big open space – well lit. There are a lot of people here. I am talking about human beings as well as those who look like human beings but are not, not in our sense. This place is very busy with everyone doing something. It is enormous and well lit but with no shadows. The light is everywhere. Everyone seems to know what they are doing but I don't know what I am doing here. There is machinery, lots of dials and controls. It has been here a while because it is so orderly, so well practiced. What am I supposed to do here?

"You are to observe and know that this exists. Know that we have plans to accommodate many."

My question is, "How are people going to know about this? It is so far down. I don't even know the way in."

"When it is important for others to know there will be an opening which will show them the way."

"My next question is who are these people you will show the way to?"

"We will show the way to those who will have something of benefit to offer the planet, without thought of selfish gain. We will know which ones genuinely wish to assist planet Earth and genuinely wish for a better world for all, not just for themselves. Those who feel they have earned a place because of position or power will not know of this entrance."

"I feel you are talking of adults here but what about families, children, innocents?"

"We look at the soul. Even children have a soul that can be seen for its true purpose. Therefore it will only be for those who, at soul level, have intentions of assisting planet Earth and the continuation of the human species. Even children may have evolved souls or inferior souls, and we will know for we have access to their innermost being when the need is there."

"My next question is why are you showing me this?"

"This is so you can make this known. So that others will look to their soul condition and take heed of what we say. We know you are safe for you do not know how to enter this place on a physical level. It will be clear when the time is right."

"It sounds a bit fancy to me but there are so many people down here. They are men down here, not ladies or children."

"These are the operators, those who are maintaining this in good order. The time is not ready yet."

They then showed me to another part, a different area. It is there that I see beings who are not humans. I can't say Extraterrestrials for they are of the earth but not as those on the surface.

"They too belong to the Earth and it is they who have assisted in this project. Without these beings from in the Earth, this project would not be possible."

SEPTEMBER 13th 2011

PREPARE AND RESOLVE DIFFICULTIES BEFORE CHANGE

"When you go into a higher state such as the Earth and humanity is going to enter, there will be a sluicing, a cleansing even after the event of any dross, anything that is contaminated, unwanted or unclean. The cleansing will take place before as well as afterwards. There will be much of this going on. It is a sort of halfway house and not a sudden transition. There is to be an interim period, not a no man's land exactly but an area beforehand, before stepping cleanly into the new world. There will also be a quarantine area – you can call it decontamination if you like.

"Family members will stay together in the changeover process and in the interim period this is where they will resolve any difficulties they may have had between them. They have to be resolved first in this, so called, no man's land. I do not have the correct word but I can't think of a suitable one. It is a second chance for everybody to sort out any family or relationship problems. They will sort them out before they can step cleanly into the new world.

"I can hear you ask, how long will this take? As you know time is not relevant. It may take a long time or it may be done very quickly. Each

370

situation is individual to that grouping so there is not one set period allowed.

"We would recommend that you try to resolve difficulties well in advance and get it sorted out sooner rather than later.

OCTOBER 12th 2011

RESCUE OF GREYS

I have finished my descent which is quite steep. I am dressed in grey, unusual for me and am in tight fitting clothes so that there is no flapping or anything to catch on something else.

"They are in grey so it blends with its surroundings and is also a cloak, a mask."

I must mask my light so it can't be seen. I look around. Not much to see. It is a bit empty like being in a big tunnel that has been made, but is just an entrance and is not itself important. I must walk along it because it obviously leads somewhere. As I go I realise that my outfit also covers my feet, padded. My feet are padded so I don't make a noise. As if I could make a noise because I am just a consciousness.

I keep going forward as the tunnel gets narrow and then widens. It is an hour glass shape. I squeeze through the narrow part and get into a lighted area. It is huge, massive, and really big. It will take me a while to walk around the area. There are lots of lights, very bright. They are artificial lights not daylight. There is a lot here, not in the middle but around the sides. I come to one area which I can't call a room but is an enclosure of some kind. Inside are many, many what you would call Greys, little people all jumbled together, all interacting with each other. I can't make out what they are saying. I am so much bigger than they are. They see me and call me, trying to get my attention. They are fingering me. They are very small and I have to be careful I don't tread on anybody. But they get out of the way as they are nimble as well.

They look at me and every time I look their way, I see their big eyes looking back at me trying to impart some information. There is not just one trying, they are all trying together. I must unify a little and I might get what they want – so many all clambering. Whichever way I look there is someone trying to tell me something. I know it sounds ridiculous, I know I am to help them get out from here. They feel physical and I am not, I am just consciousness. I know that but I feel physical here. I am so much bigger than they are.

I deliberately expand my energy field. I know this is what I have to do. I deliberately increase my energy field so it covers them and

372

surrounds them so they are now enclosed. I can excite the field so it is more powerful and they are included in this. Quite interesting! With the energy field completely enclosing them I walk out of the enclosure and back along where I have come from and through the gap. It is like squeezing a balloon through but my energy field is intact and they all come through with me. They are still with me, all of them. Some are clinging to me. I go back up the steps, dragging this load I have with me and get to the surface. I stand with the huge energy field around me and the beings inside the field. They are protected and invisible while they are within the field.

Then it is odd and it sounds so much like science fiction – there is a beam coming down from I do not know where. They all join inside the beam, collect in it and it is as if they are vacuumed up into it until my energy field is empty of them and I can bring it back to normal. The beam they have gone up in begins to fade. They have been rescued.

I feel good. I have a headache, that's all. I am on my own now and have done what they have asked me to do. I don't know where they have come or where they have gone. They are so small, like children and very vulnerable. I had to protect them. No-one is ever going to believe this but I must transcribe it just the same. Whether anybody believes it or not is irrelevant. It happened.

OCTOBER 17th 2011

SPACE CRAFT IN JUNGLE

I go down on what appears to be a bamboo ladder, the sort you get from a hut in the jungle set up high in the trees or built up high. This is a ladder that can be pulled up to make the places secure and let down when the need is there. I am going down the ladder. It is not very steady. I am going backward until I reach the ground. It is not exactly jungle but is native type land, a clearing, beaten earth. So now I am on the ground. Where do I go? I wander around a little bit but I do not see anybody.

I see a pathway off. I take the path which soon gets into undergrowth. It is like being in the rainforest. It is more rainforest than dry arid land. I keep walking but I can't see much on either side because the growth is quite high and dense. I come to another path so I follow that one. I don't know where it is taking me. Very quickly, very soon I come to a huge clearing. This hasn't been cleared by natives. It is massive. This is nothing to do with clearing the jungle for anything minor. It has been done for a specific purpose.

There is a craft and men who are nothing to do with the jungle. They are watching the craft, patrolling and safeguarding it. Very odd! I am trying to describe the craft but my mind is going in all directions now. I call it a craft because it is not an aeroplane. An aeroplane couldn't land in this jungle. It is not a helicopter. This is different. I don't know what to call it. You can hardly call it a flying saucer but it is very similar to that. It is humming and is active. That's the word. It is not dead. It is not a craft that has landed and is still. It can move at any moment, I feel.

I walk past all the guards and they don't see me or don't appear to. They are military because they have that sort of uniform, camouflage uniform. They are all around this thing and I walk straight through them. I go up to the craft. As I do a portion of it opens. Oh God, it sounds so science fiction! It opens and there is a way in for me. I walk straight in. I get inside. It is a bit cramped. The Beings, for they are not from this world, see me. They do see me. They beckon me over. They are tall and what I would call gangly. They are not the short tiny greys. I feel very nice with them, very comfortable with them. They show me to a seat. I almost recline in the seat but I feel OK. I feel fine.

"What is this all about, please?"

"You are to go on a trip. You are to go outside of your world and see the bigger picture. This is why you are here. You are here to see the big picture, not the little events that everybody is concerned about. So many on your planet are concerned about their own portion of their existence, their own private worlds and are not truly bothered about the big picture. They may say they are but when it comes down to it they are not. As long as they are alright, as long as it doesn't touch them then the rest is unimportant to them, or so it seems. That is how it seems [to us]."

So I am in. I am lying down. It is odd because I know we are travelling but I also know that this craft is still there in the centre of the clearing. I just know that. To those guards outside it appears as if nothing has happened. Yet I know it has. Very odd! What I am doing now is looking through a screen, an all round screen. I get up and go close and can see our planet and the colours from it. I see areas that are muddy and grey, that need help, that need healing.

I am not sure if I am seeing reality or an illustration of what can be because the planet is entering a beam from the sun, from other influences. I don't know the words for them. Rays of this, particles of that – entering a field of all manner of interferences and influences. The whole planet is in this, going deeper and deeper and deeper in until it is totally immersed in it. It will come out of the other side of the beam but this will take a long time. While we are in it things are going to change. It is a regenerating beam. Things will change but it is not an overnight process because the beam is very wide and vast. I'll be long gone by the time we come out the other side.

"We are showing you this so that you know that this is just a period in your Earth time. It is an age it goes through. When you come out you humans will be more responsible. What happens in your future is that you will be even more responsible than before. You will take greater charge and greater care of the entire body of your planet, instead of being self interested to the extent that you ignore external events."

I think this is already happening now on the planet.

"Yes people are being disturbed, which is as it should be. They have been complacent and stagnant for too long. We need agitation to get things moving. To change things we need you to come alive and put things where they are meant to be."

"I don't understand why you are showing me this because I can't really do much."

"Yes you can. You can help people to see what is happening. You may feel it is only in a small way but small things have a way of growing, developing and spreading. Whatever you do or say will have an effect and will spread. Don't give up. Don't give up. You will be travelling more."

"I don't think I could travel more this year than I have done already."

"You will be directed and the ways will be opened for you, so do not be concerned over where and when and how. We are opening the doors and you will walk through into where we have planned."

"Ah, a mystery tour eh?"

"Don't worry about it, it will work. There is no alternative for you."

"What do I do now?"

They release me from the seat and point to the door which is opening. I go down past the guards who have not noticed a single thing happening. As I go back down the pathway the whole thing disappears. I am back here recording this. How very weird! A true mind journey. I didn't get a chance to ask all the questions but I feel that is my fault. I could have asked more.

I don't know if that was a flight of fancy or real. I feel spaced out. I feel it happened but is it odd.

This was one of many visits to space craft but as they were not recorded I cannot include them here.

NOVEMBER 4th 2011

EXPECTATIONS OF OTHERS

The stairs are wide and clearly not meant just for one person, but for many. There is nothing terribly grand about them but is an entrance for many. There is nothing to hold on to. It is a huge wide staircase similar to steps you get outside a church or cathedral where the steps are wide so that masses can go in and out. I am to go up not down. I get to the top and there appears to be what I would call ushers welcoming. I would say, us, but I can't see anybody else. They are inviting me to go in. It is the dwelling of the Council of Nine. There are many avenues I can go into from here in the entrance hall. It has a vaulted ceiling, so high I can't see it clearly. I am drawn to the left which is my normal way anyway. I am just going to follow my nose. I can hear sweet, gentle music. I follow a corridor which feels OK. There is a rich feel about this place. I am drawn to go into my right – another pathway. It has a church-like feel.

As I go in I ask: "Take me where I need to be, tell me what I need to know. I am looking for confirmation of my abilities that everybody seems to think I have, when I don't think I have them at all. Expectations are always great and greater than I think I can deliver. I need some sort of encouragement, confirmation, something of that nature to reassure that I can deliver, even when I don't know how.

"I feel uncomfortable with the promotion side of things of what I do. I would rather just do. I can't get to grips with promotions. Self promoting doesn't sit right."

I am feeling very emotional as I say this. I am really emotional over this as if I am baring my soul.

BOOK IMPORTANT

I am down now, standing on rush matting on an uneven floor. I suspect it is an earthy floor underneath the mat. There is nothing constructed here. It is as if the open space has been made out of natural surroundings. I look for my passage. There is a sort of dug out tunnel which extends into some sort of habitat. I go along and know there has to be another opening for this is how I enter. It is smooth. I am reminded of Coober Pedy, where it is dug out for opals underground. Nice living quarters can be dug out this way. It is all very comfortable even if it is a bit rugged. It needs finishing touches.

I enter now the right turn. This is where I need to be to get some resolution to the things going round in my head. I see a central figure with an extremely long exaggerated quill pen. He has a pointed hat. He is trying to write but he is being bothered by others with their pens. They keep nudging him, trying to take him away from what he is doing. He keeps fending them off. They are all interested in writing but my attention is on the main one because he is clearly central to my work as well.

"Who are these others?"

"These are those who would write their books and who are trying to get as much attention for themselves. They are not looking at the bigger picture but their own particular journeys."

"I suppose there is nothing wrong with that. That is what I am doing after all."

"The book you are working on now will be more important than the ones you have already written, even though you cannot see that this may be. This is true."

I have an opportunity to have someone manage my work and I am not at all sure I can come up to scratch and could let others down.

PUT YOUR TRUST IN US

I have gone down a very long way on a vertical ladder. It is a bit like going down a drain but a long way past any drain level. The last step I have to jump off as the ladder doesn't touch the bottom. There is not much space, a bit like the bottom of a well. It is like being at the centre of a wheel because there are passages going off like spokes in all directions. There are seven of them. I don't know which one to take because they are fanning out from where I stand. I am looking at each one in turn to see which passage can be different. I can't possibly go down them all. I have done a complete circle and come back to where I started.

I detect a very faint glimmer down one, so that is the one I am going to take. It is not right or left but the one where there is a glimmer. It is not a big passage and I can get through it, no problem at all. It is quite closed in. I have my usual coughing fit which seems to happen when I am going somewhere special. I wish it wouldn't! I pad along because either I have something on my feet or the ground is soft and doesn't make any noise. It is smooth as you get in caves when water has been through.

I go along carefully because it is not very bright. I keep my eye on the glimmer ahead. It has a green hue to it. As I get closer it gets stronger. It fills the passage and is not just a speck any more. It is circular, a pale green. It reminds me of something and I can't think what. I reach it and it is a bit like a mist.

I have come this far so I walk into the green mist. I am surrounded by the mist now. Walking through. It is long. Walking through. I am free of it. Suddenly I am in a completely different world. It is outside.

It is a completely different world. There is activity, a bustle. I am outside and the air smells sweet, sweeter than I have ever sensed before, ever. There is sweetness about it, pure. It is a long time since the air has been this pure. Yes, there are birds singing. Quite a lot, not like the silent spring we have these days. There is re-growth, fresh and pure. It feels happy.

I entered this meditation asking if the direction I have been led to is the one I should go. I don't know if this answers. I don't think it does but is another journey. Three people come towards me. I don't know if they are men or women. It is difficult to tell, but they too are sweet. The centre one is definitely a man. He extends his hands towards me and takes mine and draws me into an embrace. Ooh it's lovely! The other two stand and watch.

"What does this mean? Should I go down this route?"

"We will provide on each occasion that which is expected of you. You need not have fear of not coming up to the expectations of others. You may feel you are on a knife edge at times. If you put your trust in us we will be there giving you what you need. Not just what you need but what the world needs to see and to hear. Trust in us then you will not need to worry about trust in yourself. For we are united, are we not? We work through you, do we not? So yes you will as you say 'come up with the goods' for that is what concerns you. It does not concern you the effort and the time which you must put in, only that you provide what others are seeking and what the world needs to hear. Maybe what they hear is not what they expected but will be what they need. Put your trust in us. Do put your trust in us for we are many. We are many."

NOVEMBER 29th 2011

I have plain wooden stairs. As I begin to go down I see a picture of me when somebody grabs me. I am watching the 'me' wanting to go forward and yet someone is trying to hold on to me to stop me. The person I am looking at, the me pulls hard and pulls away. He/me is determined to go. I am determined to go and can hear the steps on the wood, the odd creak. Pressure is building in me, building up as I go down. I feel pressure. It keeps getting bigger. I feel male. I am a male.

I am observing me. As I get to the bottom I see I have boots on, working clothes and sturdy boots. I land on a path through a dense forest. The path is narrow. I don't understand this. It is straight ahead, no turnings when my usual way is to have turnings. I still feel very determined, to keep going and not to stop.

"Keep going and do not stop. Do not be diverted. Keep the goal in site."

380

The forest is still dense and large. It is still. Not much going on. I keep marching forward. I am not taking it slowly but as fast as I can go. It is urgent that I get through this.

"You must not be put off whatever happens to you. Keep your goal in site."

I am trying not to think for if I think I will get diverted by my thoughts. I keep going and there are things on either side clutching at me, trying to stop me.

"What is this referring to?"

"This is referring to your work of course. What is it that you have in mind? Whatever it is you must keep going towards it. Do not be afraid."

"I am not afraid."

"You are afraid of many things. You are afraid that you cannot deliver. Why do you not trust us more? We will make sure that you deliver when you arrive out into the public world."

My head hurts. I can't seem to relieve it. My head hurts.

DECEMBER 5ᵗʰ 2011

I have a long conversation with the spirit world.

"Do not use your age as an excuse to slow down. You should be speeding up now, not slowing down."

I am given many stairs. It is a joke because I am given red clothes all the way down to my feet. It is a Santa type gown. Not a Santa outfit but is in that same material. Very funny! They want me to be jolly and keep saying 'ho ho ho'. I think they are playing with me a bit.

I go down carefully. They are not big or wide stairs. There is not a lot of tread which is why I am going carefully. The energy is increasing and getting more connected as I go. I am lost in the pressure of the intense energy. I can't focus properly. I am not fixed anywhere.

DECEMBER 6th 2011

"Remember what we told you this morning. Remember that we told that we were making great changes within you, preparing you for greater things. Remember our conversation."

DECEMBER 14th 2011

A message direct from spirit.

"How far do we go when we want to present something we have discovered to others? How far do we go? How do we know if what we wish to share will be understood, may be kicked aside as not being understood or not interested? Does it matter? How far do we go in pushing our own discoveries onto others? Or should we allow others to discover for themselves? For when they do this it stays with them. It is more real to them if discoveries are made by themselves. So just how far do we go in presenting what we know? It is a question that I am never quite sure about.

"Or do their discoveries come about as a result of our putting forward what we know? Is it the first link in the chain, the first opening so that they then may discover for themselves?"

My own view is that when I discover something amazing, heart-warming or whatever feels right; my first instinct is to share it. To share it with others so that they too may feel the same. Am I wrong or am I right?

DECEMBER 24th 2011

UNSAFE RADIATION BOXES

The stairs are old and worn with no carpeting. There is a sort of lino, broken in parts and uncared for. I am in a derelict place. It echoes as I go down. There is a wall on either side painted a horrible green in painted plaster. I keep going down quite a long flight of stairs considering wherever I am it is in an old building.

At the bottom it is like being in a warehouse. It is not a house but a warehouse. It is big with huge empty spaces. It could be used as it is quite dry, painted floor like concrete that has been painted smooth. It has been used in the past. I look around for my exit from this. Yes there is a passage going somewhere else. We are rather deep below ground somewhere. There are no windows.

I walk along. Gosh this is not a nice place. It is old, uncared for. It has been used and is not now. I am looking for my door on the right hand side. It has to be at some point. I come to a door that has wooden slats nailed across it to stop entry. It has been boarded up with wooden planks. How on earth am I going to get in there? I start to tug at the boards. They come away quite easily. I finish pulling them all down. The door inside is rotting on its hinges. As I push it falls inwards.

I clamber over all the bits and pieces to get inside. What an odd journey this is! Oh, that is interesting. There is something glowing. Not a celestial glow but one which feels radioactive. I don't know if it really is radioactive but that is the impression I get. There is a glow from some element. I don't know my elements but this is not a safe glow. I suddenly realise this is why this place has been boarded up. This is why a perfectly good building is now unused. It is because there is an unsafe radiation in it. Nobody would dare go near.

Well, I am only a mind so I can go near. It isn't going to affect me. I move over to whatever it is, a fairly large box. It is difficult to see through it for it has a reddish haze over it. It is not safe for most physical beings. What am I supposed to do with this? I haven't a clue. So I ask for information.

"What we are showing you is not an isolated place. That is to say there are other areas, other houses, other buildings that contain unsafe elements within them, that we have isolated, forbidden entry to. That is

383

authorities have forbidden entry to. This is much more widespread than this one building and the general public have no idea. They are in areas of the world such as Eastern Europe, China, even the Philippines. In many other parts of the world there are these buildings which we have boarded up and restricted entrance to."

"I want to know what I am doing here then. What can I do?"

"You must now use your mind. When you complete this one task it will have an effect on all these other places we have told you about. We want you to use your mind. Put out both hands and lay them on this box. As you do with your mind the glow will subside. Send your thoughts so that the danger element in this box is nullified. It reduces the radioactivity. This you must do. Create a mind picture of the other aspects of yourself doing this in many other places. You are not restricted to one place when you use your mind."

I have a picture of me many times over laying hands on the container and see the glow diminishing, fading, fading and leaving the box completely free. I see pictures of me everywhere doing the same. It takes quite a long time.

"When this is done we can use these buildings safely. All these areas will become safe as a result of your action."

"Well it is done but I don't know how I can put that into my book. It is too difficult to put into the book."

"You can type it up just the same for it needs to be a record of the actions taken by those such as yourself for reference later."

"Why couldn't you do this yourselves?"

"You are very well aware that if change is to come about on your planet the change must come from those who inhabit the planet, whether they use their minds alone or their physicality. You human beings have to make the changes, not us."

It is obvious that changes on the planet and in ourselves are taking place and that we as human beings need to take responsibility for our actions. We need to realise that we are more than our physical bodies and can travel wherever our minds take us. It is clear that whatever travel we take we can change things using our minds. We are more connected with other intelligences than we ever thought possible.

These journeys may seem unbelievable and fantasy to you, but to me they have been as real as my everyday existence. I recommend you try for yourself using the method described at the end of this book. Enjoy the ride.

MEDITATION TRAINING AND EXERCISE

GOING INTO RELAXATION

It is important you do not try to meditate too late in the day. Your body is already programmed and conditioned to sleep at the end of the day and you may drop off to sleep instead of taking it further.

Get into the state where you forget your body and where only the mind is alert? Remember this is an inter-active process. Being comfortable is a must.

Switch off any phones and ensure you will not be disturbed for at least fifteen minutes.

Before you begin, say a prayer. This is your safeguard whilst you are in that open receptive state.

THE PRAYER

Your own prayer could be something like this, though it can be modified frequently according to the purpose for the sitting.

"Dear Father, I come to you in love. I ask for your help with the work I have pledged to do. *(Insert whatever it is you want).* May there be no invading negative influences, whether it be from within me or without. May the White Light of the Divine surround me. I invite all those guides, teachers, angels or any who wish to come to communicate with me for the betterment of all. Amen."

Close your eyes. Relax. Feel your feet on the floor anchoring you, keeping you safe.
Feel the tension ease out of your limbs. Starting with the legs allow the muscles to relax and the flesh to become loose. Mentally check that there is no tension in your thighs.
Consciously relax the muscles.
Go up the body and feel heaviness of your arms and hands on your lap.
Loosen any tension.
Breathe gently and become aware of breathing.

Allow your shoulders to sag down with the gravity.

Feel the energy increase around your throat. Allow your jaw to hang loose and slightly ajar. Feel your cheeks sagging.

Your eyelids are heavy. Feel as if you are just dropping off to sleep in a soft feather bed. You do not even want to open your eyes.

Relax the forehead. Ease away frowns or tension.

Loosen the scalp. Double check your whole body to ensure it is relaxed, heavy and loose.

MEDITATION TO CONTACT YOUR SOUL GUIDE

Turn off the phone and get comfortable.

Go through the relaxation process.

Say your prayer to reassure you that all will be well and will bring an increase of energy to flow through you.

Remembering that these are mind experiences, feel or see yourself standing at the top of a flight of stairs.

Feel the ground beneath your toes. Mentally wriggle them to sense what you are standing on.

Accept immediately what comes into the mind. Do not think about it beforehand. Be as sensory as you can.

There is a rail to one side. Pretend it is there if you can't image it.

Put your hand out to touch it. Is it a banister, rope or something else?

Let your mind supply the thoughts.

Look at the stairs. Are they steep or shallow? Are they wide or narrow?

Can you see the bottom? These stairs will take you into the space where your soul resides or where guides wait for you.

It is time to do down. Use all your inner senses. Three steps to go: one – two – three – At the bottom now.

Look around. Take a few steps **forward** until you turn off to the **left**.

Note the type of passage. Soon you will come to a door on the **right**.

This is your door. What is it made of? Touch it, feel it.

It is time to open it and step inside. This is your space.

Step in and look around. Note your surroundings.

Whatever you see go towards it, even if it is a drop of water on the wall.

Interact with it. You might see a table. Go towards it.

There might be a book or a small chest there.

Open it. You might see a glimmer of light ahead. Go towards it.

If you see nothing then ask to be shown what you need to see. Most of your input will come in the form of ideas, thoughts, impressions and images.

Ask to be told what you need to know. Ask, ask, ask. Question. Make your requests.

You might not see your soul or receive a guide at first, but he will be there.

Keep asking. If you don't understand what comes to you, say so. Try not to edit what comes to your mind.

You might see an animal. Note how you feel towards the animal. An animal is often used for you to follow. It frequently is the guide himself.

Your mind will use soul memory to assist you. Trust whatever comes to show the way. When you see a spirit form it could well be your soul guide. Talk to it in your mind and ask to be shown more. You can use such words as; 'tell me what I need to know', or 'show me what I need to see'. This is giving your soul guide permission to work with you, which it needs.

CLOSING DOWN

When you successfully get into the desired deeper state and having such a good time, it sometimes happens that when the session has ended you fail to come back to a 'normal feet on the ground' vibration. You may feel floaty or spaced out.

It is easy to deal with this. You will be please to read that eating a piece of chocolate or biscuit is very good for grounding you. When you decide that it is time to finish, deliberately bring the energy levels down by telling yourself to do so. Consciously feel the weight of your body on the chair, feel the weight of your arms on your lap. Wriggle your fingers and toes. This brings your mind back to physical reality.

You can also say 'CUT' to indicate you are finished, as in filming. And finally please say thank you to your unseen friends who have helped during your journeys.

ACKNOWLEDGEMENTS

Thank you all my friends and family who have encouraged and taught me to hold fast when I doubted myself. Without your belief in me I may not have completed this book.

I thank all my spirit helpers for their patience and teaching. There would be no book without you.

I thank Paul Dobree-Carey who has interviewed me for YouTube which has helped put this book forward.